THE OTHER
FACE OF
AMERICA

Translated from the Spanish by Patricia J. Duncan

rayo *An Imprint of* HarperCollins*Publishers*

THE OTHER FACE OF AMERICA

CHRONICLES OF THE IMMIGRANTS SHAPING OUR FUTURE

JORGE RAMOS

HarperCollins books may be purchased for educational, business, or sales promotional use. For information, please write: Special Markets Department, HarperCollins Publishers Inc., 10 East 53rd Street, New York, NY 10022.

Originally published in 2000 in Mexico by Grijalbo as *La Otra Cara de America*.

FIRST EDITION

Designed by Shubhani Sarkar

Library of Congress Cataloging-in-Publication Data has been requested.

ISBN 0-06-621416-5

02 03 04 05 06   10 9 8 7 6 5 4 3 2 1

FOR ALL THOSE FORCED TO LEAVE THE COUNTRY WHERE
THEY WERE BORN. . . .

FOR ALL THOSE WHO HAVE HAD TO BEGIN THEIR LIVES
AGAIN. . . .

The collapse of walls to let people out has given rise to new walls to keep people out.

LEOPOLDO ZEA

Ethnicity seems to be destiny in the politics of the third century [of American Democracy].

HAROLD EVANS, *THE AMERICAN CENTURY*

The United States is a multiracial, multicultural country . . . This is the great historical challenge of the United States.

OCTAVIO PAZ

CONTENTS

ACKNOWLEDGMENTS

The United States has given me opportunities that Mexico could not. I left Mexico because of censorship in the press, because of the lack of political and economic choices, because I did not believe in its leaders, and because from there it would have been almost impossible for me to find my place in the world. Strangely enough, the longer I am away from Mexico, the more Mexican I feel. I didn't really want to be an immigrant; but I had to become one, and I found a country ready to welcome my passions and to rechannel the pent-up energy of my frustrations. My gratitude to the United States is enormous— gratitude for not allowing me to get stuck in the present and for giving me a push toward the future.

What really saved me in my new life as a Mexican immigrant in the United States, however, were certain individuals. Shawnesee Colaw let me sleep in the living room of his tiny apartment hours after I landed in Los Angeles the night of January 2, 1983. Thank you for the warmth, the shelter, and my first English lessons.

Marco Mendoza lent me a hand when my checkbook was lean. If it hadn't been for him, I would have returned to Mexico bearing the burden of my failure. Marco gave me the time I needed to get back on my feet. Marco is no longer with us, and I don't know how to repay him.

Without even knowing me, Pete Moraga gave me my first job in U.S. television. I still wonder why he did it. Pete, a thousand thanks.

Then there are my supporters.

I have always suspected that my family never understood all the reasons behind my leaving Mexico. I don't really know how to justify those two decades away from Lourdes, my mother, and Lourdes, my sister and confidante, and Alex, Eduardo, and Gerardo, my brothers and cardinal points. During the adventure I even lost my father. But I feel as close to him as if I had left yesterday.

Lisa, Paola, and Nicolás teach me every day what is important in life. They know that in this subject, I will always be a student.

My great friend Benjamin Beckhart, who for twenty-five years never failed to ask: How are you? Ben, I will always thank you for your question, but especially for your patience, affection, and understanding in listening to my response.

José Luis Betancourt and Angélica Arriga, Benito Martínez, and María Amparo Escandón never left me alone, sad, or hungry in the United States. I could not have asked for a more supportive, courageous, fun group of friends.

Patsy Loris knows my work best, and at times she startles me by telling me things that not even I had noticed: the instinct of a guardian angel, I guess. Thank you for your observations, suggestions, and corrections. That, and your friendship, are invaluable.

And thanks to Gian Carlo and Ariel Rosales for keeping their lines of communication open to my worries and for letting me write what I wished.

What more can I ask?

INTRODUCTION

I am an immigrant
In a country of immigrants;
And the place where I live looks more and more like me.

Everything was changed on Tuesday, September 11, 2001, when the World Trade Center was destroyed. The day was a disaster for immigrants especially, and for many years an anti-immigrant zeal will be felt. On that day, the way many in America view immigrants was changed. Forever.

For the past few months, even years, prior to that day, we in America experienced a renewed sense of optimism toward immigrants and immigration policy—the immigrant's role as a worker and contributor to American culture was recognized as integral to what makes America what it is. Sadly, this view has ceased, and through this terror and tragedy, we have emerged with a new view of immigration that ultimately will hurt more than protect the country.

The terrorist attack on the World Trade Center erased some of the things that have transpired, transforming the spirit of welcome into one of suspicion. This I find saddening. Everything that we as immigrants have worked so hard to establish has been lost. Every little gain, every little step, has been erased, changing the attitude on immigration to sentiments not felt in America since the Communist witch-hunts of the 1950s.

We have gone from discussing the beginning of a new dawn in partnership between the United States and foreign nations to discussing the possibility of closing our borders in order to guard against future terrorist incidents.

So much work has gone into erasing the concept of an "us and them" mentality between Americans and immigrants that it is a shock to see all this work collapse just as quickly as the 110-story buildings did on September 11.

With so many immigrants having worked hard to become American citizens, it is a shame that the sentiment of American patriotism within the immigrant community has been called into question. Immigrants are American patriots, and many will, and do, sacrifice their lives for the rights and opportunities this country has provided. American citizenship has given many immigrants and their families the opportunity to fulfill countless dreams. From Cubans to Central Americans to Mexicans, American citizenship is a privilege worth the sacrifice of life. It is hard to imagine people questioning this loyalty and exuberance. Even more, it is hard not to feel angry about it.

As a reporter, I've covered three wars. I have never seen anything like what I've seen in downtown Manhattan since September 11. The concentration of rubble and death was horrific, and two months later, it still is; I'm sure the experience will plague me for the rest of my life. I'm not alone in this feeling. America itself has changed. Yet the view toward America from immigrants who want nothing more than to feed and clothe and educate their children remains intact and as strong as ever. To most, America is still the country where human rights, opportunity, and success are possibilities; it inherently inspires hope in those who want nothing more than to make their contribution. I hope and pray that previously planned improvements in immigration policy are not forgotten, and even more, I hope and pray that immigrants themselves are seen not as a problem in America, but rather a solution. We will see.

THE LATINIZATION OF THE UNITED STATES

The United States is undergoing a Latinization, and there is no turning back. It is an overwhelming, definitive, and irreversible phenomenon that is changing the face of America, to the dismay of many. The racial and ethnic fibers that make up this nation have been changing at an alarming rate. Parts of this country are unrecognizable. The United States is not a country made up of whites, and this is more true today than ever before. It is a nation of mixed races, multiethnic and multiracial. A complicated diversification process is transforming this nation, and in fewer than sixty years non-Hispanic whites will simply be one more minority. The United States, however, is afraid to take a good look at itself in the mirror.

The 2000 census figures are overwhelming proof of this phenomenon: There are 35,305,818 Hispanics in the United States (U.S. Bureau of the Census, *Overview of Race and Hispanic Origin, 2000*). Latinos are now the largest minority in the country, surpassing African Americans, despite the fact that there were at least 3 million people who were not accounted for in this census, many of whom were most likely Hispanics and immigrants.

These figures, however, cannot be viewed as static. In the case of Hispanics, the 2000 census is like a photograph of a river about to overflow its banks. Latinos and immigrants are changing the United States in ways unforeseen.

For example:

- The purchasing power of Hispanics will reach $1 trillion in 2010. Economically, Latinos today produce more than countries like Argentina, Colombia, Chile, Peru, and Venezuela (*Hispanic Consumer Market Growth to 2010*, DRI/McGraw Hill, 1998; Univisión: A Market with Real Purchasing Power).
- McDonald's, "the world's largest fast-food chain," wants to be numero uno with their Latin customers. In South Florida, McDonald's is adding to its menu the classic Cuban sandwich, the Latin McOmelet, and a pineapple-mango dipping sauce for McNugget lovers (*ABC News One*, "Cuban McDonald's," 8/2/01).

- Some of the most famous baseball players in the United States have the following names on their jerseys: Mercado, Sosa, Reyes, Bocachica, Rivera, Rodriguez (without an acute accent on the "i"), and Nunez (without the tilde on the second "n").

- Spanish-language media in the United States is beginning to contest or win the battle over newspaper, radio, and television ratings in markets such as Los Angeles, Houston, San Antonio, Chicago, and New York.

- In the largest one hundred cities in the United States, non-Hispanic whites make up less than 50 percent of the population. In the last decade, one million whites left cities like New York, Los Angeles, Chicago, Houston, and Philadelphia for other areas. Anaheim, for example, lost 21 percent of its non-Hispanic white population, while the Latino population rose by a surprising 61 percent in ultra-white Charlotte, North Carolina.

- Singers and performers of Hispanic origin—such as Ricky Martin, Jennifer Lopez, Gloria Estefan, Antonio Banderas, Penelope Cruz, Edward James Olmos, and Christina Aguilera—have imposed, with extraordinary success, their Latin rhythms in territories once reserved only for non-Hispanic whites and African Americans.

- Liz Claiborne Fragrances has a new perfume called Mambo, and those in charge of the M&M brand found themselves forced to innovate in order to produce their famous chocolate candy with the flavor of *dulce de leche* (caramel). The California Milk Processors Board came out with another one of its famous "Got Milk?" advertisements, this time featuring a father and daughter in a supermarket buying the ingredients to make a *dulce de tres leches* (*Miami Herald*, 8/12/01). In many areas of the country more tortillas and *salsa picante* are sold than bagels and ketchup.

- Spanish is heard more than ever before. One of every five U.S. residents over the age of five speaks a language other than English at home, and 60 percent of these speak Spanish (*New York Times*, 8/6/01).

- In addition to the states where immigrants have typically settled—such as California, Texas, Florida, New York, and Illinois—the Hispanic population is also showing remarkable growth in other states. From 1990 to 1998, the Latino population grew by 148 percent in Arkansas, 110 percent in North Carolina, 90 percent in Tennessee, 74 percent in Iowa, 72 percent in Alabama, and 68 percent in Utah (Associated Press 9/14/99).

- George W. Bush became the first president to speak Spanish, and he got to the White House thanks to the Cuban-American voters in Florida.
- By July 1, 2059, the United States will be a nation composed exclusively of minorities.

There is not a single corner of the United States or a single activity where the presence and cultural influence of Hispanics are not being felt. This phenomenon, this "boom," is transforming the oldest democracy in the world.

BABIES, IMMIGRANTS, AND THE NUMBERS GAME

The changes come from both inside and out. Every day one thousand undocumented immigrants cross the border from Mexico illegally. Every day. Nothing is going to stop the steady flow of immigrants— not higher fences or new laws or a new border patrol budget or the army or immigration agreements.

Rather than a legal problem or a problem of national security, the immigration problem stems from the laws of supply and demand. As long as there are jobs in the United States and unemployed workers south of the border, undocumented immigration will continue. As long as an immigrant working in the United States earns in one hour what would take him one or two days to earn in Mexico, El Salvador, and Nicaragua, undocumented immigration will continue.

We must add to this undocumented immigration—which is unofficially calculated to be between 300,000 and 350,00 people per year—the one million immigrants who enter the United States legally each year. "There are already too many immigrants in this country," complain some. Not really. I suspect that these people have other motivations and fears.

There are 30.5 million immigrants in the United States, almost 11 percent of the population. Compared to the percentage of people born outside the United States in 1870 (14 percent) or in 1910 (14.7 percent), these immigration levels are far from being the highest in history. The problem is the anti-immigrant sentiment that surfaces when dealing with immigrants from Latin America, Africa, or Asia, a problem immigrants from Europe and Canada do not face. Is this racism?

What is certain is that in recent decades, the percentage of immigrants has grown. In 1970 immigrants composed 4.7 percent of the population; this rose to 8.7 percent in 1994 and now stands at 10.8 percent, according to 2000 census figures. So, the immigration flow to the North intensified in the last three decades of the twentieth century and the early twenty-first century. The greatest number of immigrants are coming from Latin America. This trend will probably continue for some time, although I doubt it will grow to the levels reached ninety years ago.

The reality is simple: Immigrants leave their countries because of push factors—lack of work, low levels of education, political repression—and they come to the United States because of pull factors— here, they are needed. If there were no jobs available in the United States, the exodus, no doubt, would be toward other countries; but here they are badly needed. A recent *USA Today* headline read, "USA just wouldn't work without immigrant labor" (*USA Today*, 7/23/01). This is true. Immigrants are indispensable to the U.S. job market; in fact, the last economic boom can be attributed to them.

Immigrants in the United States account for 34 percent of domestic employees, 23 percent of farmers and fishermen, 21 percent of assembly line workers, and 18 percent of those in the service industry (*USA Today*, 7/23/01). In other words, the houses in which Americans live, the food they eat, and the services they receive depend in large part on the work of immigrants, both legal and undocumented.

In his book *The Buried Mirror*, Carlos Fuentes wrote that undocumented immigrants are accused of displacing American workers, harming the economy and the nation, and even threatening the cultural integrity of the United States. Fuentes concludes, however, that these immigrants continue to come because nobody wants to do the jobs they do, and without them the entire labor structure in the United States would be severely affected.

Furthermore, welcoming immigrants is a profitable business. Contrary to what many Americans think, immigrants contribute much more to the U.S. economy than they take. A highly respected study carried out by the National Academy of Sciences in 1997 concluded that immigrants add roughly $10 billion a year to the nation's economic production, and that does not take into account the millions of dollars in remittances they send back to their homelands. The United States is undergoing a transformation and benefiting from the growing number of both legal and undocumented immigrants.

There are also internal factors that can explain the dramatic change taking place. One out of every five births in the United States occurs in a Hispanic family. According to the National Center for Health Statistics, the number of babies born to Hispanic mothers rose from 14 percent of the total in 1989 to 18 percent in 1995. Latinas, on average, tend to have more children than African Americans or whites. So even though Hispanics accounted for 12.5 percent of the U.S. population in 2000, nearly twenty of every hundred births occur in our families.

According to the 2000 census, from 1990 to 2000, the Hispanic population in the United States rose by 58 percent. The proportion of the Hispanic population in this country will no doubt continue to grow, due to both legal and undocumented immigration as well as the high birthrate among Latina women.

LATINOS ARE DIFFERENT

The melting pot dried up. We, the Hispanic community, did not integrate into U.S. society as other ethnic groups had before us; we did so in our own way. Latino immigration to the United States differs from the immigration of groups that came from Europe, and the reasons are many.

To begin with, there is a geographic factor that has kept us in constant contact with our homelands. It is not the same to fly from Los Angeles to Hermosillo, Mexico, as it is to go by boat from New York to Naples or Kraków.

Technology has also created the illusion of proximity. Making a long-distance telephone call no longer requires a great deal of money or the complicated systems that the European immigrants in the middle of the last century had to deal with in order to communicate with their loved ones. Letters are now easily replaced by e-mail messages sent on the Internet.

Most important, however, our sense of identity as Latinos is intrinsically linked to where we came from and what language we speak. There are Hispanic families that continue to consider themselves as being from Mexico, Cuba, or Puerto Rico, despite having lived in the United States for generations. Speaking Spanish implies belonging. Even those who do not have a good knowledge of the language tend to throw a few Spanish words they learned at home into their conversation to indicate what their roots are to the person with whom they are speaking. Every conversation in Spanish reinforces their sense of identity.

This link between language and identity is very important. A couple of decades ago, the debate among academics was whether Spanish had a future in the United States. They assumed, mistakenly, that Latinos would assimilate into American culture without resistance, just as the Irish, Italians, and Poles had done before us. Something, however, went very wrong. We did, in fact, assimilate; every year our earning power, educational level, and access to health care are improving. We are integrating more quickly than ever into the business and political worlds. However, we are often insulted and made to feel different from the rest of the population.

Our identity is tied to the land where we were born, or where our families were born, and to the language, Spanish, that has woven one generation to another. Spanish is more alive than ever in the United States. Nine out of every ten Hispanics speak Spanish at home, and this has allowed Spanish language radio, television, newspapers, and magazines to flourish.

The Italians and the Poles, for example, never had national television networks in their own language in the United States. Hispanics, however, do, and they are very successful; the Noticiero Univisión, which airs at 6:30 P.M., averages ten times the viewers that CNN does at that hour. Univisión is the fifth largest television network in the United States, after ABC, CBS, NBC, and Fox. Few people outside of the Hispanic market, however, are aware of this.

Hispanics have built their identity on cultural roots and origins that are different from those of the rest of the population. That sets us apart from all other immigrant groups in the history of the United States.

"It is the first time in history that an immigrant community has not had to go through the process of the melting pot which is that of conforming to the customs of the English-speaking population in order to be recognized as Americans," said Peruvian writer Mario Vargas Llosa. "Hispanics have not had to lose their language or their culture in order to feel as if they have assimilated; in fact, many have taken a stand in defense of that culture."

The melting pot ran out of steam.

Because of these reasons, because we are different, because we defend, as few do, our roots and our right to speak Spanish, because our process of assimilation to the United States is playing out unlike that of any other ethnic group, for many we are *los otros*, the other ones. Combined with the overwhelming increase in the number of Hispanics, this has generated tension with other groups.

Gore Vidal pointed out in 1994 the inevitable problems that would arise in the face of the transforming nation: "Now, here at home, people fret about invasions from the Hispanic world, from Haiti, from the boat people of Asia. But, like it or not, we are changing from a white, Protestant country governed by males, to a mixed polity, and in this time of change there is bound to be conflict."

ANTI-HISPANIC RACISM—FROM PÉREZ TO BUSH

The best thing the United States has to offer is opportunity, and the worst is racism. In this day and age there are no signs in parks that say "No Mexicans, No Indians, No Dogs," like the ones Professor Julian Samora saw as a boy in Colorado. Rejection of those who are different and those who have just arrived in this country, though, is still very much alive.

It is ironic that in a country where we are all immigrants, there is still such a great lack of understanding of the new wave of immigration. Those who have already arrived now want to close the door to those behind them, and at times it is hard to make them see that it is thanks to these new immigrants that the country is progressing. According to a Gallup poll, only 13 percent of Americans feel that current immigration levels should be raised (*Hispanic Trends*, 9/27/00).

No one in this country, however, has the right to be here, except the Native Americans, of course, who preceded all waves of immigration. Everyone else earned the right to be here through effort and hard work. Now it is our turn; it is time for Latin-American immigrants to receive that same recognition.

Anti-immigrant and anti-Hispanic racism pervade the daily life of all Americans. One need only look, for example, at the case of the ranchers in Arizona who took justice into their own hands and set out to hunt down undocumented immigrants as if they were animals. "We're getting invaded," one rancher complained in a recent *New York Times* article. "If the government was serious, they'd bring in the U.S. Army" (*New York Times*, 6/18/00). Likewise, there are frequent complaints of immigrants who are stopped by various government officials solely because of the color of their skin or how they look, and who are victims of racial crimes, most of which are never reported (National Network for Immigrants and Refugee Rights, 8/1/01).

In most cases, however, the racism and discrimination are more subtle. Not being properly waited on in a restaurant, losing a job to a less qualified candidate, or receiving smirks of disapproval because of the way we look are experiences that many Latino immigrants share. No, Hispanics are no longer prohibited from entering public parks, but Latinos still have not been allowed to occupy their proper place in U.S. society. Three examples illustrate this.

Of all the fictional characters on American television, only 2 percent are Latino. Things are even worse in the world of television news: In 2000, only 1.3 percent of the news reported on English language television stations was presented by Hispanic correspondents.[1] Of all advertising dollars spent by U.S. companies, not even 2 percent is spent on Hispanic media.

Even the Bush family has not escaped racism and discrimination. During the 2000 Republican National Convention in Philadelphia, George P. Bush, son of Florida governor Jeb Bush and his Mexican wife, Columba, told me that he had been a victim of discrimination.

"I have encountered a lot of discrimination in my life," the young man, then twenty-four years old, told me. The statement caught me by surprise.

"A member of the Bush family was a victim of discrimination in the United States?" I replied.

"Of course," he said, "because in our society, unfortunately, people judge you by the color of your skin. I have encountered discrimination my whole life, all around the country."

"How have you been a victim of discrimination?" I pressed him.

"With words like wetback, or ugly words like tar baby that people

[1] According to the 2000 census, Hispanic Americans number 35 million, or 12.5 percent of the population, a nearly 58 percent jump since 1990. But on TV? A report by the advocacy group Children Now found that in prime time, the number of Hispanic characters dropped since last season from 3 percent, to 2 percent. (Blacks make up 17 percent, the study found, Asian Americans 3 percent, and Native Americans 0.2 percent; they are 12.3 percent, 3.6 percent, and 0.9 percent of the population, respectively.) In prime time, Hispanic characters account for only 47 out of 2,251 characters. As for nonfiction TV, the Center for Media and Public Affairs found that Latino correspondents reported only 1.4 percent of all network evening news stories in 2000 (*Time* magazine, 5/28/01).

say to Latinos," he responded, without losing his composure, as if this were the most normal thing in the world.

Even the nephew of the president of the United States, the grandson of former president George Bush and the great-grandson of former senator Prescott Bush, was a victim of discrimination—because of the color of his skin, because he was Latino. If this can happen to a Bush, it is easy to imagine what can happen to a Sanchez, a Pérez, or a Domínguez.

"P," as he is called, is one of the "little brown ones" or *cafecitos*, as his grandfather, when he was president, used to call him and his siblings. Even though at the time the comment generated some controversy for being politically questionable—emphasizing the skin color when referring to his grandchildren—the fact of the matter is that the entire United States (just as the Bush family) is undergoing a process of racial and cultural fusion.

New York is becoming Mexicanized, Miami Colombianized, Los Angeles Honduranized and Salvadoranized, and Orlando Puerto Ricanized and Cubanized. The real challenge for the United States is to recognize that it is now a multiethnic, multicultural nation. This has yet to happen. The United States is afraid to look into the mirror and see a racially mixed country.

Will the United States somehow manage to integrate all the ethnic groups within its borders? In 1978, Mexican writer and poet Octavio Paz warned, "The United States has always ignored everyone else. At home, the black, the Chicano and the Puerto Rican; abroad, marginal cultures and societies."

The challenge the United States faces is twofold. First, it must admit that it is a multicultural society; second, it must accept that reality and fully embrace its diversity.

WHAT LATINO POWER?

There is no doubt that Latinos are transforming the face of the United States, but we still face enormous barriers that range from xenophobia to racism. The real challenge for the Hispanic community, then, is to transform its astonishing growth in numbers, its importance to the economy, and its cultural influence into political power. This is a road as yet untraveled.

We make up 12 percent of the U.S. population, but we do not have a single senator in Washington.

We make up 12 percent of the U.S. population, but we do not have a single judge on the U.S. Supreme Court.

We make up 12 percent of the U.S. population, but we do not have a single Hispanic governor.

We make up 12 percent of the population and we have only nineteen members in Congress (or 4 percent of the seats). At least fifty-two of those seats should belong to us. Although we outnumber African Americans, there are thirty-nine African-American members of Congress.

The lack of political power is just as serious on the local level. Of the 3.7 million inhabitants of Los Angeles in 2001, 46 percent were Latino. The number of Latino voters who voted in the election that could have made Antonio Villaraigosa the first Hispanic mayor of Los Angeles since 1872, however, barely surpassed 20 percent. The number of Hispanic voters registered nationally continues to increase, but the disparities between our rising percentage in the total population and the lack of power of our votes is evident.

Nevertheless, in other cities like Miami, Hispanic power *is* being felt. Cubans control the most important political positions in the city, including that of mayor. Other cities with large Latino populations are following—albeit a little late—the Cuban-American example of political mobilization.

To take a case in point, because of the Cuban-American vote in Florida in the past presidential election, George W. Bush reached the White House. In Florida, the so-called "Elián factor"[2] proved decisive, banding Cubans together in opposition to Democratic candidate Al Gore. The decision to return the six-year-old boat child to his father in Cuba—after the death of his mother in Florida waters—and the extreme force with which the young boy was removed from his Miami relatives' home in Pequeña Havana, motivated the Cuban community to vote against Al Gore.

The Democratic presidential candidate had maintained an ambivalent position with respect to Elián, and he refused to publicly criticize the operation to return the boy to Cuba which had been

---

[2] Elián González was one of three survivors of a shipwreck off the Florida coast. He floated in the ocean for fifty hours until he was rescued by two fishermen on November 25, 1999. One hundred and fifty days later, INS agents stormed the González house in Miami and took Elián by force in order to reunite him with his father.

endorsed by then-president Bill Clinton. The one who came out ahead was Bush, and he is well aware of it.

In his first television interview as president, George W. Bush told me that the Cuban vote was key to his winning the controversial election.

"Do you think you won the election because of the Cuban vote in Florida?" I asked him.

"Yes, I think they had a lot to do with it. And I'm most proud and very thankful and very grateful for the strong support I received *de los cubanos en el estado de Florida. Y por eso no voy a olvidarlos.*"

And he has not forgotten them. As president, Bush has promised to maintain the embargo against Cuba and not to establish new diplomatic or commercial contacts with Fidel Castro's dictatorship. This too, however, forms part of a long-term strategy to court the Latino vote for the 2004 elections.

Cubans are not the only ones being courted. Bush also ordered the U.S. Navy to leave the island of Vieques in 2003, an issue of great importance to Puerto Ricans. Furthermore, he began negotiations with the new government of Mexican president Vicente Fox with the intention of legalizing the status of millions of undocumented immigrants in the United States; almost every Mexican family or Mexican-American family includes someone with immigration problems.

Bush's calculations were correct. He obtained 31 percent of the Hispanic vote on November 7, 2000. If Bush is able to get 37 percent of the Latino vote in 2004, as Ronald Reagan did, the Democratic Party will be hard-pressed to find a candidate who can derail his reelection.

THE REASON FOR THIS BOOK

I make up part of the 20 million Mexicans who decided to live abroad because of the corruption and lack of opportunities; and of the more than one million Cubans who didn't want to be accomplices to Fidel Castro's dictatorship; and of the millions of Salvadorans, Guatemalans, and Nicaraguans who fled from war; and of the hundreds of thousands of Colombians who didn't want their children to live with the violence of drug traffickers, rebels, soldiers, and the paramilitary; and of the Venezuelans who distrusted their populist, authoritarian governments; and the South Americans who didn't want to get a kick in the head; and the Haitians and Dominicans who tried to escape poverty in a small boat or yawl. I am one of the 150 million people in this world who live in a country other than the country in which they were born. This is the group to which I belong, the group that is depicted in this book: immigrants, Hispanics, Latin Americans, those who have just arrived in this country.

This is not a history book but rather a book of many histories. In this book, as narrator and journalist, I am often the voice of those who have none, of those who are afraid, of those who work—and suffer—in silence.

I must confess that each time I thought I had put the final period on this book, another idea came to mind, another story to tell, another statistic, another abuse to denounce, another suspicion that I am not treating everyone fairly. I am left with that strange feeling that this is only a glimpse at a phenomenon—that of the immigrant—that is overtaking us and that we are just beginning to understand.

What I am presenting here is the other face of America, the one that many Americans and foreigners alike do not see, the one that is a victim of discrimination and exploitation just for being different, just for coming from somewhere else, and the one that is essential for understanding how to live—and survive—in the United States.

THE OTHER
FACE OF
AMERICA

FROM THE SOUTH TO THE NORTH:
STORIES OF MEXICAN IMMIGRANTS

1 THE BORDER

Tijuana, Baja, California. It was cold, very cold. I was walking toward the border like a zombie, as if a magnet were pulling me to the other side and I had no will to resist. I was here, but I didn't really want to be here. Others just like me were also approaching the border, slowly, gently, but firmly, their eyes fixed on the horizon of bushes and plains. That is where I had to go. Over there. Then, just before we got there, we stopped dead in our tracks. There it was in front of us, the fence, and on the other side, the United States. The fence was a mass of metal about three yards high and full of holes. They spent all that money for that? I thought. In the places where the wire fence wasn't broken, it would have been easy to dig a hole and crawl underneath. No problem. "This fence won't stop anyone," I said aloud. About three hundred yards in front of us, a few men dressed in green, who were standing next to a patrol car, were staring at us through some binoculars. They were so far away that it was like watching characters on a television screen. But they could surely see our fatigue, detect our red, fearful eyes, and read our determination to outwit them. The people next to me squatted, like when you want to go to the bathroom and there is none. They waited. The plan of each one there—and there were hundreds—was quite simple: wait for the immigration police to get tired and leave, or wait for the change of shift. After all, there was nowhere else to go and it was only ten o'clock at night. I sat down too. Now the only thing I wanted to know was how did they think they were going to cross the border and where, when, who to stick with and who to lose. I felt the cold through my pants. My jacket was thick but was not keeping me warm. It was then that I remembered the words of my sister, Lourdes: "I was cold inside." I was cold inside too. I drank some watered-down coffee, but it didn't help. Damn cold, damn cold, damn cold, I repeated over and over, as if hoping that the repetition would warm me. I began to shiver. Others were shivering too, but I don't know if it was because of the cold or because they were thinking about what they had left behind. Families had been reduced to black-and-white photographs in a wallet. There were the photos of the little boy who no longer cried and the wife who no longer kissed and the father who no longer smiled, right next to the card showing the image of the Virgin. They didn't really want to leave. Later on, though, they would remember why they were there—the lack of work: "In Mexico *no hay jale*." In the meantime, all eyes continued to wait, watching for the man in green to blink, the jeep to move, a moment of carelessness. The bright lights from the U.S. side—which reminded me of those in Azteca stadium in Mexico City—fought against the moonless night. All of a sudden, jaws clenched, stomachs became flat as boards, and veins bulged from necks. I was uneasy and began to breathe quickly. The moment to cross had come. Change of shift. You could hear clearly the sound of the jeep starting, and soon the vroom of the engine disappeared. Everyone on our side began to move, as if choreographed; first bent over, and then, once standing, they took off running. I stopped. I touched my pants pocket, and at once I felt different. It was the lump from my Mexican passport and my green card. Just in case. The others moved off until they were only shadows, and I stood there, thinking how screwed up life is.

THE NIGHT I APPROACHED the border, still on the Mexican side, there was a man selling plastic bags.

"Plastic bags to cross the border?" I asked one of the boys there. "What for?"

"So you don't get your pants wet, *ñero*," he replied. Then he added that when you are in Gringoland it's not a good idea if the *migra* realizes that you have just crossed the border. That could mean a ticket straight to jail.

The sale of bags was not a great business, but it provided enough to live on. Likewise, on small charcoal grills and in buckets filled with ice, others were selling *taquitos* and drinks to remedy the hunger of those about to cross *el bordo*. That's what it was called there. It must be one of those words that found its way into the new Spanglish dictionary due to so much repetition.

It's not difficult to find someone to talk to on the border. Hundreds of people, scattered along the border, looked toward the north as if they were waiting for a signal to cross. There is, however, a nervousness in the air, the tension of those who know that in a few minutes they are going to risk their necks, something akin to how soldiers must feel when they are about to initiate an attack.

The conversations are about only one thing: When are you going to cross? Has the *migra* caught you before? Where is it the easiest? Are you going alone or with a coyote? Strangely, the most relaxed time is when they can see the border police on the other side, which means that at that moment no one can cross.

"Why are you leaving Mexico?" I asked a young man who had several day's growth of hair on his face and wore a white shirt that had not been white for some time.

"You can't live on the minimum wage here," he said. "Anyone with one or two children can't support himself," he said, his eyes projecting the conviction of knowing one is facing the inevitable. Many undertook the risk alone. But others preferred the help of a coyote or *pollero*. They are easy to spot. People approach them, they give instructions, and they almost never look you in the eye.

It was not difficult to win the trust of one of them. Moreover, the one I spoke with seemed to be quite proud of what he was doing. "The deal is made here," he confided to me, "and then over there, after you deliver the immigrant to his house, he gives you the cash."

The *polleros* do not work alone. They have their helpers. One of them was Antonio, a ten-year-old boy wearing a red T-shirt. The coyotes would give him forty dollars to distract the *migra* so a group could cross. Antonio explained his job to me: "I make the agents chase me, so they move off their spots."

The coyotes are known for being abusive, for causing many deaths, and for leaving hungry, thirsty, penniless immigrants in the middle of the desert. But the police are not looked upon much more favorably. One Mexican who was preparing to cross the border told me straight out, "Instead of protecting you, the police [in Tijuana] abuse you so they can take your money and everything else."

There has been a disturbing change in the profile of the immigrant in recent years. Here I not only saw young men, I saw entire families with children, single women, and old people. Researchers suggest, too, that the stereotype of the Mexican emigrant from the countryside or Mexican farmer has changed. Immigrants nowadays are more urban, they have more schooling and more resources than those who came before them, and if possible, they travel with the entire family.

On the other side, in San Ysidro, California, a well-armed agent, Ray Ortega, took me with him in his jeep to show me how they pursue undocumented immigrants. The contrast was powerful. Cameras with infrared rays, telescopic lenses, armored vehicles, support helicopters, continuous communication. As we drove along and saw the shadows trying to hide from us on the border, I asked agent Ortega about the accusations of abuse against immigrants by the U.S. border patrol. His answer was well rehearsed. "They are allegations," he said, "but when those allegations are made we investigate them."

(I would like to explain here that I do not believe that the Immigration and Naturalization Service [INS] is filled with evil or ill-intentioned people. Of course not. But I do believe that their work is ephemeral, futile, loaded with power, and in some cases useless.)

As Carlos Fuentes said, the border between Mexico and the United States is a scar. It is a wound that won't heal. It was imposed by force, it bleeds continuously, and it is violated millions of times a year.

The abuses by the border patrol are difficult to document. However, Roberto Martinez, of the American Friends Service Committee, was able to do so. In his office, he showed me several cases he had investigated. Nevertheless, his work has taken a high personal toll. Shortly after our interview, he received threats against his life.

"What did they say to you?" I asked.

"That if I don't stop denouncing and criticizing the border patrol they will kill me."

Jorge Bustamante, the director of the Colegio de la Frontera Norte, agrees with Martinez that undocumented immigrants are often mistreated. "Racism," he said, "is a permanent element of U.S. society." Bustamante believes that the most dangerous time for undocumented Mexicans and Central Americans is when the United States is in a recession. Then, he stated, the immigrant becomes a scapegoat. "They begin to blame us for all the problems and disasters, from the economic crises, unemployment, drug trafficking, AIDS, to the common cold. They blame us for everything."

But regardless of the danger and the abuse, every afternoon on the border that separates Tijuana from San Ysidro, hundreds of people gather, ready to change their fate with a leap, or two, or three.

"And what will you do if they catch you?" I asked a Mexican boy who was about to try and flee to the North.

"They just send us back," he said. "They throw us out once, and we go back again."

POSTSCRIPT: Throughout the combined history of Mexico and the United States, there have been many different attempts by the U.S. government to control the flow of undocumented Mexicans to the north. They have all failed. What has remained constant, however, is the experimenting with different methods to fill in some of the holes on the border.

One of those experiments was Operation Gatekeeper, announced on October 2, 1994. The operation was based on a very simple assumption: If you put more agents on the border, the number of undocumented immigrants who attempt to cross will decline. Hundreds of agents were hired, and others were transferred from office jobs to the field. Similar experiments had had relative success in Tucson, Arizona, and El Paso, Texas. Success for the INS meant a greater number of arrests.

There were, in fact, more arrests. But just as a torrent of water can find its way around a brick, the immigrants skirted the most heavily guarded spots. What Operation Gatekeeper did do was to force the immigrants to use more dangerous routes: deserts, mountains, areas without water or means of communication. The immigrants kept crossing anyway, and the deaths along the border, due to dehydration, cold, thirst, hunger or crime, began to multiply.

Operation Gatekeeper was based on the false premise that undocumented immigration is a problem of the law and its enforcement. It doesn't matter how many officers the United States puts on its border or how many fences they build; as long as there are jobs in the north for workers from the south, there will continue to be undocumented immigration.

President George W. Bush, two-time governor of the border state of Texas, did not indulge in wishful thinking regarding migration to the north. In a 1999 interview he told me:

> I understand why their parents are here. Their parents are here to put food on the table. People come from Mexico to all across America to work. Family values do not stop at *la frontera*. Family values, dads and moms love their sons and daughters in Mexico as well as in the United States and other places. And so if you've got a child that's going hungry and you're looking for work, and you can make fifty cents in the interior of Mexico or fifty dollars in the interior of the United States, you're gonna come for fifty dollars if you are a hardworking, loving dad. And so I understand.

The continuous flow from south to north across the Mexican–U.S. border has shown no sign of abating. The first fifteen days of the year are essential for the INS in determining how the flow of undocumented immigrants from south to north will unfold throughout the year. The first fifteen days in January 2000 broke all previous records. On the more than twenty-five miles of border between the towns of Agua Prieta and Douglas, Arizona, for example, 14,664 undocumented immigrants were arrested during the first two weeks in January 2000 (according to figures provided by the INS and reported by the *New York Times*). This is almost double the number recorded in 1999.

The Mexican government keeps other statistics. Since Operation Gatekeeper went into effect along the Mexican–U.S. border, the number of arrests has increased, as has the number of Mexicans who die trying to enter the United States illegally. From 1995 to early

2000, there were at least 717 deaths. This occurred because the rein-
forced vigilance and the considerable increase in border patrol officers, who guarded certain spots on the border, forced the future
immigrant to take more risks. Therefore, they attempted to cross in
places where extreme temperatures prevailed and where it was necessary to walk for several days in order to reach a U.S. town. This is
the domain of the coyote.

2 AMELIA AND SAN GUIVI

Compton, California. Every time I heard the former governor of California, Pete Wilson, speak, I knew that she was going to suffer. It was a kind of anti-migration voodoo. Wilson's threats made Amelia's first few years in the United States much more difficult.

Amelia lives near Los Angeles, and she came to the United States in the early 1980s. Like millions before her, she crossed the border between Tijuana and San Diego, outwitting the helicopters and the border patrol officers. She crossed with the help of a coyote, as she pulled her ten-year-old daughter by the hand. (Even today, she gets nervous when she hears the noise of helicopter propellers overhead.)

Amelia used to live in Michoacán, Mexico, on what she called a *ranchito*. She remembers vividly how her father was murdered over a dispute involving land. She also well remembers the time her husband told her he was going to the north. And he did, never to return, leaving her with two children to support. It was then that she made the most difficult decision of her life: She too would head north.

Sobbing and barely able to breathe, Amelia asked her mother to take care of her younger child, and she left for California with her daughter. When she arrived, she was lucky to have the support of her sister and her family, who had come to California before her. But she didn't stop worrying until she was able to send for her son and her mother.

She worked for more than two years to earn enough money to send for them. As a team, grandmother and grandson followed the route that Amelia had mapped out for them, and they walked for miles, dodging the *migra*, until they crossed over into the United States.

The boy has still not forgiven Amelia for leaving him in Mexico. The grandmother spoke of how he would sit at the front door of their house every day, waiting for his mother to come for him.

I am telling you Amelia's story because there are millions like her in the United States. I was surprised when Mr. Wilson, using warlike terminology, said that California was in a state of siege because of the undocumented immigrants, and the face I associated with that group was Amelia's. Why did Pete Wilson want to wage war against that woman?

WILSON'S NUMBERS DON'T ADD UP

When things are going badly, any trick is fair game for some politicians. The economic situation in California was not good during Wilson's administration, but this was not because of the immigrants, as many would have liked us to believe. According to Wilson, undocumented immigrants were costing the state much more than what they were contributing to it. But he was wrong.

Forgive me, but I am going to have to do a bit of math in order to demonstrate that Wilson and other xenophobes were mistaken. To remove any doubt, we are going to use a study, published in 1992, carried out by Los Angeles County itself. The study said that immigrants who arrived here after 1980 cost the county of Los Angeles $2.5 billion in medical services, education, and other benefits during the 1991 fiscal year. That is what the anti-immigrant demagogues shouted from the rooftops.

They had subtracted very well, but they had forgotten to add.

Those very same immigrants whom they had been so quick to criticize contributed $4.3 billion in taxes that same year. So Los Angeles County, the state of California, and the federal government wound up earning $1.8 billion, thanks to the immigrants in that region. It is a matter of adding and subtracting. It seems to me like a very profitable business. Of course, the pie is not divided evenly among the different government agencies, but the immigrants are not to blame for that, either.

Many in the United States think that the real motive behind the persecution of undocumented immigrants is racism and ignorance. But there is more. It seems that many politicians—Democrats and Republicans alike—have found no better scapegoat for their incompetence than to blame a segment of the population that will not complain for fear of being deported.

Perhaps former governor Wilson was alarmed because California was changing so much. The fact is, the skin color of its inhabitants has not been white for quite some time. But there was nothing he could do about it. Hispanics already are the largest minority in the United States. What's more, without the help of immigrants, California would come to a standstill. We need only bear in mind the thousands of jobs generated by the mere presence of immigrants in this country.

Contrary to popular belief, undocumented immigrants do not take jobs away from U.S. citizens. Without those immigrants, the United States would cease to be the leading agricultural power in the world. Nor do immigrants take advantage of the state. Only 4 percent of those who have just arrived apply for welfare or federal assistance. They are loyal customers. They work as few others do, and they pay taxes every time they buy something. They create businesses. They impart vitality to the cities where they live, and they contribute an incalculable cultural richness.

Sometimes Mr. Wilson forgets that his family came from another country, too. He wanted to prohibit children of immigrants from becoming U.S. citizens automatically, even though they were born on U.S. soil. To start with, he would have had to change the Constitution. But in the meantime, like it or not, Wilsons, Reagans, Clintons, and Bushes were blending in with Rodriguezes, Gonzaleses, Suarezes, and Gomezes.

As long as the economic disparity between north and south exists,

there will continue to be immigrants like Amelia. She is a courageous, hardworking, dedicated person who is an excellent example of
a Latina fighting for a better life for herself and her children. The former governor was afraid of her and wanted to send her back home.

In the end, as things turned out, it was Wilson who left and
Amelia who stayed.

THE CHILDREN

We'll call them Margarita and Enrique, just to be safe, just in case
the *migra* (as some affectionately call the U.S. Immigration and
Naturalization Service) decides to play detective and looks for
them in order to deport them. They live with their mother in Los
Angeles County. The father had left them years before, telling
them he was going to the north. He never returned, nor did he
send any money.

Margarita is twenty-one years old. It was ten years ago that her
mother, with very little emotion, announced that they were going to
the United States. They gathered together some of their things from
their *ranchito* in Michoacán, and early one morning set off in a bus
for Tijuana. After many anguishing moments, dodging helicopters
and "a few men dressed in green wearing dark glasses," they arrived
in Los Angeles. It was there I met them.

Enrique is sixteen years old. He was very small when his mother
and sister came to California, so he was left in the care of his grandmother. Enrique would wait, but his mother never came back. So, in
a moment of desperation, his grandmother nailed a few pieces of
wood over the doors and windows of the house, hid the dollars she
had in her shirt, clutched her grandson by the hand, and took off for
California.

Enrique followed the same route that his sister Margarita had,
only with his grandmother and without a coyote, for which they did
not have enough money. Enrique and his grandmother crossed the
border successfully on their first attempt. When Enrique finally saw
his mother after the two-year absence, the first thing he did was scold
her: "Why didn't you come for me?" he asked.

She just hugged him and said nothing.

We stayed in touch over the years. One day I spoke with them by
phone and noticed that Margarita and Enrique were losing their
Spanish. Margarita proudly told me in Spanglish that she wanted to

get into "college," and Enrique couldn't bear the idea of going to "high school."

Since she was a little girl, there was always one thing on Margarita's mind: She wanted a party for her fifteenth birthday, a *quinceañera*. "That's my dream," she told me. Well, thanks to the efforts of her mother and the help of several godparents, Margarita celebrated her fifteenth birthday in a big way. She sent me a photo of the party, and she looked beautiful, so happy. There was mole and *pozole*, technomusic and *quebradita*.

With memories of the party still fresh in her mind, a new obsession overtook Margarita. She wanted to be the first person in her family to attend a university. But how was she going to study at a university if undocumented immigrants like her were not allowed to enroll?

Years later, she was accepted by the prestigious University of California in Los Angeles (UCLA), but since she had no Social Security number, she could not enroll. When she told me this, I didn't know what to say. I put her in touch with a lawyer I knew, and when I hung up, there was a lump in my throat.

What politician would think of proposing a law that prohibits the most qualified young people in the state from studying because their parents don't have the correct documentation? Where are all the names of the legislators who prevented Margarita of Michoacán from being able to attend UCLA? Who among them would dare to look her in the face and tell her she does not have the right to continue studying? Who?

No one is questioning the right of the United States to control its borders. But there are millions of undocumented immigrants in this country who have already contributed to U.S. society with their taxes, their work, and their culture. They deserve to be treated with respect and to be considered for amnesty.

Amnesty would allow Margarita to continue studying. Thousands of young people are in the United States illegally, not because of a decision they made, but because their parents brought them here. Perhaps they should be held responsible, as minors, for the acts committed by adults? What they need is to be given legal status, not to be prohibited from continuing their education. That is not the way. Margarita and Enrique, Amelia's children, have earned the right to live with respect in the United States, even though many may not like it.

ENRIQUE AND THE GANGS

It was inevitable that things would not turn out well for Enrique. He was reprimanded several times by his school for truancy as well as for tardiness. He stopped doing his homework and one day just decided that he didn't want to study anymore. He eventually dropped out of school. His mother, his aunts and uncles, everyone tried to make him think it over, but it was no use.

Enrique gets up late, wears pants that are two or three sizes too big, and doesn't work. When he's hungry, he grabs something from the kitchen and goes out to meet his friends. Those who care about him most feared he was involved with a gang. Those who care about him least believe he could be mixed up with drugs. Everyone knew he was in trouble.

He was still a minor, and his mother didn't dare kick him out of the house. "Where would he go?" Amelia said to me. When he became violent and defied his family, his mother didn't know what to do. "Who can I call?" Amelia, worried, told me one night. "If I call the police, they will treat him like a criminal, or they will deport him because he doesn't even have a Social Security number. They'll send him back home and he'll be even angrier."

I spoke with him on the phone one day, and I told him that if he kept getting into trouble with his friends and with the police, he ran the risk of being deported to Mexico, where he now had no one. "Yeah, yeah," he said. But his sister told me that after talking to me, he left the house without looking back. He didn't even turn to say good-bye.

Many gave up on Enrique. But his mother, Amelia, who had not finished grammar school but who had infallible instincts, did not, and she came up with a solution. Move away, far away, from Enrique's friends, so that going to see them would be a marathon journey.

So far, the solution has worked like a charm. For now, Enrique has stopped seeing his pals. He has not gone back to school, but he is working part-time in a store. Only time will tell if it will last. In the meantime, Amelia prays to San Guivi, the patron saint of immigrants.

SAN GUIVI

Amelia had never imagined that one of her children would be a "gringo." (She uses this word innocently, with no intention of offending anyone.) She was further surprised that she, with her thick, dark brown hair, would now have a little blond boy. What can you do; the boy looks like his father.

Amelia is one of the best examples in the United States today of what it means to be a hard-working immigrant, with ideals but without "papers." Amelia and her large family—as I mentioned before she was welcomed with open arms when she arrived from Mexico—still eat *pozole* on holidays. They have not lost that tradition, nor that of piñatas, baptizing their babies, or going to church on Sundays. Normally, they gather at Amelia's sister Felicidad's house. Felicidad always has tortillas and one or two hot salsas in the refrigerator. *Muy hot*, as one of the many children running around the house says. They brought their recipes and their religion from Mexico. But in other areas, they have quickly adapted to this country.

Until fairly recently, several families were living together in the two rooms of Felicidad's house, from newborns to a grandmother who could never remember how old she was. It was a house where three generations—two Mexican and the other half-American—searched for their space. The children and three teenagers spoke English with each other, and with their parents they used an amusing Spanglish. The girls plucked their eyebrows so they were pencil thin. I had the feeling they were trying to look like the singer, Selena.

Little by little the roles have changed. Until not long ago it was the adults who had control. But as many of them speak no English, the children have become official translators. Every time there is a problem with the electric company or they want to buy something on the Internet or look for work, it is the children who pick up the phone or sit in front of the computer and take care of it. They have grown up faster than they would have liked, but they had no choice. Sometimes they are translators, sometimes they look after babies, and other times they are psychologists consoling their parents when they argue or have problems. In such tight quarters, you hear everything.

When the mothers or aunts answer the phone, they no longer say *"Bueno?"* like in Mexico. Now they say "Hello?" They buy their clothing at Kmart and in neighborhood shops. The men are more reluctant to change. They continue to wear hats and boots, as if they were still in the fields of Michoacán.

Amelia's family has it all—undocumented immigrants, legal residents, and U.S. citizens. Those who were eligible for and availed themselves of the 1986 amnesty flaunt their green cards. Amelia's youngest son is a U.S. citizen by birth, even though she has not been able to legalize her own status. Nevertheless, she soon intends to marry the son's father, Luis, who already has his legal documents. It looks like Amelia will have a baby, a husband, and a green card, all at the same time.

I tell you this story so that you can see how, little by little, they have all integrated into life in the United States. Amelia and her famliy are a perfect example of what was revealed in a study carried out by the University of Southern California. The study concluded that immigrants in California are acclimating quickly to life in the U.S., learning English, and escaping poverty at an unprecedented rate. Seven of every ten children who came from Latin America in the 1970s can speak and write in English today without any problems.

Furthermore, immigrant families like Amelia's are a profitable business for the United States. Every immigrant family contributes annually much more to the government than what it receives in social services. And far from taking jobs away from others in the United States, they create jobs. In short, immigrants in the United States are improving their standard of living and adapting quickly to this society, despite the attacks and laws that are frequently used in an attempt to hold them back.

One of the most telling examples I have of the adaptation process was given to me by Amelia several years ago. The story goes like this. Amelia was about to celebrate Thanksgiving Day here in the United States. She had just arrived in the United States, but she was very interested in the upcoming holiday and wanted to know what I was planning to do for San Guivi.

"San Guivi?" I asked, puzzled.

"Yes, San Guivi, that saint that they pay tribute to here," she replied.

Amelia, who did not know any English then, had changed Thanksgiving to San Guivi, because phonetically the words are similar. That was how she joined the most traditional lay celebration in this country to her world, which was full of saints. She wanted to integrate quickly, and she did, in her way. It was the only way she could give meaning to something so new.

Of course, today Amelia knows that Thanksgiving Day has nothing to do with any saint. But for me the story of San Guivi has become the best example of how immigrants adapt to life in the north. She may have been a bit confused, but Amelia had turkey and cranberries on her first Thanksgiving Day in the United States.

POSTSCRIPT: 1993 and 1994 must have been the worst years for immigrants in the United States. A survey conducted in July of 1993 by *Newsweek* magazine reflected the anti-immigrant sentiment of the time. Of those surveyed, 59 percent thought that immigration had been a good or positive thing in the United States in the past. However, 60 percent thought that current immigration was a bad thing.

The context of the answers was the disappearance of the idea of the melting pot, where all immigrants would put aside their innate differences and so transform the United States into a united country. Of those surveyed, 66 percent believed that immigrants today maintain their identity and do not integrate into the rest of the nation.

Time magazine published a similar survey in November 1993. It reported that "immigrant backlash is particularly strong," and stated that 64 percent of those surveyed believed that immigrants took jobs away from U.S. citizens; 59 percent were convinced that new immigrants were contributing to the crime problem. Moreover, three out of every four (73 percent) felt it necessary to "strictly limit immigration" to the United States, an increase from 67 percent, who felt that way in 1985.

3 FALSIFYING THE FUTURE

Los Angeles. Ricardo and Jorge Alberto are counterfeiters. For $80 they can make you a green card and give you a Social Security number. If you drive along Alvarado Street, across from Mac-Arthur Park in central L.A., you'll find them there. In just twenty-four hours, they can transform an undocumented immigrant into a documented one—with forged papers, but documented, nonetheless.

The other day, as I was waiting to make a television appearance, they approached me. The camera did not scare them.

"Hey, Ramos, what are you doing around here?" they asked.

"Not much," I said, "just a report about immigration."

"Ah, that's good."

"What about you?" I asked, raising the ante.

"Here we are, *en el jale*."

For them, *"el jale"* meant giving someone who has no papers the chance to work, and earning a few dollars in the process. Ricardo and Jorge Alberto do not see themselves as criminals, rather they feel they are artists, missionaries, and businessmen, all at the same time.

"The *migra* doesn't come around here?" I asked.

"No, they never show up around here."

"What about the police?"

"Well, they come by, but they don't bother us."

Technological advances don't worry them. The immigration service has been experimenting with a small machine that can identify forged green cards on the spot. A well-known taquería in Los Angeles is already using it to verify the documents of those applying for jobs. But Ricardo and Jorge Alberto have a knack for their work. They make photocopies of legitimate green cards and, according to them, the new system can't detect them.

"When they go, we come," one of them said proudly. His mocking smile revealed his rotting teeth.

"What about the Social Security numbers? How do you come up with those?" I asked.

"Well, we get the number of a family member or a friend who has already left the country, or we get it from some dead guy, and that's that."

In recent years, a new California state law has given Jorge and Ricardo more work. The law prohibits drivers' licenses from being issued to those who cannot prove they are in the United States legally. So, naturally, they now forge drivers' licenses, too.

Their business is well organized. Ricardo is the boss. His neat, slicked-back hair falls to his neck. When I spoke with him, his bright green shirt was open to his belly. From behind his dark glasses he controls his boys, three or four of them. Jorge Alberto is his hanger-on, his assistant. Their territory is only half a block of Alvarado Street, but they work it hard. The merchants on the other side of the street know them well.

Their body language gives them away. With the thumb and index finger they make the shape of a card and shout *"mica!"* to everyone who passes by, whether in a car or on foot. They carry samples of their work in their pockets. Not even the best trained eye can detect that the *micas* they are offering are fake.

Whoever is in need of their services must first have a photo taken at a place that only they know. Later, the photo is given to another guy who makes the card or the license or whatever it is they need. They didn't tell me who the other guy was. They protect him like gold.

"The most important thing is that the photo not look like it's glued on," Jorge Alberto told me. A professional secret, I suppose. In just a day or two, they can fix your "situation," and for everyone who arrives without papers, the "situation" is being unable to work.

The law of supply and demand is on their side. It is estimated that more than 300,000 people remain in the United States each year illegally. With or without the Free Trade Agreement, they keep coming. With or without earthquakes. They come for dollars, for themselves, and for their families. Their priority is not that the U.S. government pay the doctors and the hospital bill in the event they get sick. They don't want charity either. They want to work.

A study by the University of California, Davis, confirms this. The study concluded that undocumented immigrants come for work, not for social services. Moreover, the majority do not request government assistance. One, because they don't speak English. Two, because they are afraid of being deported. And, three, because they don't even know how to get access to these services. Period. So for starters, we must put aside these myths. Undocumented immigrants do not take jobs away from U.S. citizens. Proportionally, there are more immigrants in Switzerland, Australia, Germany, and Canada than there are in the United States. The problem is pure xenophobia.

The long-term solution lies in tying U.S. foreign policy to the immigration problem. Not to do so is to follow the ostrich policy, burying its head in the face of a monumental problem. But in the short term, those who are profiting are people like Ricardo and Jorge Alberto. No, they are not angels. They are breaking the law. But I can't forget what they said to me before they left: "We are just giving people a chance to work." That is the first thing someone who comes to the north wants.

POSTSCRIPT: Those who do not properly counterfeit their future—or those who are caught doing so—can end up like the Salvadoran Julio Pérez, whom I met at a detention center for undocumented immigrants in El Centro, California. He was one of the more than four hundred immigrants recently arrested in roundups. His fate was inevitable. He would be sent back to his country as soon as possible. He lamented, "I don't want to be deported because my country is so bad off now." No one properly counterfeited Julio's future.

4 A DAY WITHOUT A MEXICAN

What would happen if all of a sudden all the Mexicans who lived in the United States disappeared? Yes, all of them, the more than 7 million Mexicans who were born in Mexico but live here in the United States.

A similar question crossed the mind of film director Sergio Arau, and through what he called a "false documentary," he tried to answer it. I saw several scenes from the movie and what stood out, with both humor and insight, was the enormous importance of the Latino population in the United States. Giving an original twist to one of the most overused sayings—"You never know what you have until you lose it"—Arau has managed to capture on film what many have thought and hinted at for years: If all the Mexicans disappeared for a day, the U.S. economy would be seriously hindered.

The movie focuses on what would happen if all the Mexicans in the state of California, where most Mexicans in the United States live, suddenly and inexplicably disappeared. Let's try and imagine this.

A day without a Mexican in California would mean losses in the millions in the orange, avocado, lettuce, and grape industries. Supermarkets would be without fruits and vegetables, and wine shops without those famous California whites and reds. (According to the 1990 census, slightly less than 15 percent of all Mexicans in the United States, legal and undocumented, work in agriculture.)

A day without a Mexican in California would mean a complete halt in the construction and garment industries, among many others. (Approximately 35 percent of Mexicans in the United States work in these sectors.)

A day without a Mexican in California would show that hotels, restaurants, stores, markets, gas stations, and offices depend on those workers who cross the southern border of the United States. (More than half of Mexicans in the United States are employed in the service industry.)

A day without a Mexican in California would mean that thousands of English-speaking men and women would not be able to go to work because their nannies would not show up to take care of their children and babies.

A day without a Mexican in California would leave the television and radio stations with the largest audiences in the Los Angeles area—which transmit in Spanish, although few are aware of this—without viewers or listeners.

A day without a Mexican in California would give the false impression that the official language in the United States is English.

A day without a Mexican in California would mean canceled operations because doctors would not arrive, unkept court appointments because lawyers would not show up, and unfulfilled commitments because of absent executives.

Contrary to the trite stereotype that all Mexicans in the United States are poorly educated and are gardeners and work in the fields, the 1990 census revealed that there were 3,869 immigrants, born in Mexico, who held doctorate degrees. That tears the stereotype to shreds. It is worth mentioning that Mexican labor, in U.S. fields and gardens, just as in the assembly plants on the border, is considered among the best and most efficient in the world.

This exercise of magical migration where we make more than

7 million Mexicans disappear just like that can be applied to other Hispanic groups in the United States with the same results. For example, what would become of Miami without the Cubans and Nicaraguans? Or New York without the Puerto Ricans and Dominicans? Or New Orleans without the Hondurans? Or Los Angeles without the Salvadorans and Guatemalans? What would become of the U.S. Army without the 7.9 percent of its soldiers who call themselves "Latinos"? Unfortunately, the positive impact of the presence of the more than 30 million Hispanics in the United States is not always recognized and appreciated by the rest of the population, despite their enormous cultural, social, and economic contributions.

Nevertheless, there are people who do not want us here in the United States. I received a phone call from a young man who had heard about the subject of Arau's movie—*A Day without a Mexican*—and he had the arrogance to tell me that, deep down, nothing would make him happier than if all Mexicans were to disappear from the map. Naturally, I hung up on him before he had finished speaking, so he would see for himself just what would happen if all Mexicans in the United States disappeared for a day. I wouldn't be surprised if the dreams of former California governor Pete Wilson and the xenophobic conservative Pat Buchanan were just like the wishes of that impertinent man who called me.

The United States has still not accepted its multiethnic and multicultural makeup. It has still not realized—or simply does not want to recognize—that the children in our families are not all white anymore. The "little brown ones," as former President George Bush said of his grandchildren of Hispanic origin—his son Jeb is married to a Mexican, Columba—are increasing in number.

It is a shame that Arau's short film was turned down by the organizers of the main film festivals in the United States. *A Day without a Mexican* would reveal to many in the United States the country they are really living in, a country far from the black-and-white one they have instilled in their minds.

POSTSCRIPT: The ultraconservative politician Pat Buchanan would enjoy a day without a Mexican in the United States. In a 1995 television interview (which was quoted by the *New York Times*), the eternally unsuccessful presidential candidate, when asked what he would do should he get to the White House, said, "I will stop illegal immigration cold by putting a double-linked security fence along the two hundred miles of the border where millions pour in every year."

There are three errors, however, in that argument. First, if Buchanan wants to put up a double-linked fence along two hundred miles of border, what will he do along the other 1,800 miles? Second, Buchanan does not understand that undocumented immigration is a problem of supply and demand of jobs, not laws and fences. Buchanan's third error is that with such racist views, he will never be president of a multicultural country such as the United States.

That is a relief.

5 ASPEN FOR THE UNDOCUMENTED

Aspen, Colorado. In the winter it is probably one of the most expensive towns in the world, and it prospers as much from the stream of dollars from its visitors as from the efforts of its undocumented immigrants. Some—the wealthy—enjoy themselves, while others—the undocumented—work so the others can enjoy themselves. Such is the division of labor in Aspen.

For those with money, Aspen is sensational. How much money? A lot. A double room in one of the best hotels—the Little Nell or the old Ritz Carlton (now an ITT Sheraton)—can cost more than $600 a night. Dining out can also be a big investment, especially if you have reservations at Kenichi, an eclectic Japanese restaurant where they serve Peking duck on something similar to a Mexican taco, or at Bang, a trendy place that combines Asian ingredients with French recipes in a cool atmosphere. If eating and sleeping are expensive, skiing requires a small fortune. The ticket alone for the lift costs over

$50 a day at one of the four mountains in the area. That, of course, does not include skis, boots, goggles, scarf, and gloves—that is all extra. How about an après ski massage? Well, it'll cost you $80 for fifty minutes at the Aspen Club, tip included. Thank goodness.

Cold? Not a chance. I've never seen more fur coats per square mile. In other cities across the country, from Los Angeles to New York, anyone who dares to wear mink or fox could end up with red paint joyfully sprayed on their coats by animal rights activists. But in Aspen, dressing in animal fur, even though it's politically incorrect and can cost over $10,000 per back, is the rule for the well-to-do.

This is the Aspen that you see—pleasant, laughing, glistening in the snow, the one that appears in music magazines and on entertainment programs. But there is another Aspen, the one you don't see, the one that is cold and works out of sight, that earns very little but enables everything to work. That is the Aspen of the undocumented.

They are everywhere. Immigrants from Mexico and Central America do the toughest jobs, the ones no U.S. citizen wants to do. Most of those immigrants do not, of course, have legal documents to work. But their employers apparently prefer to risk getting a fine from the U.S. Immigration Service than to have to pay higher wages. It is an unwritten agreement: I'll hire you and pay you a pittance; you will work, and no one will say anything to immigration authorities.

These immigrants are invisible to the Aspen visitors. Nevertheless, you need only open your eyes to realize that thanks to them the daily machine remains well oiled. For example, I met some girls from Michoacán who worked hard cleaning cabins for tourists, a group of Salvadorans who cooked cheeseburgers for skiers at the top of one of the mountains, and a couple of *chilangos* (as northern Mexicans call those from Mexico City) taking out the trash at one of the area's supermarkets.

Who looks after the skiers' children? Undocumented women, of course. They are unmistakable. They wear huge polyester jackets, tight jeans, cover their dark hair with wool hats, and they push their blond babies in strollers, red-faced and expressionless from the cold, wearing so much clothing it looks like their arms and legs are in casts.

These immigrants, who take care of babies, clean hotels and offices, and work in construction, would rather experience the cold in Aspen than hunger in Latin America. It is easy to understand. The minimum wage in Mexico barely reached four dollars a day at the turn of this century. They can make the same amount in less than an hour in the United States.

The cold, even if it falls below freezing, as it does in Aspen, is better than hunger. There is no mystery behind this: As long as there are millions of unemployed people in Latin American and a surplus of jobs in the United States, there will continue to be illegal immigration to the north. It is a question of supply and demand, not laws and borders.

Initially, the migration flow only reached certain places, like Seattle, San Antonio, and Chicago. But it has now spread like oil across the entire United States, and today there are undocumented immigrants in places like Omaha and Anchorage, as well as in Little Rock and Aspen.

Aspen has benefited enormously from these immigrants, despite the rednecks who still look at them with contempt and the pseudo-aristocracy who openly criticize them but use and abuse them without a second thought. As the last published study by the U.S. Census Bureau indicated, every place that has immigrants, including Aspen, is growing economically and generating new jobs. Without undocumented immigrants, this ski town would be stuck in the snow, even though many don't even know it.

POSTSCRIPT: An editorial in the *Denver Post*, reacting to a series of raids of undocumented immigrants in Colorado, reported that the undocumented immigrants were actually keeping our economy afloat. It was right. Without these workers, the United States would not be able to sustain the greatest economic growth in its history.

Ironically, in the not too distant future, the country with the most immigrants could be the one with the greatest probability of economic survival, maintaining its productivity and distribution of social benefits. According to an article in *Foreign Affairs* magazine (January–February 1999) by writer and businessman Peter G. Peterson, the oldest and richest of developed societies are going to need young immigrant workers in order to maintain their high standard of living and social benefits.

As Peterson predicted, the aging of societies is already occurring in the United States and in Europe, where fertility rates have fallen and the older population is increasing. In 2000, people older than sixty-five years of age made up 13 percent of the U.S. population; in 2033, this same group will constitute 20 percent of the total population.

Given this, who will work? Who will keep the economies' engines running? Who will pay for the retirement programs for the elderly? Young people and immigrants. Peterson said that "in many European countries, non-European foreigners already make up roughly 10 percent of the population." And about Germany he said, "Foreigners will make up 30 percent of the total population by 2030."

6 MATAMOROS, NEW YORK

New York. If things were all right in Matamoros, Puebla, there wouldn't be so many Mexicans in New York. But the reality is that things are not all right in Matamoros, or in Michoacán or in Monterrey or in . . .

Mexicans, poorly led by President Ernesto Zedillo—who refused to publicly discuss the country's great problems and who became increasingly immersed in the rigidness of his office—would no sooner find their way out of one crisis before encountering another. It has been this way since the early 1980s, when President José López Portillo vowed to defend the Mexican peso "like a dog." His success was such—the peso plummeted—that even today there are people who bark at him when he appears in a restaurant or some other public place.

With these periodic crises, I am not surprised that the exodus north continues, and particularly to a city like New York, where the

U.S. Immigration Service is having trouble distinguishing the legal immigrants from the undocumented ones, regardless of whether they are from Mexico or China. New York is a huge city where anyone can feel relatively safe from the INS, even though they may have swum across the Bravo River or come on a barge from Hong Kong. Of course, there are raids by the *migra*, but they are nothing compared to what takes place in Texas and California.

Oddly enough—and defying all stereotypes—I ran into dozens of my fellow countrymen in a bookstore on the Upper West Side of Manhattan. We were all looking for books, and we were freezing cold, our coats and jackets pulled up to our ears. The only difference was that I was *chilango* (from Mexico City), and they were from Matamoros, in Puebla. Most of them were young, single men who had left behind wives, girlfriends, parents, or children in Mexico, three, thirteen, or twenty-three years ago. Over the past decade, a route has been created, a kind of chain of family and friends, that has influenced entire generations of *Poblanos* to come to New York. (I have heard many times that the best *mole poblano* outside of Puebla can be found in New York restaurants.) There, in the bookstore, reliving the aromas and flavors of the past, the conversation naturally turned to Mexico.

"I miss it a lot," said one. "But we're better off here." I asked another if after ten years he felt like returning home, and he replied, "What for, if there is no work?"

These *Poblanos* have bet their dollars and their sweat on the chance to get a piece of the American dream, and their balloon hasn't burst yet. What about Mexico? Mexico was for before and maybe for later, for retirement, for showing photos to the grandchildren, for remembering the hotness and sweetness of mole. But not for now.

This group of Mexican immigrants in New York continue to cling, however, to their traditions. One December twelfth, when we all happened to be in New York, many of these Mexicans went to mass. Mass on Saturday afternoon? I asked them. "Well, it's the day of the Virgin of Guadalupe," one woman, who was well on in years, told me. "Where else are we going to go?" I found it strange that she would say that, for if there is a city where there are places to go, it is New York. But for her and her family, the options that Saturday afternoon were reduced to one: praying to the Virgin of Guadalupe.

Without a second thought, they passed up a shocking and tortu-
ous exhibition of the tormented alcoholic painter, Jackson Pollock, at
the Museum of Modern Art (MOMA). I didn't run into anyone from
Matamoros, Puebla, at the MOMA. Nor did they rush to see a show
that was causing quite a sensation on Broadway, *The Blue Room*, in
which the fair-skinned ex-wife of Tom Cruise, Nicole Kidman,
appeared naked. (I didn't see the show. It was sold out, and scalpers
were asking $1,400 per ticket. But I did read that several of the lucky
attendees arrived at the theater with binoculars in order to appreciate
every single freckle on the talented Australian actress.) No, Pollock
and Kidman are not part of the cultural language of most of the
Poblanos I ran into in New York. But it doesn't matter. They, along
with the Puerto Ricans, Dominicans, Ecuadoreans, Peruvians, and
Central Americans, are slowly transforming one of the most vibrant
metropolises in the world.

Entire sections of the United States are dominated by Spanish
and different versions of Spanglish. Hispanic media competes with
the English language media with growing success. There are an
increasing number of Latinos in elected offices, and those who think
that the United States is a country of white people should go to Central Park or Fifth Avenue to see that brown is the predominant shade.
The future of the United States depends on its recognizing itself as a
multiethnic and multicultural nation, and one of the first cities to
learn that lesson was New York.

After speaking with the *Poblanos* for a while, Matamoros, Puebla,
did not seem so far away. I don't know what it is like, although from
what they told me, I picture it to be a town with a plaza, lots of
women, and few jobs. With so many of its inhabitants here, however,
for a moment I felt as if I had immersed myself in a refuge of the
imagination called Matamoros, New York.

POSTSCRIPT: How many Mexicans are in the United States? According to a study carried out by the governments of both countries
(Binational Study on Migration), there are between 7.0 and 7.3 million Mexicans born in Mexico who are living in the United States. Of
these, there could be as many as 4.9 million legal residents and
approximately 2.4 million undocumented ones. The study concluded
that between 1990 and 1996, the number of undocumented immigrants who remained in the United States to live was 630,000. That

is to say, each year, 105,000 Mexicans made the United States their place of permanent residency.

However, there are many more Mexican workers who come and go. A study carried out by Jorge Bustamante for the Colegio de la Frontera Norte and the University of Notre Dame ("Immigration from Mexico and the Devaluation of the Peso; The Unveiling of the Myth," September 29, 1995) established the circular nature of migration from Mexico to the United States and then back to Mexico. That is to say, Mexican workers cross the border to the north in order to earn eight, nine, ten times more than in Mexico and then tend to return home on important dates, especially during Christmas and New Year's. Some, as we saw before, remain in the United States.

According to Bustamante, there was no increase in the flow of Mexican immigration to the United States after the devaluation of the peso on December 19, 1994. He wrote, "This last devaluation of the Mexican peso has been linked by some public officials and prominent politicians in the United States to an increase in the flow of undocumented immigrants from Mexico to the United States. More than six months after the devaluation, two independent sources of statistical data show that such a link is operating, if any, in a reverse manner than what is a virtual consensus in the United States." The study breaks the myth about the supposed circumstantial causes that increase immigration and, on the other hand, points out and describes the real circular nature of Mexican migration.

On the political level, a figure of at least 20 million is used for the number of Mexicans living in the United States This would include, however, those who are U.S. citizens and residents, but who are considered Mexican under Mexican law.

7 THE RAID

Los Angeles. The raid was staged is if it were a movie, and, in fact, it took place very close to Hollywood. Early one morning, an INS agent called the news directors of the major media to inform them that in a few hours they were going to be arresting a group of undocumented immigrants. We were called to a street corner, and as soon as a group of reporters had gathered, we left for the site of the raid—a furniture factory.

Forty INS agents circled the factory. Several pairs of worried eyes peered out from the shadows. They surely knew what awaited them. As soon as the agents had blocked all access to the building, the pursuit began. During the operation, workers took off running, and the television cameras were rolling. The Immigration Service had prepared a show for the journalists; they were the Immigration gladiators, armed to the hilt, hunting down defenseless, confused Latin American workers.

Some workers tried to escape, but most put up no resistance and were arrested without incident. It was easy to figure out who the immigration agents were arresting: a dark complexion, black hair, and a mustache were the three common denominators. Not a single blonde was arrested.

About an hour after the operation had begun, a group of Mexican workers stood, lined up, next to the INS buses. One by one, they gave their personal information to the agents and got on the bus, resigned to being deported. I had the chance to speak with two of them.

"Is this the first time you have been arrested by immigration agents?" I asked a young man not more than thirty years old.

"No, this is the second time," he told me.

"Will you try to return to the United States again?"

"I don't know. I haven't been home for eleven years," he replied. Maybe he will make the most of the *migra* paying for his return ticket to Mexico so he can see his family. He didn't look very upset, actually.

The other young man, however, was much more aggressive. I wanted to know why he had left Mexico, and I asked him, "How are things there?"

"Very hard, that's why everyone comes here," he said. Then, thinking about what was bothering him most, he went on, "I just paid off my debt for getting here. Pay it again? It's not worth it."

It was clear what was on his mind—the $250 he had to pay the coyote to help him cross from Baja California to the other California. It simply wasn't worth it. Just like the three dozen undocumented immigrants arrested in the raid, he earned $3.35 an hour. To pay another coyote to cross the border again, he would have to use the equivalent of two weeks pay. It wasn't worth it.

Outside the factory, a proud regional director of the INS was justifying the raid in an impromptu news conference. "We received a lot of calls from the public indicating that they could not get a job in this factory," he stated.

What he never said was, what U.S. citizen would be willing to work for the $3.35 an hour that these arrested immigrants were earning?

POSTSCRIPT: From June 1997 to June 1998, an association called the National Network for Immigrant and Refugee Rights studied the effects of 235 raids carried out in thirty-one U.S. states and the District of Columbia. The conclusions were startling:

- Raids violate constitutional and civil rights. INS officials have used physical, verbal, and psychological abuse, relied on racial and ethnic stereotyping, and denied rights of due process in conducting raids.
- Raids involving collaboration with other law-enforcement agencies undermine civil rights and community trust. INS involvement in gang-and-drug interdictions has intruded upon the civil rights of Latinos, in particular, heightened emotional stress in families, and disrupted the stability of community life. Joint INS/local law enforcement actions have further undermined community trust and confidence in reporting crimes.
- Raids destabilize families. Children and other family members have been traumatized by raids. Often, parents are removed in shackles and children are left unattended or orphaned because their parents have been quickly deported as the result of a raid.
- Raids undermine fair wages and safe working conditions. Unscrupulous employers have used raids or the threat of raids to destroy workers organizing for better wages and working conditions, creating an atmosphere of intimidation that affects all employees, regardless of immigration status.
- Raids do not significantly impact migration patterns. INS raids are a punitive, ineffective, and inhumane approach to regulating immigration, and fail in their stated purpose of deterring undocumented migration. Many economic sectors remain heavily dependent on undocumented immigrant labor, and raids have no impact on the broader economic, political, and social factors that propel undocumented migration across international borders.

The association reached one single conclusion: "The problems with raids are so fundamental that the INS should end such operations." The raids, of course, continue.

In 1997, approximately 22,000 undocumented immigrants were arrested and deported (*New York Times*, March 9, 2000). According to Immigration Service figures, in 1999, arrests fell to just 8,000. In fact, immigrants managed to keep inflation under control during the entire Clinton presidency by maintaining a cheap cost of labor. Without the legal and undocumented immigrants, the economic history of the late twentieth century would have been quite different. Most experts on this subject, however, pointed out that as soon as the economic boom that characterized Bill Clinton's presidency ended, the number of undocumented immigrants to be arrested and deported would rise again. Now that the boom has in fact ended, it will be interesting to see if their predictions were correct.

So when the United States needs workers, the undocumented immigrant is lured and tolerated. When he is not needed, however, the United States tries to throw him out, just like a disposable object.

8 NANNIES

They gather in parks in the afternoon with our children. They are their substitute mothers. They get them up, dress them, feed them, protect them from dogs and from catching a cold, they bathe them, comb their hair, hug them and put them to bed. They take care of them as if they were their own.

The children probably remind them of their own children who they wanted to bring with them to the United States but who they had to leave behind. The risk of illegally crossing the border with a minor is great. Moreover, they know that if they do manage to bring their children here, they might not be able to get a job. Who is going to hire a nanny who, in turn, needs someone to take care of her children? That is their tragedy. That is why they pour their affection on the *locos bajitos* (as the Serrat song says), whom they are hired to take care of.

They are the impromptu doctors of our homes. In their memories and in their hands they bring the remedies from their towns and their grandparents. They know the properties of fruits and vegetables because they used to grow them. "Don't give plums to the baby, señora; it won't stop the runs," I've heard said. "It's better to give him chicken soup with rice, and you'll see how much better he feels tomorrow." What about the hiccups? "Put a wet cloth on his forehead."

They are the Spanish teachers for children who speak only English. I know children of English-speaking parents who communicate perfectly with their baby-sitters in Spanish. But more than teaching a new language, their mere presence is the best lesson these children can receive on the ethnic and cultural diversity that characterizes the United States. It is unlikely that a child who grows up with a Latin American nanny will become a person who hates those who speak Spanish and are different from him.

They come from everywhere, but especially from the south. There are, of course, more Mexicans in Los Angeles, more Nicaraguans in Miami, and more Columbians in New York. And there is even a noticeable national pride when they say that they come from a country where "children are well cared for." Which are better? "The Hondurans are wonderful," one friend told me. "No, for me none is as good as the Mexicans," said another.

The lawyer Zoe Baird lost the chance to become the first woman U.S. attorney general because she had hired an undocumented immigrant. That was a scandal. But no one is shocked when a lawyer from Peru looks for employment as a housekeeper, or a doctor from the Dominican Republic offers to clean houses, or when an engineer from Costa Rica has to take care of children because she does not have permission to work in the United States.

They are easy to find because they are acquaintances of the girl who helps the neighbor of the assistant who works with the brother of your cousin. Sometimes the relationship is even more complicated. References are almost impossible, so one must depend on instincts to determine that the woman who will spend twelve, thirteen, or fourteen hours a day with the person you love most in the world will not harm your child and will be a positive influence in his or her life.

There are, naturally, people who abuse children. There have been reports on television—often dramatic—about nannies who hit the children in their care. But they are the exceptions. Likewise, there are people who treat nannies as if they were modern-day slaves, giving them little food, insulting them constantly, spying on them when they are on the phone, limiting their contact with others, and paying them wages that are poor compensation for their two weeks of work without rest.

They are the chefs of the house. In what restaurant in the United States can you eat freshly made tortillas, hot *arepas* or *pupusas* of cracklings and cheese? We eat the best ceviche, the best mole, and the best *lomo saltado* in our friends' houses, and the cook is often the same person who just minutes before was cleaning the dirt from the ears of some mischievous little pip-squeak.

They are the impromptu administrators of what is not theirs. They are there when the carpenter comes, or the plumber, or the refrigerator repairman. They enable the man and the lady of the house to spend half the day away in order to pay for the big house, the second car, and the three weeks of vacation a year. They take messages and give advice. They can be silent, but they know the family secrets—the husband who didn't come home, the uncle they got out of jail, the pregnant teenager, the friend who wants to borrow money, or the teenage son who gets stoned. At times, they have to be invisible, particularly when there is tension in the house. Other times, they must be readily available, even if they have a stomachache or headache or are suffering from the flu that the little girl gave them.

They look after the cat and the dog, and they are amazed when they see that what is spent on the family pets is several times more than what a family in Mexico, Costa Rica, Venezuela, or El Salvador spends on food.

Considering all that they do, they do not earn much. Some receive as little as one hundred dollars a week. Others may earn up to $300 a week, plus room and board. If they are lucky, they will have two days off a week. They get up at the crack of dawn, and often stay up late ironing or washing the dishes from dinner. They do not have set schedules. They are jacks-of-all-trades. Few complain and none takes legal action; they know that if they make trouble for the señora of the house they will end up in the street with all their things . . . or worse, arrested by an immigration agent.

A large part of what they make is sent back home. For the house.

For the land. So that the children can go to school. For their clothes. For my parents. So my sister can look after my kids. Another part is put aside to pay the phone bill. Those who know how use prepaid calling cards; that way they can determine beforehand how much they will spend. The worst thing, without a doubt, is when the call is cut off just like that, halfway through the conversation.

What they do complain about, though, is not having anyone to complain to. They were sold a telephone card without any time on it. The money they sent three weeks ago never arrived. They got a very low exchange rate for their dollars. The commission is so high that it's not worth sending money. They were sold an old lottery ticket. The bus driver charged them double.

Early Monday morning, after a short weekend, you'll find them getting off the bus. Only those who have been in the United States for a long time own their own old car. The rest have to travel two or three hours by subway or bus to make a trip that would take only twenty minutes by car. As in their towns, many of them walk. Sometimes in the summer I see them walking with umbrellas to block the sun. I imagine that some time ago, they also battled the sun in Managua, Tegus, San Pedro, Zacatecas, or Barranquilla.

REBECA — "IT'S A BIBLICAL NAME that my father chose"—takes care of small children in the United States because she can't take care of her own in Mexico. She is only twenty-four years old, but the children she left behind in San Luis Potosí are already grown. "My girl is seven and my boy is five," she told me with a smile that encompassed her face.

The father of her children, like many immigrants from the state of Hidalgo, came to the United States because there was no work back home. First, he said it would only be for a year, and then it was two, and now he doesn't know when he'll go back. With what he earns here, he can live several years there.

At first, Rebeca waited for him, but then she grew tired of the waiting. So one day when they were on the phone she said, "I'm coming there, and I'll help clean your clothes." She left her children in the care of an aunt, and got in touch with a *pollero* to help her cross the border into Texas.

When they set out, there were several women in the group, but when they got to the border, Rebeca was the only one left. She didn't know anyone, so she befriended a man "who looked nice" and told the others he was her uncle. No one touched her.

The crossing was not the most difficult part. The most difficult part was the roundabout route they had to take to avoid passing through Louisiana. The immigration agents there are very smart, because they know that almost everyone who crosses through Texas and is headed for the fields in Florida takes the short route. Rebeca's group took the long route. So long, in fact, that they went from Texas to Virginia, near Washington, D.C., and then back down through the Carolinas until finally reaching southern Florida.

Once there, she paid the coyote, said goodbye to her phony uncle, and reunited with her husband. She quickly realized that it would be better to take care of other people's children than to wash her husband's shirts. Now she earns almost as much as her husband, and together they are sending money back to Mexico to pay for a house. "It has a bathroom, so you don't have to go outside to the patio at night," she said.

Rebeca is a determined and affectionate woman. The love she can't give her own children—with whom she speaks by phone every two weeks—she gives to whoever is lucky enough to fall into her hands.

One day her boy in Mexico fell ill. His nose was bleeding and no doctor in San Luis knew what was wrong. A few frightening days went by, and she considered returning to Mexico. There is nothing more agonizing than knowing that your child might die and you're not there to help him. Fortunately, a doctor from another state was able to control the boy's hemorrhage and he recovered completely.

Rebeca wants to return to Mexico to be with her children when they begin school. But the other day, she was telling her husband that she might go to Mexico for a while and then return to the United States. Rebeca is now used to life in the United States and she likes it. She was born in a place where there was no light or telephone or drinkable water, and she spent her days working in the fields. So she is not afraid of the hard work or long hours required for taking care of children, even if they aren't her own.

Rebeca's dilemma is what to do with her children—leave them in Mexico or bring them here. She is afraid to cross the border with them, but she is not counting it out yet. It would be the only way to reunite the family. "They are still so young, but when they are older, who knows," she said.

In the meantime, the children who Rebeca takes care of in the United States, who without her would only speak English, today know how to say thank you in Spanish. That brightens her day and helps her to forget, for a little while, a boy and a girl who live in Mexico and who ask almost every day, "When is Mommy coming home?"

9 THE RECONQUEST OF CALIFORNIA

Los Angeles. The following story has taken on a life of its own, and some people have taken it out of context in order to use it to suit their purposes. In a speech he gave in mid-1998, the former consul general of Mexico in Los Angeles, José Angel Pescador, referred to the "reconquest of California." His comment, said jokingly and intended to promote discussion, fell like a bomb on ultraconservative circles in the United States.

The diplomat was clearly not proposing a military invasion to recover the land that Mexico lost in the mid-nineteenth century, or a suicide mission, or anything of the sort. That would have been absolute foolishness. (After the conflict between Mexico and the United States in 1848, the States kept half a million square miles of Mexican territory, which is now part or all of California, Nevada, Utah, Arizona, New Mexico, Wyoming, Texas, and Colorado.)

As many before him, the diplomat was merely remarking on how the number of Hispanics of Mexican origin had been steadily increasing in California. The truth is that the matter of "the reconquest" has been manipulated and exploited by anti-immigrant activists. But the interesting thing about this story is that it brings to light two strong currents that are clashing right now in California.

We have, however, strength in numbers. One of every three people living in California is Hispanic. The majority is of Mexican origin. As the Willy Chirino song goes, ". . . and they keep on coming."

The border between Mexico and the United States is a sieve. No matter how many laws and fences are made, as long as there is a surplus of manpower in Mexico and a scarcity in the United States, there will be migration, both legal and illegal. Every year, 105,000 undocumented immigrants arrive and stay in the United States, according to the findings of a binational commission. Other less rigorous studies put the figure at 300,000 a year. Whatever the correct number may be, most of those Mexican immigrants decide to stay in California. It is a silent, continuous migration.

En masse, these immigrants are very powerful. With their growing purchasing power, they exercise influence not only in what is eaten in California but in what is broadcast by the media. For example, the most listened-to radio station in Los Angeles broadcasts in Spanish, and in the afternoon, when the news is on TV, the Latino audience is often larger than the English-speaking audience.

Hispanics in California, however, trail in politics. Latinos represent more than one third of the population in California, but they are far from having equivalent political representation. That is changing, though. More and more Mexicans are becoming U.S. citizens and, therefore, are able to vote. But it will take years, and maybe even decades, for those votes to have an impact.

All of these things—the rising Hispanic demographic, the steady immigration, the increased economic power of Latinos, and the expectation of greater political influence—constitute what many, off the record, call "the reconquest" of California. Others speak of the "Mexicanization" or "Latinization" of the state. But any label runs the risk of being interpreted as politically incorrect. Whatever you choose to call it, it describes the large-scale presence of Mexicans in California.

The countercurrent has taken different forms. Sometimes it is anti-immigrant, other times anti-Latino or anti-Mexican, and in most cases, all of the above. Those who make up that countercurrent want, in short, to stop "the reconquest."

This xenophobic endeavor also has numbers. Proposition 187 is the law that would have taken away all medical and educational services from undocumented immigrants, had it not been deemed unconstitutional by the court. Proposition 209 eliminated the affirmative action programs in California that helped Hispanics, among others, to get jobs and to enroll in public universities. The immediate consequences are already being felt. For example, the number of Latino students accepted by UCLA decreased from 1,010 to just 458 for the 1999–2000 academic year.

The final threat was Proposition 227, which sought to prohibit Spanish from begin spoken in California classrooms, thereby negatively affecting the bilingual education programs that served 1,400,000 students, mostly of Mexican origin.

The sum of 187 + 209 + 227 = 0—zero tolerance for those from abroad. This is the new math of the anti-immigrant, anti-Latino, anti-Mexican movement in California.

These are the two currents that are clashing in California and causing sparks to fly. It is not really about reconquering anything. Mexicans stopped fighting for California a long time ago. The United States has the real conflict, for it has yet to realize that the face of its country has changed. It is not white nor is it pure. Looking in the mirror, it would find a mestizo face with mixed features and skin browned from the sun. The immigration of Mexicans, Cubans, Central Americans has changed the face of the United States forever.

Americans, and Californians in particular, must accept, even if reluctantly, that they live in a multicultural, multiethnic, and multiracial society. Anything else would be a futile effort.

POSTSCRIPT: Are there more immigrants in the United States now than at any other time? No, definitely not.

According to information cited by Julian L. Simon in his study *Immigration: The Demographic and Economic Facts*, the present migration rates are not the highest in history. In 1870, 14 percent of the population was born outside of the United States. In 1910, that figure had increased to 14.7 percent. However, from that time until 1970, the number of inhabitants in the United States who were born abroad declined considerably.

In 1994, the number of immigrants living in the United States was 8.7 percent, a figure in line with others of the same decade, and in March 2000, Census Bureau figures indicated that 10.4 percent of U.S. residents, or 28.4 million people, were born in another country. So we can conclude that, presently, there are not more immigrants in the United States than at any other time in history. What has changed is the country of origin of those immigrants.

In the mid-nineteenth century, the first immigrants who arrived en masse came from Ireland. From 1880 until 1920, emigration to the United States came from southern Europe, Italy in particular. Little by little this changed to include people from northern and western Europe. As immigration originating from Europe decreased, immigration from the southern border of the United States increased. After the Mexican Revolution in 1910, massive migrations to the north were reported. By the end of the twentieth century, it was clear that Mexican and Central American immigration was predominant.

It is troublesome that as the profile of immigrants to the United States changed, so did acceptance of them. During the height of Irish and Italian immigration, never was there an anti-immigrant sentiment so noticeable and so great as in 1994. That was the year that Proposition 187 was approved by California voters. Proposition 187 constituted a blatant attack on immigrants coming from Mexico and the rest of Latin America.

10 THE INDISPENSABLE

What would become of the United States without the undocumented immigrants? Well, to start with, it would be a much less productive nation with higher inflation and the serious problem of finding cheap labor. Furthermore, it would lack the energy and cultural diversity that every one of those immigrants contributes. Let's be frank, undocumented immigrants are indispensable for the United States in maintaining its lifestyle and its current economic levels. Who in this country works for less than minimum wage and without medical insurance? The undocumented. Who harvests the fruits and vegetables eaten at American tables? The undocumented. Who takes the jobs that no one else in the United States wants? The undocumented. Who takes care of the children of the working parents? The undocumented.

In October 1996, there were 5 million undocumented immigrants in the United States, according to figures from the Justice Department. This is an increase from the 3.9 million recorded in 1992. The irony is that in the period of the greatest xenophobia that has existed in the United States since World War II, the number of undocumented immigrants has increased dramatically. Despite the barriers, the undocumented continue to come to the United States for two very simple reasons: in their countries there are not enough jobs, and here, there are.

Far from being a burden to the United States, these undocumented immigrants make an enormous contribution to the country's economy. They do so by paying taxes every time they buy something, creating new businesses and providing cheap labor. That cheap labor is one of the many elements that has kept inflation in the United States under control for years.

Furthermore, the undocumented take the jobs that the blacks and English-speaking whites don't want. For example, who harvests the tomatoes in Homestead, Florida, for $1.95 per hour? The undocumented. Who has worked the vineyards in California for decades so that its wines could be known around the world? The undocumented. Who cleans the country's hotel rooms for $5.50 an hour? The undocumented.

Despite all of this, arrests and deportations only seem to increase. In early 1997, in Albuquerque, New Mexico, sixty-seven cleaning women from the Holiday Inn, Best Western, Ramada Inn, and Motel Super 8 were arrested in a raid. Question: How much would it now cost those hotels to find employees with legal documents to do the exact same job that the arrested undocumented immigrants did? Much, much more. I wouldn't be at all surprised if after hiring new employees, the Albuquerque hotels were forced to raise their prices.

In one case that might be amusing, if it weren't for the tragedy that is now affecting several families, twenty mariachis were arrested in El Paso, Texas. Apparently none was a legal resident. What is amusing is that Dan Kane, spokesman for the INS, said that they arrested those mariachis "in order to return their jobs to American workers." It sounds strange, because in the twenty years that I have lived in the United States, I have never met a single American mariachi . . . or one who knows how to sing *rancheras*.

Undocumented immigration to the United States is an economic problem more than a political problem. That's why it is incomprehensible that politicians on both sides of the border avoid discussing the subject when they meet. It's very comfortable for them, but it is irresponsible.

Granting another amnesty to the undocumented who are living in the United States is a very unpopular idea in some political circles these days, but it is the only idea that can temporarily resolve the serious cases of discrimination the Latino population is facing. In 1986, more than 3 million undocumented immigrants benefited from the amnesty. Along with another amnesty, the governments of Mexico and the United States should be urged to tackle the taboo subject of undocumented immigration and design a program so that workers from the south can enter legally and safely to do the jobs that are most needed in the north.

Undocumented immigrants are clearly indispensable for the United States. That fact must be acknowledged. The only sin committed by these immigrants is not having the documents required to live in this country. Because of their many contributions to the U.S. economy and culture, they are, single-handedly, earning the right to remain.

POSTSCRIPT: Exactly how many undocumented immigrants are living in the United States has always been the subject of much debate. Any given figure will be questioned. So, we can only cite the most reliable information. In February 1998, the Justice Department reported that the number of undocumented immigrants in the country had increased from 3.9 million in 1992 to 5 million in 1996. In early 2000, the AFL-CIO (American Federation of Labor and the Congress of Industrial Organizations) calculated that there were approximately 6 million undocumented people. That is to say, 2 percent of the United States population does not have the documents necessary to remain in the country legally, and each year, approximately 300,000 more undocumented immigrants join those that are already here.

Eighty percent of these immigrants are concentrated in California, Texas, New York, Florida, Illinois, New Jersey, and Arizona. In October 1996, according to the Justice Department, 2 million undocumented immigrants were living in California and 700,000 in Texas. Likewise, immigration lawyer Priscilla Labovitz calculated that 42 percent of all the undocumented in the United States live in California.

More than half the undocumented residents come from Mexico, according to Justice Department figures. The rest, in descending order, come from El Salvador, Guatemala, Canada, and Haiti.

11 FROM CHICAGO WITH SKEPTICISM

Chicago. In the heart of the Latino community in Chicago, on Eighteenth Street in the Pilsen neighborhood, I ran into a group of Mexicans, and we began to talk about—what else?—Mexico. With the subtlety, diplomacy, and sharp eye that all Mexicans have for sizing up someone they just met, we began to talk about what we missed most about our country—our families, the mole, the tacos *al pastor*, the parties, old friends—and finally we got around to soccer. "Who are you for?" I asked them. "Chivas," said most. A few mumbled "America" and another shouted "Cruz Azul." We burst out laughing. We then got into the inevitable topic of politics, and there was no turning back.

The first step for politically sizing up your fellow countryman is to find out whether or not he supported the PRI (Partido Revolucionario Institucional) and the government. Depending on the answer, conversations were either broken off or friendships strengthened. I was not surprised that in this little corner of Chicago, almost everyone I asked had some complaint about the government.

It's funny that by saying "the government," the almost 20 million Mexicans who live outside of Mexico lump together all the past PRI governments. They think not just of the government of Ernesto Zedillo, but also that of Carlos Salinas de Gortari, Miguel de la Madrid, José López Portillo, Luis Echeverría, et al. The complaints against "the government" range from corruption and scheming in small towns to the most typical—the lack of job opportunities in Mexico. "It's very hard there," was the most common remark.

The conversations of Mexicans living abroad are peppered with nostalgia and resentment—resentment for having had to look to another nation for the opportunities they could not find in Mexico. When Mexicans here are told that things are changing quickly back in Mexico—like the economy, freedom of the press, television, political choice—it is not surprising that many are suspicious. It is difficult to imagine a Mexico different from the one we left.

I have come across enormous skepticism in Mexican communities abroad every time there are elections in Mexico and opportunities for the opposition. "No, *hombre*," I have often heard, "those guys from the PRI are a bunch of crooks." Well, there are a lot of ways to explain how a single political party has held the presidency in Mexico for more than seventy years, and that was one way.

For these Mexicans—rural beings from a hot climate who have become icy urban beings—it is hard to imagine that a party like the PRI, which has used every kind of fraud, deceit, and trickery to retain power, proclaimed itself, as it did in several paid advertisements, to be the most democratic party in Mexico. Almost nobody abroad buys that. What I can tell you is that on that street corner in Chicago, what happens south of the border is closely followed, and here very few Mexicans believe that the most anti-democratic party that Mexico has had can teach us a few lessons in democracy.

That was the theme on that cold afternoon on Eighteenth Street in Chicago.

POSTSCRIPT: The Chicago school district enacted a program in the year 2000 that could be used throughout the country and, if it proves successful, could simultaneously resolve the combined problems of the United States and Latin America.

The problem in Chicago was a shortage of teachers, while there were too many in other parts of the world. So the Chicago school district came up with a pilot program that requested special permission from the INS and the Department of Labor to bring teachers in from other countries. Permission was granted, applications were accepted at U.S. embassies around the world, and by early 2000, there were forty-seven foreign teachers working in Chicago public schools. In this way, many openings that had existed in the U.S. educational system were filled with first-rate teachers from other countries. These teachers earn much more in Chicago than in their own countries, and at the same time they do not financially burden the school district. Most importantly, hundreds of students now have teachers.

All of the teachers entered the country as tourists with the promise of becoming permanent residents if the program were successful. Problem resolved.

Question: Could not a similar program be established with the government of Mexico to resolve the problem of the shortage of workers in the United States and the surplus that exists south of the border? Why not, if it worked in Chicago?

12 THE BETRAYAL (OR HOW THE VOTES OF 10 MILLION MEXICANS WERE STOLEN)

The Mexican government, and the Partido Revolucionario Institucional in particular, sent a clear message to Mexicans living abroad: Your dollars are welcome but your votes are not.

The 10 million Mexicans of voting age living outside of Mexico were betrayed by the PRI senators who took away our chance to vote in the presidential elections on July 2, 2000. Betrayal is the first word that comes to mind to describe how a group of PRI politicians violated their commitment to represent all Mexicans in the senate in return for protecting their party's interests and their increasingly fragile control of the political system. Instead of representing Mexicans at home and abroad, they chose to defend their pals in power.

Some will say that that is politics; it sounds to me like trickery and dishonesty. If the PRI was not really in favor of political reform and giving the vote to Mexicans abroad, then why did it wait three years to say so? Back in 1996, when the principal Mexican parties approved a proposal for political reform, the PRI could have said: We do not agree that Mexicans abroad should vote because we are afraid that most of those votes will be cast against us. But they said nothing. They played the game and then they backtracked. That is dishonesty. They bought themselves time so they could cheat us later.

This is the brief history of that betrayal. On Thursday, July 1, 1999 at 11 A.M., the Mexican senate should have been discussing political reforms, including the vote of Mexicans abroad, which had been previously approved by the house of representatives. However, capitalizing on its majority in the senate, the president of the executive committee decided, at 12:40 P.M., that there was no quorum, and he cancelled the session. "Period," said the PRI senator Eduardo Andrade, and with that word, the hopes of 10 million Mexicans living abroad, who only wanted to exercise a right that the Mexican constitution granted them, died.

The PRI senators went to the extreme, turning their backs on the Mexican constitution in order to exclude the vote from abroad. There is no doubt about the fact that the house of representatives (on July 30, 1996) and the senate (on July 31, 1996) approved the third clause of Article 36 of the constitution, which establishes a Mexican's duty "to vote in popular elections under the terms dictated by law and no longer in one's electoral district as previously stipulated." The PRI senators who argued that the vote of Mexicans abroad would be unconstitutional had obviously not read the constitution, or they had read it selectively.

Another argument used by PRI senators was that organizing a vote outside of Mexico would pose enormous logistical problems. That is true, but a commission of specialists from the Federal Electoral Institute (IFE) presented not one but six different ways to organize the Mexican vote abroad, each one guaranteeing the integrity of the electoral process. Once again, the PRI senators turned their backs on the conclusions of the IFE expert commission in order to protect their own power.

We Mexicans will now have to wait until the year 2006 to see if we will be allowed to exercise a constitutional right that belongs to us. That is not fair; that is not right. Before its shady legislative maneuvers, the PRI suspected that more than half the Mexican votes from abroad would go to the opposition. They may have been right. But the main duty of any congressman is to protect the interests of the country, before that of his party.

There are many questions left unanswered with this partisan decision. For instance, if there are more Mexicans living in Los Angeles than in most cities in Mexico, why can't they vote in federal elections? Why can't they choose their own candidates? The option of dual nationality is not enough. The more than 20 million Mexicans living abroad contribute $8 billion a year to Mexico's economy. The least we should receive in exchange is the right to vote and to choose who will represent us in congress.

It is absolutely foolish and a fallacy to argue, as many congressman have done, that Mexicans abroad can in fact participate in elections. To do so would require returning to Mexico twice—once to register and then once to vote. Almost no one, especially the undocumented, has the economic resources to do this, and the purpose of the argument, I fear, is to dilute the force of millions of votes that would probably go against them.

Former president Ernesto Zedillo is not blameless in this matter either. The senators who denied us the vote were from his party. Even worse, when I was living in California in 1999, Zedillo did not have the courage to come out and say that his party, the PRI, was against Mexicans abroad having the right to vote. Why was he silent? Why was he two-faced? Was he afraid of being booed?

What is clear is that, whether for or against the PRI, some day Mexicans abroad will have the chance to vote, just as the citizens of forty other countries do. Since it was the PRI who took the vote away from 10 million Mexicans, they shouldn't be surprised in 2006 where most of our votes will go: against those who first created the conditions that made it necessary for us to leave our country, and then denied us the vote in 2000. Our vote will go against those who betrayed us.

POSTSCRIPT: Mexicans abroad want not only to exercise the right to vote granted us by the constitution, we also want to be represented in the Mexican congress. So the fight for the right to vote abroad must be linked to the desire to have our own representatives and senators in the Mexican congress. Why not? There are more Mexicans living abroad than the total number of Mexicans living in several Mexican states combined. The right to vote and the right to political representation, therefore, belong to us.

13 ANGEL, "THE DISCRIMINATED ONE"

Angel was discriminated against from the moment he was born. Just for being Hispanic; just because his mother and father were Mexicans without work permits in the United States.

According to his parents, Angel was born in New York City on January 1, 2000, at twelve A.M. sharp. That would make him the first baby born in the United States in the new millennium. His parents were supposedly informed by a staff member at Lincoln Hospital that Angel had been the first baby born that year. Bertha, the mother, recalls: "They told us there were prizes and money." Besides that, they were expecting a visit from New York mayor Rudolph Giuliani to congratulate them publicly. But then something happened.

The hospital realized that Gabriel and Bertha Barrientos, Angel's parents, were undocumented immigrants from Mexico. Gabriel told me that after the initial excitement of realizing that Angel was the "first baby of the new millennium" in the United States, the hospital found out that he and his wife had entered the United States illegally, and the attitude of the doctors, nurses, and staff at Lincoln Hospital changed.

Angel did not receive any gifts or money, and Mayor Giuliani did not visit him. No one had told Gabriel and Bertha that their son was not the first born that year. In their eyes, Angel went from being the first baby of the new millennium in the United States to being a child forgotten and disriminated against. "I believe what they did to us is because of racism or discrimination," Gabriel told me by phone. He and his wife are convinced that Angel was born at the stroke of midnight. As proof, besides having had their watch in hand in the delivery room, they have the plastic bracelet that was put on the baby's wrist that Gabriel said read, "1/1/2000 time of birth 12 A.M."

The version from Lincoln Hospital is quite different. Nydia Negrón, director of public relations for the hospital, assured me that Angel was not born at twelve A.M. sharp, but rather twelve seconds after midnight. That would make Angel the third baby to be born in the United States in 2000, not the first. (Rebekah, a baby girl born one second after midnight, is officially considered to be the first of 2000. The mayor of New York did go to visit Rebekah and her mother Yunhee Yi, at a hospital in Long Island, and Rebekah's family received close to $25,000 in gifts.)

What's more, Nydia Negrón is adamant that "at no time did I tell them [the Barrientoses] that their baby was the first one of the year." When I asked if it was possible that Angel had not been considered the first baby of the year because his parents were undocumented immigrants, she replied, "No, it's not. We support immigrants regardless of their legal status."

The hospital stated publicly that it did not publicize Angel's birth in order to "respect the right to privacy." According to the hospital's public relations office, it was the mother, Bertha, who asked not to publicly announce Angel's birth to avoid problems with immigration. The baby is a U.S. citizen by birth, but the parents could be deported. Both parents, however, told me a totally different story from the one released by the hospital.

"I'm not afraid of anything," the father, Gabriel, told me. The mother's tone was identical. Recognition for being the first baby of the year "is something that belongs to him," Bertha confided to me. In fact, they both appeared on national television in the United

States denouncing what they felt to be an injustice on the part of the medical center. That is not generally something that is done by someone who is afraid of being deported.

Someone was not telling the whole truth. No matter what really happened, the case was forgotten. There are many things we will never know. For example, at what point were the births of baby Angel and baby Rebekah recorded? When you could see the head or the feet? Who recorded the exact time? What clock was used?

This case really has nothing to do with who was born first. Angel's case has to do with the perception that Hispanics— especially undocumented immigrants—are still discriminated against in the United States because of their last name or the language they speak or their legal status. Maybe Angel wasn't the first baby of the year. Maybe not. But his parents did not deserve the treatment they received. First, filled with hopes; then, treated with almost complete indifference. I wonder if the family of a blue-eyed, blond-haired, fair-skinned baby with the last name of Miller or Johnson—and with enough money to hire a lawyer—would have been treated the same way.

Despite their negative experience, Gabriel and Bertha have no regrets. They crossed from the Mexican border state of Chihuahua into Arizona by foot. "The crossing was very hard because we had to walk for a long time," Bertha told me. "It was ugly; the hardest part was walking." It took them six days to arrive, safe and sound, on the U.S. side. They did not want to tell me how much they paid the coyote who helped them across.

Once in Arizona, they took a plane to New York, where Gabriel found work as a waiter in a seafood restaurant. "This is the best place for me to build a future," he said. Bertha, twenty-four, is from Michoacán, and Gabriel, twenty-two, is a native of Veracruz. Both, however, were living an existence with little promise in the Mexican provinces. So when Bertha found out she was pregnant, they decided to head to the north. Bertha crossed the border when she was two months pregnant.

"Do you regret leaving Mexico?" I asked Bertha.

"Not at all," she replied. "The future of our child is here."

Angel's beginning in this world may not have been so nice, but it will be many years before we can know if the effort of his parents was worthwhile.

POSTSCRIPT: In 1992, 96,000 babies were born to undocumented mothers in California, according to American congressman Buck McKeon. Based on this information, an effort got under way in the House of Representatives to amend the Constitution and take U.S. citizenship away from children of undocumented immigrants. The proposal suggested that only those babies born in U.S. territory, who had at least one parent who was a legal resident, could become U.S. citizens. The argument was that the United States did not have enough money to pay for the medical and educational benefits that some of these children were going to receive as U.S. citizens. What those who supported this proposal in Congress forgot was that those 96,000 babies are as much U.S. citizens as they are.

The proposal did not gain the necessary support, and it died in Washington. But it was a reflection, in all its rawness, of the xenophobic sentiment of many members of the U.S. Congress.

14 HELIODORO'S LETTERS

Proposition 187 in California demonstrated that a large part of the U.S. population erroneously considered the undocumented immigrants to be responsible for the main problems in the United States. When Californians approved Proposition 187 on November 8, 1994, their vote approved one of the most radical and unfair anti-immigrant laws in recent memory. Despite having been approved by voters, Proposition 187 was overturned in the courts for being unconstitutional. Nevertheless, had it taken effect, it would have denied education and medical attention to hundreds of thousands of undocumented immigrants.

Then-governor Pete Wilson was quickly identified with Proposition 187. The proposition was based on the idea that immigrants were coming to California to take advantage of free education and medical services. Studies, however, indicated something much different.

According to a study carried out by *U.S. News & World Report* (October 4, 1993), which included the analysis of 12.5 million documents from the Census Bureau: "Contrary to popular belief, immigrants do not rob citizens of jobs but either expand employment niches or take jobs few Americans want." Likewise, the magazine stated, "Most newcomers do not rely on welfare . . . overall only about four percent of new immigrants receive welfare aid."

This kind of reasoning had no impact. Only a judge was able to put an end to the most radical anti-immigration law in the history of California and, possibly, the history of the United States.

While all this was going on, I received copies of two letters that a Mexican, whom I will refer to only as Heliodoro, sent to the then-governor of California and to former Mexican president Carlo Salinas de Gortari. Both letters were written in 1993. He asked me to share them:

Mr. Governor Pete Wilson:

My greatest wish is that you read this letter that expresses what I feel. As a Mexican, I came to this country at the age of fifteen. I have now been working here for eighteen years and earning minimum wage. I began to work at the age of sixteen because I didn't want to be a burden to anyone. I have kept almost every pay stub from all these years. I have always tried not to be a burden to society. And many of my race, just like me, have done the same.

But sometimes you can't cope with so many bills, and hospitals that charge you without regard. With the little that we earn, we have no other choice but to ask for public assistance in order to survive and to not let our children or ourselves die. How I wish you and others like you were in our shoes.

It is not true that the women come to give birth here because of the great fortune that welfare gives them. I have two children. If what you say is true, I would have twelve children. I accept that among my race we have everything . . . just like the other races. No race is perfect. If you believe that the illegal Mexicans are to blame for the problems in this country, we should be living like kings and not like we are, working from sun up to sundown for a miserable wages, without paid vacations or holidays and, on top of that, being treated poorly by our bosses. We have no job security, and they pay us minimum wage . . . if we want it. And if not, they say *"allí está la puerta abierta."* And they say it just like that because most do not know English and even less a high school diploma, which is what is needed to get a better paying job.

Mr. Governor, if the illegals stopped coming, do you think the problems would end? I don't. Who would the bad leaders blame then?

Sincerely,
Heliodoro R.

Mr. Carlos Salinas de Gortari
President of the Republic of Mexico

Mr. President:

I am writing this letter with the hope that you will read it. I have been living in California since 1975. I came with the hope of returning to Mexico as soon as we had an honest and fair president in office, a president who would remove the bad leaders from cities and towns, a president who could establish order and rid the country of corruption.

I was compelled to write this letter because here in the United States we are insulted and humiliated. We, the Mexican immigrants, are looked down on. It is not right that we must suffer so many injustices at the hands of the employers who make us work without job security and pay us minimum wage. If they can, they pay us less than if they were doing us a favor giving us work. Aside from that, the American government is accusing us of coming to exploit this country. They want to make us look like sewer rats. We can't take it anymore.

With our work we are enriching this country, which is not ours thanks to Mexico's former presidents. We, the poor, don't even have the freedom to chose them, even though we are the majority. Let the people decide which party and which religion they want, and let them have freedom of speech. Now, at the end of the twentieth century, do not impose leaders on us.

We need someone who will lead us with honesty and fairness,

someone who will help us save the country with our effort and our will. Our Mexico will no longer be a mediocre country that does not know when it can repay the debts that every president has been increasing. That is why we want a president who loves the people and his race as he loves himself.

Think about it. It's difficult, but not impossible.

Sincerely,
A fellow countryman.
Heliodoro R.

POSTSCRIPT: In his letters, Heliodoro hit the nail on the head. There are two main causes for immigration from Mexico to the United States—one that pushes the Mexican to the north and the other that draws him to the United States. But as the Mexican crosses the border, the problems are just beginning. Far from being the earthly paradise that was imagined, the United States turns into a kind of labyrinth, an obstacle course. Heliodoro's letters reflect the resentment and frustration of an immigrant, as much with the homeland he left behind as with the circumstances he must face after his arrival in the north.

15 THE MEXICAN GIRL WHO WROTE TO PRESIDENT CLINTON

In 1997, I received a letter that a Mexican girl had written to the then-president of the United States, Bill Clinton. She did not want her name to be revealed, but she did want Clinton and Americans to know how the immigration laws were negatively affecting the future of many immigrant families like hers in the United States. She had been living with her family in Texas for six years, until the climate of persecution, and the impossibility of resolving their legal status, forced them to return to the Mexican state of Puebla.

This is the letter from a little girl who had the courage to tell the president what many others just like her were experiencing. The letter said:

Dear President Clinton:
    I do not know if anyone will ever read this letter, but I hope that someone does. Whenever someone reads this let-

ter, hopefully it will be Mr. Clinton, by then I will be back in my native country, Mexico.

I was born in Puebla, in Mexico, in the year 1981. I will be sixteen years old in June, and in June it will have been six years that I am here in the United States. I am a straight-A student and have been ever since I began school. I have earned the respect of my peers and of other people whom I love, and they love me, too. I have received many academic awards as well as athletic awards. I have even won a Presidential Award. I have been involved in many basketball, volleyball, soccer, softball, and track teams. I keep my grades up and at the same time I'm involved in other programs, such as student council. I was also the president of D-FYIT, a program to keep kids off of drugs, and you name it. I've been enrolled in many other programs.

When I got to the United States, I looked at the United States as the place where one could make their dreams come true. The "place" of liberty and freedom. When my family and I migrated into the United States, it was only my mom, my dad, my brother, and me. Now I have a three-year-old brother who was born here and is an American citizen and has all the privilages [sic] and rights any American citizen has. We were finally beginning to get stable in one place, and finally living a "nice life," but because of all the new laws that have been approved and the ones that are to come, we have to return to our country, Mexico. As you can now tell, we don't "belong here." My parents, one of my brothers, and me, are illegal aliens that came to the United States in search of a better life, and to find freedom. I was ten years old when we came to the United States and I guess that one could say that a ten-year-old cannot distinguish right from wrong.

But now, I am a mature sixteen-year-old who can distinguish right from wrong, now I can say that I was "wrong" to believe in what I did as a child. A child that dreamed too much and a child that knew "nothing" about "anything."

One cannot blame anyone for certain situations, but because laws have been passed and approved, I have to leave behind good friends that I made, and I have to forget those goals and dreams that I had for my future. It is going to be very hard for all of my family, but because my family is strong mentally, physically, and spiritually, we believe that we will survive this adversity. Now we have to go back and start "living" once again. All I want you to know is that we never came in search of your money. All my family and I wanted was a chance to become individuals that were worthy citizens.

Thank you for your time.

M.G.

POSTSCRIPT: I sent a copy of this letter to the White House. But I do not know if President Clinton ever read it.

WE COME FROM EVERYWHERE

16 ELIÁN: HIS FIRST 150 DAYS IN THE UNITED STATES

In this chapter, you will not find Elián's present or his future. You will only find a report on Elián González's first critical 150 days in the United States, from Thursday, November 25, 1999, when he was rescued at sea, to Saturday, April 22, 2000, when agents from the U.S. Immigration and Naturalization Service burst violently into the Gonzálezes' house in Miami and forcibly took Elián so he could be reunited with his father.

STRANGE COINCIDENCE

Miami. There were very few occasions when the Cuban government agreed with the Cuban exile community in this city. But because of a strange circumstance, the government, as well as the Cuban exile community, turned a six-year-old boy into a symbol of struggle. Elián symbolized the two faces of Cuba.

He was one of three survivors of a shipwreck off the coast of

Florida. For fifty hours he floated in an inner tube, until he was found by two fishermen. Eleven people died in the tragedy, including his mother, Elisabet, and her boyfriend. They were all fleeing Cuba in an aluminum boat only five yards long. The fishermen, Donato Dalrymple and San Ciancio, who found him in the normally shark-infested waters, reported that Elián had been surrounded by dolphins. No one has been able to prove this, but it now forms part of the mythology that has grown around Elián.

I have two photographs of Elián. In one photograph, his eyes are lifeless, as if his soul were dead. Maybe this was moments after he was rescued, hours after the shipwreck. Or maybe this is what happens when it is impossible to erase the image of your mother drowning. In the other photograph, the sparkle in his eyes seems to be trying to reappear as he plays with a little toy truck. In that photo he is wearing a Reebok T-shirt, and he could be easily mistaken for any American child.

The Cuban exile community took up Elián's cause at once. Some of Miami's most important politicians rushed to have their photograph taken with the boy, and radio programs promoted the idea of keeping the boy here. The argument was simple: Even though Elián is far from his father, it is better he live in a free country than under a dictatorship. Naturally, that idea did not catch on in Cuba. Elián's father, Juan Miguel González, reported that the boy had been kidnapped by his mother, that the child had left the island without his authorization, and through the Ministry of Foreign Affairs, demanded that his son be returned immediately.

The father's words hit hard those in Miami. He was accused of being pressured by Fidel Castro's government. Juan Miguel González was working as a cashier in a tourist resort in Varadero, and that kind of work, with access to foreigners' dollars, was not available to someone outside of the Communist party.

The photograph of Elián's father at his home in Cardenas, with a portrait of Che Guevara behind him, automatically transformed him into a contemptible person in some sectors of the Cuban exile community. Likewise, seeing Elián in Disneyworld, next to Mickey Mouse, must surely have turned the anti-imperialist stomachs of many Cuban socialists. The propaganda war, and the rumors, had begun.

In a scathing editorial, Cuba's official newspaper, *Granma*, stated:

"We will free you, Elián, from that inferno of selfishness, alienation, abuse and injustice, where they have so brutally and illegally taken you. You will return to the bosom of your family, your people and your homeland, boy symbol, boy hero."

The spokesman for the Cuban Ministry of Foreign Affairs, Alejandro González (no relation to the boy), followed the same line when he said: "The scenes of the kidnapped Cuban boy, surrounded by toys intended to buy his innocent conscience, as if he were a twenty-year-old man, are repugnant. That we know of, this has never occurred anywhere else. That is the empire that so cynically speaks of human rights."

These statements were followed by mass demonstrations outside the U.S. Interest Section in Havana, demanding the immediate return of Elián. It was said, no doubt, to be among the largest protests since the beginning of the revolution.

THE UNITED STATES AND CUBA: MORE THAN AN OCEAN APART

Castro's government asserted that it was the "wet feet—dry feet" policy that was causing hundreds of Cubans each year to set out to sea in rafts and small boats in the hopes of reaching Florida. That policy allowed any Cuban who managed to touch U.S. soil to remain. The U.S. government, on the other hand, was convinced that it was the high level of repression, and the lack of food, democracy, and freedom in Cuba, that drove the exodus to the sea. No matter what the reason, many Cubans—and we will never know exactly how many—died trying to reach the United States.

The likelihood of Cuba and the United States coming to an agreement that would prevent all those deaths at sea was not very good. Both countries were very set in their positions—one, by sustaining the economic embargo, and the other, by showing no signs of opening up to democracy or respecting human rights. There was no room to negotiate. In fact, the two primary presidential candidates in the United States at the time (George W. Bush and Al Gore) said that there would not be any major changes in U.S. policy toward the island. That is to say, for the time being, Cuban boat people will continue to die in the Caribbean. Just like Elián's mother.

POLITICIANS AND SURVEYS

As a father, I understood a child's need to grow up with a loving and supportive father figure. As a resident of a free country, I would not have wanted Elián or anyone else to grow up in a dictatorship. The decision was not an easy one.

Elián quickly became a diplomatic pawn between the United States and Cuba, and everyone got involved. In just a matter of days, then-president Bill Clinton was personally involved, as were Fidel Castro, several members of the U.S. Congress, the president of the Asamblea del Poder Popular on the island, Ricardo Alarcón, the Cuban-American National Foundation, Attorney General Janet Reno, the Immigration and Naturalization Service, a judge from Miami (who granted temporary custody of the minor to his family members in Miami), a federal judge, a court of appeals, psychologists, and countless civic organizations, both in the United States and Cuba. The central question of this dilemma was: Who could legally speak for Elián? His family members in Miami or his father?

On January 3, 2000, the INS decided that the only person who could speak for Elián was his father, Juan Miguel González, and it set January 14 as the date by which the boy had to be returned to Cuba. However, the controversial decision was followed by protests in Miami led by groups of Cuban exiles. Streets and highways were blocked, and dozens of people were arrested. But the strategy worked. The pressure was felt, and the case was sent to the federal court.

Opinion polls spoke of one city—Miami—and one country—the United States—divided over the Elián case. One poll conducted on January 7, 2000, by Channel 23 in Miami showed that 86 percent of Hispanics did not agree with the decision of the INS to return Elián to Cuba. On the other hand, 70 percent of nonHispanic whites and 79 percent of blacks in the city supported the decision to send him back. Once again, in times of crisis, the Cuban-American community was at odds with the rest of the population. Accusations of extremism and intransigence began to circulate, and racial prejudice against Hispanics appeared in statements made in newspapers and on radio and television.

Critics of the behavior of the Cuban-American majority also came from within the Hispanic community: "Fear is not allowing them to

think," an influential Cuban exile, who did not share the idea of letting Elián remain in the United States, told me. But this important
figure, like many others, did not publicly express his opinion for fear
of retaliation.

For the Cuban community living in exile, Elián's case was a
chance to score a victory, no matter how small, over Castro. Few hesitated in taking away from Elián the chance to live with his father.
After all, close to 16,000 Cuban children had come to the United
States in the so-called Operation Peter Pan, and they survived. There
was no reason to think that Elián couldn't also survive. For Castro,
Elián's case was a rare opportunity to distract world attention from
the real problems of his country.

During the Latin American summit, held in Havana in November
1999, the protagonists were the dissidents, not the invited presidents. The anti-Castro movement within Cuba began to gain
strength under the watchful eye of the Latin American leaders; they
asked Castro for a democratic gesture in order to keep his country
from becoming even more isolated. All that was overshadowed, however, by Elián. In early 2000, when talk turned to Cuba, the obligatory
reference was no longer the lack of democracy and the reappearance
of internal opposition but rather the case of "Eliáncito," as it was
called in Cuba.

MOTHER AND FATHER

Everything leads us to believe that Elián was born to a married couple that waited for him longingly. For years, Elisabet, his mother, had
had many problems getting pregnant. So, when she finally gave birth
to a son on December 6, 1993, he was called Elián; that is, the first
three letters of Elisabet with the last two of Juan.

With so much propaganda both for and against him, it is practically impossible to know if Juan Miguel González had been a good
father before, during, and after the definitive separation from his
wife, Elisabet, in 1997. What was easy to see, however, was Juan
Miguel's anger over not being able to recover his son. In an interview
via satellite on ABC's *Nightline*, he threatened to break the neck of
anyone who got in the way of bringing Elián back to Cuba. In Miami,
that was viewed as an act by someone trained by Cuban state security agents. The official version of the Cuban government was that
Juan Miguel was never aware that his son was going to Miami and

therefore they considered Elián to be kidnapped, first by his mother, and then by his family members in Miami.

ELIÁN'S HOUSE

Little Havana. The driver of the car must have seen me looking lost. He stopped his car next to me and, without my asking, he pointed: "There is Elián's house."

I had expected a circus atmosphere: television trucks, journalists everywhere, annoyed neighbors, busybodies hanging around the sidewalk. But that afternoon of January 22, 2000, I saw nothing like that. Elián was still at school, taking intensive English classes, and his relatives had gone to federal court to attempt to stop his repatriation to Cuba. Instead, I found a very modest house. It belonged to Lázaro González, Elián's great uncle who, for a short time, had temporary custody of the boy. At that time, the two windows that looked onto the street had the curtains permanently drawn to avoid the peering eyes of the cameramen. The house was completely white, except for four steps of red tile which led to a double door—one to enter the house and the other to keep the mosquitoes out. The family paid $600 a month in rent.

The grass in the square yard was worn down by the frequent passing of an old car that they kept in the back of the yard. But there was enough space for the little black dog that Congressman Lincoln Díaz-Balart had given the boy to play with. Christmas lights, which no one had had time to take down, still hung from the roof. They were more worried about other things in that house where Elián was living.

Ding-a-ling, ding-a-ling—the bell of a rickety ice cream truck could be heard; it made its usual stop in front of number 2319 of the second most famous street in this part of Little Havana. (Sorry, but Calle Ocho is still number one.) Not a child came running. But three Cuban exiles did.

"What are you doing around here?" I asked them.

"We're on guard duty," said Dagoberto Avilés, who introduced himself as a former Cuban political prisoner. The gray stubble on his face indicated that he had been in front of the house for many hours, the bags under his eyes that he had slept little.

"On guard duty? Why?" I kept on.

"We have to be on the alert," he responded, as if the reason could not be more obvious.

The other two exiles—a woman and a man, both middle-aged—
were much more talkative. They began to tell me all the rumors: that
Elián was being protected by FBI agents, that he avoided reporters by
leaving out the back way, that one of the neighbors was charging television reporters $500 a day to use his yard—"That house is already
paid for"—and that the INS had already come to an agreement with
Castro to send the boy back to Cuba.

Dagoberto kept watching.

"What would happen if they send the boy back to Cuba?" I asked
him.

"Personally, I think Miami would go up in flames," he told me.
"We would shut down the airport and a million other things."

Standing there next to the fence that surrounded the house
where Elián was living, it was easy to believe what many Cuban
Americans think. "The future for Elián is much better in this country. In Cuba there is poverty, hardship, and a lack of opportunity to
live a good life," said black letters on one piece of white cardboard,
and just beyond that, "Elián must live here!" Another message,
hung from the fence by a string, was almost a prediction. It suggested that sooner or later Elián would be sent into the arms of the
tyrant.

From far away, it was hard to understand what Elián signified for
many of the Cuban exiles in Miami. Not only did they see in him an
extraordinary opportunity to show their hatred of Castro's dictatorship, but they identified with Elián on a personal level. I heard many
people say, "That boy looks like one of mine." It was not just his alert
eyes, his quick smile, or his playfulness that touched their hearts.
Deep down, many exiled Cubans saw a part of themselves in Elián,
and their first instinct was to try to defend him against what had
done so much harm to them.

No one along that gray fence that shielded Elián's fragile interior
world, no one wanted to give credit to the statements of the two
grandmothers who had come to the United States hoping to bring
the boy back to Cuba. They did not want to read the national opinion
polls that went against Cuban-American sentiment in Miami. Nor
did they want to listen to the opinions of those like the psychologist
from Yale University, Preston Miles, who appeared on television saying that the separation from both parents would be a tragic and
unimaginable loss for Elián. Miles conceded that freedom is very

important for an individual, but he stated that after the death of his mother, what Elián needed most was the emotional security that only his father and his grandparents could give. In Miami, those arguments never stood a chance.

That very night, I returned to Little Havana hoping to look into Elián's eyes. I still did not understand his eyes; they were an enigma. I didn't know what they wanted. But I never saw them. Elián was locked up in his house, in his Miami world. Through the curtains, I could see a television on in a dark room. It was the only little light coming from the house where Elián was living—the Cuban boat child who was still fighting to stay afloat in this, his second shipwreck.

THE GRANDMOTHERS

Miami Beach. In mid-January 2000, Elián's two grandmothers, Raquel Rodríguez and Mariela Quintana, came to the United States. They landed in New York because they were afraid of how they would be received in Miami. Their arrival was broadcast live by several U.S. television stations.

The grandmothers were clearly not favorites among the Cuban exile community. After they were seen on TV conversing with Fidel Castro in Cuba, before leaving for the United States, for many it was clear that they were not acting freely but on instructions from the government in Havana.

With the assistance of employees from the Cuban Interest Section in Washington, the grandmothers sought to gain support in New York as well as in Washington D.C., where they met with several members of Congress. The question hanging in the air was this: Are the grandmothers acting of their own will, or are they receiving instructions, directly or indirectly, from Fidel Castro's government? If they were truly acting independently, then what was Cuban ambassador Fernando Ramírez doing so close to the U.S. Congressman's office where the meeting with the grandmothers was taking place?

Suddenly, on Monday, January 24, the strategy changed, and Raquel and Mariela boarded a private jet—one of those that costs an average of $2,200 per hour—and flew to Miami. (The National Council of Churches, which supported the grandmothers' visit, insists that they only paid for one of the flights and that the rest were paid for with private donations. From whom, they did not want to say.)

The jet landed in Tamiami airport. The logical thing to do, now that they were in Miami, would have been to go to Lázaro's house to see Elián. But logic was never a factor in this case. The grandmothers waited at the airport for five hours. Apparently they wanted to see the boy alone, in a neutral place. Was that really the decision of the grandmothers, who obviously longed to see the boy, or was it the decision of the entourage from the Cuban government that accompanied them? I heard at least one radio station report that a flood of telephone calls were made from the airport in Tamiami to Cuba.

Lázaro González and his family had prepared a dinner at their home to welcome the grandmothers. The menu included roast suckling pig, Cuban-style rice and beans, and fried cassava. The grandmothers, however, never showed up.

That same afternoon, Elián had asked for one of those small disposable cameras sold at drugstores for the reunion that night. Outside his house there were dozens of journalists and hundreds of Cuban exiles with carnations in their hands; but they were all waiting in vain.

When he realized that the grandmothers were not coming, Lázaro headed for the Tamiami airport to speak with them in person. When he was just a minute and a half from the airport, however, the grandmothers' jet took off for Washington. The women stated, through the highly visible and egocentric president of the National Council of Churches, that they had refused to go to Lázaro's house for security reasons. Whatever the case, the food went cold, the flowers that Elián was going to give his grandmothers wilted, and the boy was left, dressed up and upset, with one more frustration in his life.

The drama of the meeting that never took place that Monday would be repeated the following Wednesday. The INS ordered Lázaro, who at that time had custody of the minor, to allow Elián to see his grandmothers in a neutral location. The family's fear, of course, was that the boy would end up in the hands of Cuban agents. That was not taken into consideration. The place chosen for the meeting was the eight-room house of Sister Jeanne O'Laughlin, rector of Barry University in Miami Beach.

The boy arrived first, accompanied by Lázaro and his daughter, Marisleysis, who had become a kind of substitute mother for Elián. The grandmothers' trip was more complicated. They woke up in Washington in the middle of a snowstorm. (Mariela and Raquel had never seen snow before.) The weather conditions improved in the afternoon, allowing the private jet, which had shuttled them all over the east coast like an air taxi, to take off. When they landed in Miami, they were taken by helicopter to Mount Sinai Hospital in Miami Beach, and from there they were finally taken to the home of Sister O'Laughlin for the meeting.

The meeting, however, began late for two reasons. First, there were members of the Cuban-American National Foundation in the house next door, and representatives from the Cuban Interest Section threatened to postpone the meeting once again if Jorge Mas Santos and other members of the Cuban exile community did not leave that house. Second, one of the grandmothers tried to bring a cellular telephone to the meeting—it was unclear whether it was for Elián in order to speak with his father or for the grandmothers to receive instructions from Havana. The telephone was finally removed by Sister O'Laughlin and the meeting proceeded.

It lasted only two hours. When the grandmothers left, they made no public statement. Elián's relatives did, however. In the car that took them from Miami Beach to his house in Little Havana, Lázaro handed Elián a cell phone so he could say, for both a radio and a television station to hear, *"Mañana me dan la ciudadanía americana,"* or: Tomorrow I will become an American citizen. I doubt very much that a six-year-old boy would say something like that without having been told to say so, but the Cuban exile community naturally interpreted the little boy's statement as a signal that Elián did not want to go back to Cuba.

Back in her house in Little Havana, Marisleysis said that after the meeting, she thought the boy had more chances here than back in Cuba. While this was going on, Elián had gone to bed.

The following day, Thursday, January 27, Elián's family in Miami would leave for Washington, D.C., in an attempt to convince the U.S. Congress to grant citizenship—or at least permanent residency—to Elián. This was the first of many trips to the nation's capital.

The Seattle Public Library
The Seattle Public Library [BR$]
Visit us on the Web: www.spl.org

Check out date: 03/24/16

xxxxxxxxx7226

The other face of America : chronicl
0010045610846   Due date: 04/14/16
book

TOTAL ITEMS: 1

Renewals: 206-386-4190
TeleCirc: 206-386-9015 / 24 hours a day
Online: myaccount.spl.org

* * * * * * * * * * * * * * * * * * * *
Pay your fines/fees online at pay.spl.org

THE MISTAKES

When the grandmothers finally returned to Cuba, they started talking, and they had a lot to say. They were interviewed for hours on Cuban television where they described, in detail, what had occurred during their meeting with Elián in Miami. The paternal grandmother, however, trying to explain how she broke the ice with her grandson, said on TV that she had bitten Elián's tongue and then opened his zipper to see if his genitals had grown. The grandmothers' statements were repeated dozens of times on local TV in Miami, and they became the cause for indignation in the Cuban exile community.

For Elián's family in Miami, things were not much better. On February 9, the *New York Times* reported that Lázaro, Elián's great uncle, who had temporary custody of the boy at the time, had been fined on at least two occasions for driving under the influence in the 1990s, and his Florida driver's license had been suspended for three years. (Lázaro later completed a rehabilitation program.) According to the same newspaper, Lázaro's brother, Delfín, a regular visitor to his home, had also been arrested at least twice for drunken driving. To complete the family portrait, the newspaper reported that in January 2000, José Cid, the son of Georgina—Lázaro and Delfín's sister—had begun to serve a thirteen-year jail sentence for robbery and fraud.

After these details were made known, the question was: What would carry more weight in court: the statements of the paternal grandmother or the past of Elián's family in Miami?

THE DEMONSTRATORS

"Freedom, Freedom!"

In front of Sister O'Laughlin's house in Miami Beach, I found dozens of demonstrators opposed to Elián's being returned to Cuba.

"Libertad, libertad!" They were crying out, and I wasn't really paying much attention until, all of a sudden, it hit me.

"Libertad, libertad!" For these exiled Cubans, the most important thing there is—more important, even, than the love of a mother or a father—is freedom. They lost their freedom under Castro's dictatorship, and they were not willing to allow someone else to lose his. On their value scale, being free was above being loved.

"Libertad, libertad!"

Orestes Lorenzo, the pilot who escaped from Cuba in his MiG-23 in 1991 (and who later returned in a dangerous secret mission for his wife and two children in another plane) agreed with the demonstrators. On February 5, 2000, the *New York Times* reported his having said that it was more important that his children grow up with freedom than with him, and he was prepared to defend this principle with his life.

Lorenzo said that, based on his experience in Cuba, Elián would have to worship a dictator, hate those who hated Communism, take part in demonstrations against exiles in Miami, rely on the government for which books to read and movies to watch, submit to censorship if one day he should want to write something, give a large part of what he earns to the government if he ended up working for a foreign company, and compromise his artistic talents—if he had any—in the name of ideology.

Family, the daring pilot concluded, is not everything in Cuba.

THE DOMINICAN NUN

Sister Jeanne O'Laughlin, rector of Barry University, who kindly offered her house as a neutral location for the meeting between Elián and his grandmothers, surprised U.S. public opinion when, after the meeting, she stated that the boy should remain in the United States. In an editorial published in the *New York Times*, Sister O'Laughlin stated that Elián had transferred the love for his mother to Marisleysis, his twenty-one-year-old cousin. Marisleysis was only one year younger than Elián's mother, Elisabet, who died in the shipwreck. The nun mentioned having seen fear in Elián and his grandmothers due to the constant presence of members of the Cuban government, who were in continuous communication with Havana via cell phone.

Sister O'Laughlin concluded, "Yes, his relationship with his father should be renewed, but he also still needed the love of his family in Miami and to live free of fear."

THE DISSIDENTS

During the Latin American summit in Havana, in November of 1999, the protagonists were, without question, the Cuban dissidents and not the participating presidents. Suddenly, covered by a mantle of protection they had never had before, opponents of Castro's government were able to express their views to the world. The presence of hundreds of foreign journalists and the visiting government leaders prevented direct repression by the Cuban government.

When the presidents left, however, Fidel Castro began to tighten the screws, and when Elián's case came up, international attention was diverted. The dissidents were no longer the most important news coming out of Cuba; attention was now turned to the future of the six-year-old Cuban boat child.

Capitalizing on this situation, while the Cuban government organized mass marches to demand Elián's return, in the darkness they arrested political dissidents. On Tuesday, January 25, it arrested two of the most well known opponents of Castro's government, Oswaldo Payá Sardiñas, of the Movimiento Cristiano Liberación, and Héctor Palacios Valdés, of the Centro de Estudios Sociales. State security agents appeared at their homes with warrants for their arrest, and took them away.

While the world was watching Elián, Castro seized his chance to arrest those who had peacefully opposed his forty-one-year-old dictatorship.

THE MEDIA

Miami. This was not Miami. This was *Eliantown.* Or maybe *Eliancity.* Everyone seemed to have something to say about Elián: that freedom is more important than love; that if his father really loved him he would have come for him; that sending him back to Cuba would be a life sentence of repression and sacrifice; that if the INS used force to try to send him back to Cuba, they would set Miami on fire and bring the highways and the airport to a standstill.

For those who were not part of the Cuban exile community, however, the Elián matter was beginning to grow old. One day I received a call at the television station where I work, and a viewer said, "If there is one more news story on Elián, I'm going to throw up." Others were a bit more refined, but the message was always the same: They were tired of hearing about Elián. Local newspapers, radio and TV stations were accused of journalistic shortsightedness for focusing their coverage on Elián and showing their bias in favor of the Gonzálezes in Miami.

OTHER VOICES

During the first few days of the international crisis, the voices of the Cuban exile community sounded off loud and clear. Three examples illustrate this.

Congressman Lincoln Díaz-Balart: "In a unipolar world, we have been able to stand up to Clinton's efforts, even though there are a million Cuban-Americans in a society of almost 300 million, and we have only three members in Congress."

Congresswoman Ileana Ros-Lehtinen: "Our community has demonstrated tremendous political power because we have kept the debate about Communism in Cuba on the front pages of newspapers around the world since the end of November 1999 when Elián was found in this free country."

Congressman Bob Menéndez: "We have followed the same process that other ethnic groups have successfully followed, and I believe we have great influence, especially in U.S. foreign policy."

But there were other more distant voices too, which did not make the news, like that of columnist Robert Steinback of the *Miami Herald*.

Steinback told me that he had not spoken with one African American, like himself, who was in favor of Elián remaining with his relatives in Miami. This, he argued, could be attributed in part to the historical problem of the absence of parents in black families. This was also, he points out, due to the fact that bridges had not been built between the black and Cuban communities in Miami. "Elián is not causing the problem," and the division between the communities, Steinback said, "is bringing the problem to the surface."

Sergio Muñoz, political analyst and member of the editorial board of the *Los Angeles Times*, explained how other Hispanic groups felt overlooked because of the preferential treatment Cubans received in the United States. "A Mexican who enters the United States illegally will probably be sent back to his country," Muñoz said. "A Cuban who enters the country illegally is given residency in a year and a day; so they do not start with the same possibilities, and other communities resent that." During those days when Elián was making the news, I heard one television station report that in 1999, close to 8,000 Mexican children had been deported from the United States.

Muñoz also pointed out that "he had never seen a consensus between whites, blacks, Hispanics, Jews, and Catholics demonstrating their annoyance with the Cuban-American community, who refused to see things like the rest of the world." But when my Cuban friends heard these points of view they exploded. "They don't understand us," said two journalists of Cuban descent, whom I respect a great deal. "They have never lived in Cuba and they don't know what it is to live in a dictatorship."

Opinion polls corroborated the belief that the Elián case had divided homes, families, communities, cities, and countries. Many Cuban-Americans with whom I spoke, however, assured me that these divisions surfaced due to the enormous ignorance that existed on the international level about the high levels of repression in the Castro government.

THE LEGAL PROCESS

On Thursday, March 9, federal judge K. Michael Moore—who had replaced another judge who had fallen ill before the first hearing was held—listened for more than three hours to those who wanted Elián to stay in Miami and to those who were convinced that he should be returned to his father. Judge Moore had to decide if he had jurisdiction over the case. If he had jurisdiction, Elián's relatives could move forward with the procedure for obtaining political asylum for the boy. If he did not, the previous decision of the INS—which was endorsed by Attorney General Janet Reno—to recognize the paternal authority of Juan González over his son Elián, meant that the boy would be one step away from leaving for Cuba.

Both sides, however, were prepared to appeal a negative decision on their behalf. While this process was moving forward, a new player appeared on the scene: Greg B. Craig, President Bill Clinton's lawyer during the Monica Lewinsky scandal, would now be responsible for trying to return Elián to Cuba and to his father. Craig had traveled to Havana and met with Elián's father before taking the case. His law firm, Williams and Connolly, was one of the most famous and expensive in Washington, charging a minimum of $400 per hour.

Judge Moore's decision would come just days later, on Tuesday, March 21. As many had expected, Moore decided that Elián could not request political asylum because he was a minor, and the only person who could speak for him was his father. In short, the previous decision of the INS and the Justice Department to return Elián to Cuba was sustained.

That same Tuesday, Attorney General Janet Reno said, "It has been almost four months since Elián has been separated from his father and lost his mother. It is time for this little boy, who has been through so much, to move on with his life at his father's side."

On hearing the decision, radio stations in the Cuban exile community ignited. I heard it said that "Elián had been saved by God and then turned over to the devil by Clinton." That was the tone of many of the comments. In Havana, there were no joyous demonstrations. Castro's government reacted with caution. They knew that Judge Moore's decision would not be the last one, and that it did not signify the boy's immediate return.

That same Tuesday afternoon, lawyers for Elián's Miami relatives announced that they would appeal Judge Moore's decision to the Court of Appeals in Atlanta and that they would go as far as the Supreme Court, if necessary. However, Elián's Miami relatives had not counted on the continuous pressure from the INS, which wanted them to agree in writing that they would hand the boy over if they lost the appeal. They were not willing to do that. They chose, instead, to win the hearts of Americans through public opinion, and so they obtained the help of journalist Diane Sawyer.

THE TELEVISION INTERVIEW

On March 27 and March 28, 2000, Diane Sawyer presented a two-part report on the ABC program *Good Morning America*, in which she appeared along with Elían and his cousin Marisleysis. In the interview, Sawyer behaved like a little girl. She took off her shoes and played with Elián before the watchful eyes of two psychologists. Her obvious objective was to win Elián's trust, and she probably did, at the cost of appearing manipulative and condescending.

If Elián's Miami relatives thought that those reports would change American public opinion in their favor, they were wrong. Far from giving a positive image, Elián was seen as a confused little boy. He made a drawing in red ink in front of the journalist, and in the drawing there was a little boy floating in the sea inside an inner tube, a dolphin, and a shipwrecked boat. Then came the surprising explanation.

Despite four months having passed since the accident, Elián still believed that his mother was alive. "My mother isn't in heaven," Elián said in the report. "She must have been picked up somewhere in Miami; she must have lost her memory and doesn't know I am here." To add to the confusion, Elián called his cousin Marisleysis, *"mamá."* Elián was clearly a traumatized little boy who was not seeing things clearly and who needed a lot of love and help. He was still in denial.

Maybe Elián's Miami relatives were hoping that journalist Diane Sawyer would include the boy's statements that he wanted to stay in Miami in the report. The ABC network, however, decided not to include them in order to prevent them from being taken out of context. Whatever the case, the damage was done. Back in Havana, Castro seized the opportunity to denounce the interview as an attempt to manipulate the boy and to say that Marisleysis was trying to corrupt Elián's mind.

On Wednesday, March 29, Castro adopted a new strategy: He would allow the boy's father, Juan Miguel, and a small support group of adults and children who were close to Elián, to travel to the United States and remain until the Court of Appeals made its final decision. Even Elián's school desk would be taken. Of the twenty-eight visas requested, the U.S. government granted only six. Havana's initial reaction was that that was not enough, but it finally accepted these conditions. On Thursday, April 6, Juan Miguel González, his wife Nersy, and Elián's half-brother Hianny arrived at Dulles Airport in Washington, D.C.

The rules of the game quickly changed. Elián's Miami relatives were informed that custody of the boy would be transferred "in an orderly manner" to the father. Among the Cuban exiles, the suspicion circulated that Elián, sooner or later, would return to Cuba with his father. The future looked bleak.

CUBA OF THE NORTH

Madrid. The Elián case was giving Miami a very negative image around the world. At that time, I was traveling in Spain, and I realized that the legal, familial, and political battle over Elián González had brought out the worst stereotypes with respect to the Cuban exile community and the residents of southern Florida.

Elián was also making news in Europe. Looking through the Spanish newspaper *El País* I came across an unusual description of the Cuban exile community in Miami: Cuba of the North, they called it. The article suggested that the laws that are applied in other parts of the United States are not always followed in Miami, and that the Elián case had intensified the challenges to authority by the Cuban exile community. In other words, it spoke of a kind of Independent Republic of Miami. Statements made by Mayor Alex Penelas, saying that the local police would not help federal agents remove the boy from his Miami home, were prominently highlighted to exemplify how isolated the city was from the rest of the country.

The newspaper *El Mundo* was not far behind. One of its correspondents wrote, "The Elián soap opera had helped to hang the label of 'Banana Republic' on Miami once again." In other reports, it was not uncommon to find the words mafia, fanaticism, or radical in the same sentence which mentioned the 800,000 Cubans living in southern Florida.

The position of most Cubans in Miami, 83 percent of whom wanted Elián to remain in the United States, was not very popular nationwide, according to the *Miami Herald* (April 9, 2000). A CNN national poll conducted in late March 2000 indicated that three out of every four Americans favored the international practice of reuniting children with their parents. But those who inferred from this unpopular position that the Cuban exile community was monolithic, that it did not have generational differences, and that all residents from south Florida were intransigent, were wrong. Miami is really an open community: multiethnic, multiracial, and multicultural.

If Miami were such a closed community, as some have tried to portray it, then why are there more and more international companies moving their headquarters to southern Florida? Why is Miami Beach at the forefront of fashion and French, Italian, and tropical cuisine? Why do new Internet companies prefer to establish their businesses in the Lincoln Road corridor and not in San Francisco, New York, London, Havana, or Hong Kong? Why do some of the most important radio and television stations broadcast in Spanish from Miami? Why? It is not just because of its beaches, tourism, and climate, but also because of its people. Especially, its people. The people in Miami have opened themselves to the world, and the world has opened itself to the people of Miami. That is why this corner of the world is so attractive.

Miami intolerant? I don't think so. Where in the United States can someone speak Spanish every day at all times without feeling discriminated against? Where is the economic progress of a superpower combined with Latin American culture and values? Where do several worlds coexist at the same time without destroying each other? Where are political refugees and foreign investors welcomed alike? Where can you see a white man married to a black woman with Latino children without drawing attention? Where, as the influential Chilean executive Joaquin Blaya often says, are Hispanics treated as first-class citizens? Where has a bridge been built between the United States, Europe, and Latin America? In Miami.

It is true that the Cuban community exerts enormous influence in Miami and on U.S. foreign policy. Cubans in Miami go to the polls and vote, and they are heard. They vote for their own to represent them, and when they don't think something is right, they complain. We cannot, however, criticize them for this; on the contrary, if only the Mexican-American community were as influential in Los Angeles, Chicago, or San Antonio as the Cuban-American community is in south Florida.

I have been living in Miami for more than a decade, and to be honest, there are times when I don't share the same ideas as my Cuban neighbors. I am sure I would find this in any other city with other groups. My Cuban neighbors, however, listen to me and respect me, and I listen to them and respect them, and there is no problem. As for their feelings about Cuba, I now understand them better than before. After visiting the island in 1998 and witnessing Castro's use of repression and fear as a form of social control, I understand the resentment and nonconformity of Cubans who were forced to flee the dictatorship. I share their frustration when I see countries like Mexico or Spain not treating Castro with the same toughness and skepticism as they do Augusto Pinochet; and it saddens me to realize that my Cuban friends cannot return to their country as I can return to mine.

Within this context, it was less difficult to understand their position with respect to Elián. It merely reflected the wish of a community—the Cuban exile community—that absolutely no one be forced to live in a dictatorship and without liberties. In the case of Elián González, we may or may not agree with them, but Cubans in Miami had every right to fight until the end for what they believed in; a right they did not have in Cuba.

THE VIDEO AND ZERO HOUR

Miami. Thursday, April 13, 2000, at two o'clock in the afternoon was the deadline set by the U.S. Justice Department for Elián's Miami relatives to turn the boy over to his father, Juan Miguel. The relatives, however, were not prepared to do so.

The previous afternoon, U.S. Attorney General Janet Reno had traveled to Miami to speak with Lázaro, Delfín, and Marisleysis González for the first time. She did not come to give them an ultimatum, but she did expect them to cooperate in turning the boy over. The scene was bizarre. Never had the attorney general of the world's only superpower gotten personally involved in the future of a six-year-old boy. Clearly, the matter was a priority for the U.S. government. The meeting took place in the spacious house of Sister Jeanne O'Laughlin. After a two-and-a-half-hour meeting, Reno was unable to achieve any compromise with the family.

On the morning of April 13, the media in Miami reported nothing but this unfolding story. The boy, it was said, could be turned over that very afternoon to his father. At the same time, Elián's little voice was heard everywhere. On a video filmed by the family, and later distributed to the media, Elián appeared for the first time speaking directly to his father. Crouching on top of a bed, Elián said, "Papá, I don't want to go to Cuba. Did you see that old lady that went to that nun's house? She wants to take me to Cuba. I am telling you now that I don't want to go to Cuba. If you want, stay here, but I don't want to go to Cuba."

The video lasted about forty seconds and was divided into three segments. The circumstances under which it was filmed were not very clear. It is not known if Elián had been rehearsed by an adult to say those things or if they had been spontaneous. What we did know was that Elián's father saw his statements in Washington and was furious.

Through his attorney, Greg Craig, Juan Miguel González stated that his relatives had exploited and manipulated his son. It was also obvious that a six-year-old boy could not understand all the repercussions—legal, emotional, and moral—of his words, and that his family in Miami was using the video as a last resort in order to try to prevent his repatriation.

As the zero hour neared, thousands of immigrants gathered outside the González home in Little Havana; in the end there were 4,000. Civic leaders asked for calm, but the crowd was defiant. Many of them would simply not allow an agent from the Justice Department or the INS or the police to enter the González home and take Elián by force, least of all after having heard the boy say, rehearsed or not, that he wanted to stay in the United States.

In support of the Cuban exile cause, many famous Cubans in Miami gathered outside the modest González house, including Gloria and Emilio Estefan, Cristina Saralegui, Willy Chirino, Arturo Sandoval, and Andy Garcia. It was clear that the boy would not leave the house that Thursday.

Aware of the volatile situation, Janet Reno held a press conference at noon. Her statements were delivered with moderation and coolness. No, there would not be agents at 2:01 P.M. ready to tear Elián away from his relatives. She made clear that she was prepared to apply the law, and that they would do so in a reasonable and measured way. Nevertheless, Janet Reno insisted on a meeting between the father and the boy's relatives to resolve the situation. But in that atmosphere—with emotions running high, the video of Elián being shown everywhere, and an annoyed father making an offensive gesture with his finger at his critics—a meeting of the Gonzálezes was not very likely. Two o'clock came and went, and Elián was not turned over.

Now what? Lázaro no longer had legal custody of the boy. His father, Juan Miguel, did, but he could not exercise it because he refused to go to Miami. The Justice Department could try to take the boy by force, but Attorney General Reno had said that it would not be done that way.

Shortly after three o'clock in the afternoon, the news that would prevent a confrontation came. The U.S. Court of Appeals, eleventh circuit, in Atlanta, ordered the Justice Department to stop all actions until it had thoroughly analyzed the case. Likewise, it prohibited

Elián from leaving the United States. The executive branch, now involved in a battle with the judicial branch, had no choice but to cross their arms and wait.

Thursday, April 13, would not be the day that Elián would be turned over to his father.

MORE ACCUSATIONS AND COUNTER ACCUSATIONS

On the evening of Friday, April 14, the Gonzálezes of Miami made their final attempt to keep Elián in the United States. They presented an affidavit signed by Orlando Rodríguez to the Court of Appeals. In that notarized and sworn statement, Orlando Rodríguez accused Juan Miguel Gonazález, Elián's father, of having struck his former wife, Elisabet Brotons, in Cuba, and that Elián, too, suffered as a result of his father's bad temper.

The affidavit, signed on April 14, 2000, in the state of Florida, said that since June 1995 until his departure from Cuba in June 1998, Orlando Rodríguez had visited Juan Miguel and his wife Elisabet in Cardenas, Cuba, and that he, Orlando, had witnessed Juan Miguel abusing his wife. "I know of my own personal knowledge that Juan mistreated Elizabet in many ways, to the point she went to the hospital for injuries [inflicted] by Juan Miguel." Orlando Rodríguez went on to say that Juan Miguel had a violent, impulsive nature and an uncontrollable anger, which was affecting Elián.

Greg Craig, Juan Miguel's attorney in Washington, immediately qualified those accusations as "insults" to his client, and later went on to explain that it was the Miami relatives' last resort for trying to keep the boy. Later, Elián's father would also deny the accusations. "They are lies," Juan Miguel González said during an interview he gave to Dan Rather on the program *60 Minutes*. He also added that he had never harmed Elián or his mother Elisabet.

In that interview, the first since Juan Miguel had arrived in the United States, Elián's father denied being a puppet of Fidel Castro, as his relatives in Miami claimed. "Why do you have to involve Fidel Castro in everything?" he wondered. "Elián is my son," he said, "not Fidel Castro's."

Juan Miguel also said that his son wanted to return to Cuba but was confused because of his relatives in south Florida. In his opinion, Elián had suffered more in Miami than at sea. "I know him better than anyone," he concluded. The interview ended with Juan Miguel blowing a kiss on TV to his son and telling him not to worry, that soon they would be together.

The accusations against Juan Miguel were not the only ones. The Cuban government was not leaving anything to chance either. They accused Lázaro of "sexually abusing his students" when he used to work as a physical education instructor in Cuba, and they called him an "alcoholic." Lázaro answered these accusations with a letter containing his criminal record that established, on July 1983, that "he had not been sentenced by any judge or court in the nation for any crime."

THE SATURDAY I SAW THE MOST FAMOUS LITTLE BOY IN THE WORLD

Little Havana. I finally saw Elián. I saw him three times, only for a few seconds, but I saw him. Nobody knew it then, but it would be the last weekend he would spend in Miami.

Elián was wearing a yellow T-shirt and denim overalls that were a little too big. The straps barely stayed on his shoulders and the short pants fell below his knees. He was barefoot.

"There he is," shouted some journalists who were with me in front of the González house. Click. Click. Click. The cameras went off, sharply, quickly, like clucking chickens. Elián was going in and out of the back yard like a whirlwind. I was surprised and held my breath. I stopped blinking; I didn't want to miss a moment. This is the boy that is causing an international commotion, I thought. The most famous boy in the world.

The first time I saw Elián, he was kicking a ball, and I wondered if he liked soccer better than baseball. There were four or five friends playing with him in the yard that Saturday, April 15. The González family of Miami was very large; forty-three relatives in Miami, compared to about twenty in Cuba, according to the Catholic priest and González family friend, Francisco Santana. The ball went flying, and Elián disappeared.

The second time I saw the boy-symbol it was only a flash. He came out of the kitchen into the yard, from the side where the washer and dryer, the barbeque grill, and the white plastic table were, grabbed one of the adults by the hand and pulled him inside the house. The house was full of politicians, psychologists, clergy, lawyers, advisers, relatives, distinguished visitors, and hangers-on who wanted to catch a glimpse of the boy. (I would later find out that that day, April 15, 2000, Elián was expecting a call from his father from Washington, and because of this he was a little agitated.)

The third time I saw Elián, he came running over to the swing and the slide—which was bright yellow, just like his T-shirt—which his great-uncle Lázaro had set up in the back of the yard. Then he vanished. That was it. A few seconds here, a few there. As a journalist, though, I couldn't keep talking about that boy without having seen him. I just couldn't.

From a distance, Elián looked smaller than the images I had seen on television. He looked fragile, breakable. I was not able to get close enough to look into his eyes, even though I realized the absurdity of trying to discover the secret of that boy through a quick glance.

Elián's every move in the yard was watched. The satellite antennas filled the sky with needles, spinning the words of the radio, newspapers, and the Internet and filling the television with images. Across from the González house, where both a Cuban and an American flag waved, I counted sixteen tents and dozens of local and international journalists. All were Elianized. All isolated from the rest of the world. For them, this was the center of the world. It used to be Kosovo. Now it was Little Havana.

In the midst of this display of technology and resources, I was saddened to think that the playful little boy I saw had not left that modest two-room house in the last four days because of the relatives' fear that he would be taken by federal agents and sent back to his father. If my son and daughter had to stay locked inside the house for four days, we would all go crazy. Elián, however, seemed to be handling the situation fairly well, with a maturity well beyond his years.

Why was this boy so special? What had he done to make an entire community come to his defense? How did Cuban-Americans end up confronting, at the same time, the government of Bill Clinton and the regime of Fidel Castro?

The answers were there, on the street, for whoever wanted to hear. Off to one side of the González home, hundreds of people were acting as Elián's personal guards. The Miami police kept them at bay behind steel barriers, but their shouts had no limits: "Elián won't go, Elián won't go, Elián . . ."

The Cuban Americans were more united than ever around this case. I had never seen so many Cubans, with so many differences of origin, social class, age, and education, unite around a single cause—never. According to a *Miami Herald* poll, fifty-five of every one hundred non-Cuban Hispanics were also in agreement that the boy should stay. In other words, the Spanish-speaking neighbors—Nicaraguans, Colombians, Venezuelans, Mexicans, Hondurans—were lending Cubans a hand.

It was also true, however, that most blacks (92 percent) and non-Hispanic whites (76 percent) in south Florida were in favor of returning Elián to his father. But according to several Cubans with whom I spoke outside the González home, those opinions and that disparity came about because of all the misinformation in the United States with regard to the abuses of Castro's dictatorship. "They do not understand our tragedy," said Ramón Cala, one of the volunteers who was protecting the González house. Then, suggesting that there had been a shade of anti-Cuban, anti-immigrant, and anti-Hispanic racism in the handling of this crisis, he said, "If the boy had been a blue-eyed German, it would be a different story."

Other volunteers, who wore T-shirts which read in English NO CASTRO, NO PROBLEM, explained to me that this was not a typical custody case. "Here we have to bear in mind that we would be destroying the boy if we allowed him to return to Cuba," he said. "And that is something that those who are not Cuban and who do not know the misfortune the Cuban people live with do not understand."

It was a little late, but I finally grasped that this case touched on the most profound meaning of Cubanness. Almost all Cuban Americans told me, in different ways, that accepting Elián's return to Cuba would be a betrayal of all those—parents, grandparents, aunts, and uncles, brothers and sisters and friends—who had done so much to leave the island, in many cases, with them on their backs.

There was much talk of betrayal in Miami those days. The Cuban-Americans felt doubly betrayed by the U.S. government, first, for not having lent air support in the tragic invasion of the Bay

of Pigs, and now, for having turned its back on Elián's Miami relatives and forging a strange alliance with their arch-enemy, Fidel
Castro.

For Cuban Americans, the Elián case was more about convictions
and being true to their past than about laws. Supporting Elián's
returning to Cuba would be tantamount, for them, to a permanent
insomnia, an unbearable guilt. They couldn't let Elián experience
what they had worked so hard to avoid. For the Cuban-American
community, supporting Elián's repatriation would have been hypocritical. That is why they fought for what they believed in until the
very end.

Regardless of the final outcome, the voice of the Cuban-American
community, internationally denouncing the oppression in Cuba,
stained the rosy image that Castro's regime still had in some countries. After the Elián case, no one could say that they had never heard
that they put people in jail in Cuba and executed them just for dis-
agreeing with Castro, just for being democrats. After the Elián case,
no one could make excuses for not hearing about the forty-one years
of abuse by Castro's dictatorship.

After five hours outside the González house, I left. I still wanted to
get a closer look at Elián, but it was no use. The boy was nowhere in
sight. Maybe he had gotten caught up in his video games. I walked
three blocks to where I had left my car. All the streets were jammed,
and there was no parking anywhere. I started the car, drove a few
yards, and suddenly I saw Lázaro, Elián's great-uncle. He was walking along, wearing a sleeveless gray T-shirt, jeans, sunglasses and Top
Siders without socks, holding a lit cigarette and bearing the weight of
the world on his shoulders. This forty-nine-year-old mechanic, an
exile since 1984, is the person who until now had made the most
important decisions with respect to Elián. I waved at him through
the window and he recognized me. I stopped my car, got out, and
asked him how he was. "Here I am, *chico*," he said. "Trying to win
freedom for this boy."

His gestures revealed the weariness of one who knows he is up
against many powerful rivals. There was, however, no hesitancy or
fear in his voice.

THE ENDLESS WAITING

Would there be justice in the end? Would a decision that really took into consideration the best interests of the boy be made? While everyone awaited the important decision from the U.S. Court of Appeals in Atlanta, several things happened that only complicated the case further. Psychologist and director of pediatrics at Montefiore Children's Hospital in New York, Irwin Redlener, was hired by the government, and in a letter he stated that Elián was being "horrendously exploited" by his relatives in Miami, where he was in "psychologically abusive surroundings." The letter concluded that the boy had to be "rescued" from Miami.

One of the González family lawyers immediately responded to Redlener's letter. José García Pedrosa stated that the doctor's comments were "absurd" because he had never even met Elián or any of the adults who were taking care of him.

At that same time, another debate arose around the enormous cost of maintaining order outside the González home. The *Miami Herald* reported that the city had spent almost a million dollars in overtime for police and control operations during the first four months. Mayor Joe Carollo did not question the newspaper's figure, but said: "The cost of freedom never comes cheap." Carollo was also the first politician in Miami to denounce a strange attack by security agents of the Cuban government on demonstrators outside the Cuban Interest Section in Washington.

THE VOTE AGAINST CUBA

The Cuban government was hoping to reap positive results from the crisis surrounding Elián in the United Nations Commission on Human Rights in Geneva. Just as there was every year, there would be a vote on Cuba. This time, though, Fidel Castro's regime seemed optimistic in achieving a reversal of the usual condemnation. However, the math did not work in favor of the Cubans that Tuesday, April 18, 2000.

When the Commission proposed a resolution of condemnation for having violated human rights in Cuba, twenty-one nations approved it, eighteen rejected it, and fourteen abstained. Among the countries that approved the condemnation were Chile and Argentina.

The spokesperson for the new Chilean president, socialist Ricardo

Lagos, said that in Cuba, "there is an unjust situation and there is no free expression of different ideas." He added that the civil and political rights of Cuban citizens "are violated." Reflecting the same position, the minister of foreign affairs of the new Argentine government of Fernando de la Rúa said, "We have not noticed any improvement" in the situation of human rights in Cuba. That is to say, the two youngest governments in the region were turning their backs on Castro.

Even more surprising was the position of Mexico, which had traditionally rejected proposals to condemn Cuba. This time, then-President Ernesto Zedillo abstained from voting. In the typically ambiguous and indirect language of some Mexican diplomats, a communiqué from the Ministry of Foreign Affairs explained that "the Mexican government reiterates that the policy that most favors democracy is dialogue, not condemnation; unity, not isolation; brotherhood, not aggressiveness." It was clear that in his last year in office, Zedillo did not want to demonstrate unconditional support of the last dictatorship on the American continent.

Cuba was counting on the votes of Mexico and the Czech Republic in the Commission on Human Rights in Geneva. But it was mistaken. When it realized its error, it became defiant. In the very moment the voting was taking place in Geneva, approximately 100,000 demonstrators staged a protest outside the Czech embassy in Havana. The Cuban demonstrators accused the Czechs of being "puppets" and "traitors." The Czechs, who had been historical allies of Cuba before the dissolution of Czechoslovakia, voted their conscience. As the vote was taking place in the Commission of the United Nations, the dissident Elizardo Sánchez counted approximately 350 political prisoners that were in Cuban jails.

After the vote was taken, Cuba stated that it was "proud" of its historical record on human rights. Apparently, however, the months of condemnations made by Cuban exiles against the Castro regime because of the Elián case were finally resulting in their first political consequences at the international level.

THE DECISION OF THE FEDERAL APPEALS COURT

Shortly before three o'clock in the afternoon on Wednesday, April 19, 2000, the Federal Appeals Court, in an unprecedented decision, ordered Elián not to leave the United States until his case could be heard the second week of May. While the court did not want to involve itself in the custody question, it did suggest that it would seriously analyze whether a six-year-old boy could apply for political asylum.

At that time, the fight over Elián reminded me of a statement made by U.S. Supreme Court Justice Warren Burger in 1992, in which he pointed out that there are a myriad of problems and matters that the court simply does not have the power to resolve, and we need to accept this. The Elián case was one of those matters, unique and historic.

When the provisional decision of the Court of Appeals was made known, there was a burst of jubilation outside the González house in Little Havana. There was a celebration on N.W. 2nd Street. Elián spent that afternoon unaware of the festivities, swinging on his swing and playing with his cousin, Marisleysis. That night a beautiful moon reigned over Miami. In Washington, however, the mood was somber. The worst was still to come.

Once again, Juan Miguel did not want to issue a statement to the press, but his lawyer, Greg Craig, asked the U.S. government to take "immediate action" to unite the father with his son. Craig pointed out that it would be "unconscionable" to wait one day more. Attorney General Janet Reno, who appeared on television shortly after, visibly shaken by the legal decision, insisted: "The court order did not preclude me from placing Elián in his father's care while he is in the United States." However, she went on to say, "We are going to take care and consider all our options and take the course of action that we deem appropriate under the circumstances."

The reality was that a U.S. court had never before encountered a case like this. The complexity of the situation was enormous; in a very special way it combined the general with the particular, politics with emotion, the local with the international, the story of a small boy and the irreconcilable differences of the Cuban exile community with Castro's dictatorship.

It was also true that, regardless of the final outcome, the Elián case provided the Cuban exile community with the best opportunity in forty-one years to explain to the world why Castro's tyranny had to end. With the Elián case, the deaf and the blind who said they were unaware of Cuba's reality were done in; for three months we had had daily lessons—in the press and on the radio, television, and the Internet—about the abuses of the regime in Havana.

Only the O. J. Simpson case had received more coverage on the main English language television stations in the United States than the Elián case. According to the Center for Media and Public Affairs, in almost five months, the three major networks, ABC, CBS, and NBC, broadcast 273 reports on the little Cuban boy, compared with 200 when Princess Diana died and 161 after the death of John F. Kennedy Jr. Whatever the final solution would be, Elián had already made history.

Some, both inside and outside of the United States, believed that the image of the Cuban-American community was negatively affected by this case. As my good Cuban friend Felipe Mourín told me at the time: "I feel very proud to be Cuban; whether or not Elián goes, many people around the world have begun to listen for the first time to the voice of the exiles."

THE STORMING OF THE GONZÁLEZ HOUSE IN MIAMI

No one in Miami thought that the federal government would be so insensitive as to storm the González house in the middle of Easter week, and as negotiations for a possible meeting between Elián and his father were still going on. But that's exactly what happened.

Friday night, April 21, stretched into the early morning of Saturday, April 22, and the González family was still unwilling to turn Elián over under the conditions imposed by Juan Miguel, his attorney, and the U.S. government. At four o'clock in the morning that Saturday, Attorney General Janet Reno ran out of patience, as she would later state.

At five o'clock sharp in the morning, John Podesta, chief of staff, woke up President Bill Clinton to inform him that the two sides of the González family had not been able to come to any agreement and that Reno was going to give the order to remove Elián from the Miami house by force. Clinton did not object.

A few minutes later, two dozen federal agents dressed in military attire, some heavily armed, pulled up to 2319 N.W. 2nd Street in four white SUVs with dark windows and no license plates. They jumped out and ran toward the house yelling, "Go, go, go." They banged on the door of the González house for thirty seconds shouting, "Open the door, open the door," and when they got no response, they kicked it in. Eight agents entered the house.

In the meantime, out in the street, about thirty people who had been camping out in an attempt to prevent Elián from being taken by force were being controlled by agents with tear gas. There was nothing they could do to stop Elián from being taken.

Inside the house, the agents were shouting and demanding that the boy be handed over. When he saw the commotion, Donato Dalrymple, the fisherman who had saved Elián from the sea, hid with the boy in one of the closets. By then, the photographer for the Associated Press news agency, Alan Díaz, had already jumped the fence and slipped into the house. He began to take photographs as soon as he was inside. That would be the only visual testimony of what went on inside the González house.

Marisleysis, Elián's cousin, said that when she saw the heavily armed agents, she asked them to hide their weapons, so as not to further traumatize the boy, and then she would hand the boy over to them. They paid no attention. One of the agents entered the room where Donato had the boy. With his rifle propped on his right arm, he demanded that the fisherman hand over the boy. "Give me the boy or I'll shoot you," the agent said to Donato. "Help me, help me," Elián cried to the fisherman.

The moment was captured by Díaz's camera. In the photograph you can see an agent dressed for war, wearing a helmet, gloves, and goggles, and aiming very close to Elián and Donato. Elián has a look of horror on his face, and the fisherman a look of disbelief. Elián was ripped from Donato's arms. (Later, in a press conference, Janet Reno would say that her agents had to be armed due to the possible existence of weapons inside or outside of the house. She also defended the action by pointing out that the agent's gun was not aimed directly at the boy and that his finger was not on the trigger.)

Elián had woken up at four-thirty in the morning—earlier than usual—and he was in his pajamas. Just like that, in his white T-shirt and checkered shorts, he was handed over to a woman who spoke Spanish and taken, heavily shielded, out of the house. A few cameras recorded those seconds: Elián was crying. They quickly put him in one of the white SUVs. Donato, powerless, ran out of the house. The car with the boy inside turned around and disappeared in the same direction it had come.

According to INS commissioner Doris Meissner, the agent who carried Elián from his house had instructions to say to him in Spanish: "You might be scared right now, but you'll feel better soon. We are going to take you to see your *papá*. We aren't going to send you back to Cuba. You aren't going to get into a boat. You are surrounded by people who want to take care of you. We are going to take care of you. Please don't be afraid." The commando-style operation lasted less than five minutes.

From the house in Little Havana, Elián was taken to a plane that would take him to Andrews Air Force Base near Washington, D.C., where he would see his father for the first time in five months. Photographs released that very same day by the father's attorney, Greg Craig, showed a smiling Elián embraced by his father.

In the end, two very different photographs told the story of that day: one, of a well-armed federal agent next to a terrified little boy; the other, of a father and son reunited and happy after a five-month separation.

REACTIONS AFTER THE STORMING

President Bill Clinton was informed at five-thirty that morning that the operation had been a success. At that moment, Elián was already on his way to see his father. That same day, Clinton stated that taking the boy by force "was the right thing" and that "when all efforts failed, there was no alternative but to enforce the decision of the INS and the federal court that Juan Miguel González should have custody of his son. The law has been upheld, and that was the right thing to do."

Agreeing with President Clinton, the Cuban leader Fidel Castro commented on Elián's "rescue" and said that "the success is shared" between Cubans, Attorney General Janet Reno, the INS, several members of Congress, and the president of the U.S. Never had a father had two such unlikely allies—-Bill Clinton and Fidel Castro— in a family custody case. Never.

A CNN poll indicated that most Americans agreed that the boy had to be returned to his father, although they criticized the excessive force used in the operation. However, in Miami, things were seen very differently. Another poll carried out on the Internet by the *Miami Herald* showed that 79 percent of those who responded were critical of the way in which the Clinton government handled the early morning operation that Saturday. The Cuban-American community felt frustrated, indignant, and betrayed. There were extensive demonstrations of discontent throughout the city of Miami. At the end of the day, the police had arrested 303 people, and firemen had responded to 304 fire alarms, according to a report from local Channel 23.

Politically, it was inevitable that the storming of the González house would have serious repercussions in the U.S. Congress and between the two presidential candidates for the upcoming November elections. Was it really necessary to go in for the boy with such a display of force?

POSTSCRIPT AND MOURNING: Elián and the entire González family, both in Cuba and in Miami, were the best example of what happens to normal people in extraordinary circumstances. One of the most shocking things during the unfolding of the Elián case was that the boy, at least publicly, did not have time to assimilate the death of his mother. He did not have time to mourn, to understand his enormous loss.

If Elián had not become a public figure, maybe his mourning process would not have stopped. But the laughs and smiles that Elián shared with us were not those of a little boy who had lost his mother. They were those of a boy who still had not realized the great tragedy he was living.

Elián was condemned to live a life so different from that of a normal six-year-old boy. The needs of his internal world faded into the background before the political clash and the desire for revenge on the part of Cubans from the island and those in exile.

So, Elián entered the land of Cuban mythology. In south Florida he became a boy-symbol. On the radio in Miami, I heard more than one person suggest that Elián was "a messenger from God," and many would indeed write that Elián really was "an angel."

In Cuba, on the other hand, Elián became a boy-hero. Managing to achieve Elián's return was a reaffirmation of its sovereignty and proof of independence from the United States. One more blow from the long, interminable, and brutal government of Fidel Castro.

Elián, who bore the face of an exile as well as that of the Cuban revolution, wound up being pulled in opposite directions. His ship-wreck was not really over.

17 CUBA ENTRENCHED IN MIAMI

—For Felipe

Miami. Cuba, so close but yet so far. I have several friends who have not spent one day of their very long exile without talking and thinking about Cuba. Some have been here ten years. Others almost forty. *Calle ocho*, downtown, Hialeah, *"la sagüecera"* (as the southwest of the city is called) . . . is not Cuba, but there are reminders of the island everywhere.

Make no mistake about it, Cuba might be ninety miles south of Florida, but it is here, now, in the everyday life of exiles in their conversations, telephone calls, letters, and numerous news programs.

The exiles' continuous obsession with the country that they cannot and do not want to return to—as long as Fidel Castro is in power—is frequently conveyed to whomever reaches this land, whether by chance or out of necessity. Few politicians, artists, businessmen, tourists, or lost souls who arrive in Miami can avoid the question: "What do you think of Castro?" The answer is used by the exile community to size up the visitor; it is a kind of test. Depending on the answer, there is either a warm welcome or a look of repudiation.

Naturally, I was unable to escape this initiation ritual. Six or seven years passed before the suspicion that some Cubans had about me, simply because I was Mexican, disappeared. "All Mexicans are *come-candela* [Communists]," they would say to me, echoing a generalization that, fortunately, began to loose credibility at the turn of this century.

Very few here can understand the reasons the Mexican government backs a dictatorship like the Cuban one. No matter how often I explain that it is a relationship that predates Castro and that, in some way, it has been used by different governments in Mexico to demonstrate its independence from the United States, rarely am I able to convince my Cuban friends that this matter is completely out of the hands of most Mexicans.

If I were unable to return to my country, I am sure that my obsession with Mexico, and with what others thought about Mexico, would be very similar to that of the exiled Cubans for Cuba. I understand because I have had to live a "light" version of exile; mine is voluntary and reversible, theirs is not . . . at least for now.

The Cuban exiles, however, do not necessarily want to return to the island, should Castro's government fall. An expert analyst on such matters told me that only 5 percent of Cuban-Americans would return to Cuba to live when Castro leaves power. What they care about is not the returning but rather the collapse of the system that forced them to leave. It's about having the option to return, if they so desire. The problem is how.

What is the most effective strategy for promoting, from abroad, a democratic change in Cuba? On this point, as with many others, the Cuban exile community is not monolithic. Yes, it opposes Castro, but it is increasingly difficult for the exiles to find a consensus on how to do away with the dictatorship.

One study by Florida International University (FIU) found that younger Cubans and Cuban-Americans favored reestablishing contacts and dialogue to deal with the government in Havana. Older people, however, continued to support the U.S. embargo on Cuba, despite the fact that for more than three decades, it has not managed to topple Castro from power; for them it is a matter of principle. But regardless of the general divisions among exiles, Cuba touches them all; it is the absent present.

I heard the words *"ausente presente"* for the first time from the Nobel prize winner Adolfo Pérez Esquivel, when he described to me the anguish and expectations of the families of those who had disappeared and been kidnapped during the military dictatorships in Argentina and Chile. They are words, however, that can be applied just as well to the Cuban case. Cuba is the absent present for Cuban exiles; it is gone, it was taken from them, but they are convinced that it is only temporary. It is very difficult for them not to think about it often.

This is in addition to the feeling that something big is about to happen. In this city, it has been announced many times that Castro had died or was terminally ill. Later, it was revealed, with sadness, that this was not the case. I remember, in particular, a so-called Cuban doctor, Elizabeth Trujillo, who stated in the summer of 1998 that Castro seemed to be mentally ill. Trujillo was discredited, and Castro came back to life again. "When I die, no one will believe it," Castro later joked.

This is not a laughing matter in Miami. Most of the radio and television stations in the city have made plans and have special budgets for when Castro, inevitably, leaves this world—by fair means or foul, by natural means or by violence. Castro and Cuba, for all these reasons, are part of what we call *mayami*.

Any exile is brutal. The most difficult part, though, must be that restlessness, that absence of internal peace, because of the call of that land that we were forced to leave. I see this every day on the faces of my Cuban friends.

POSTSCRIPT: Miami has one of the highest concentrations of any U.S. city of residents born outside the United States. According to census figures, in 1990, 59.7 percent of residents were immigrants, compared to 9.7 percent in 1940. (Between 1990 and 1999, 337,174 new immigrants arrived in Miami-Dade County.)

In Houston, the number of residents born outside the United States increased from 11.3 percent in 1890 to 17.8 percent a century

later. In Los Angeles, in 1990, 38.4 percent were immigrants, compared to 25.3 percent a century earlier.

Just over one hundred years ago, ninety of every hundred immigrants came from Europe. Today, out of every 100 immigrants, 45
come from Latin America, 26 from Asia, 23 from Europe, and the
remaining 6 from other regions.

18 LÁZARO: A DISSIDENT IN EXILE

"Hi, good evening," I said. "Is Lázaro home?"

"No, he's not here," his wife, Daula, replied. "He's finally found a job, and today is his first day."

I was overjoyed because Lázaro had been out of work for several months. Since his arrival in Miami on December 7, 1999, Lázaro had not been able to find a job, and he was getting by with the help of his friends in the exile community.

Lázaro's first job in the States must surely have brought much happiness to his family, because I don't know Daula, and despite being a total stranger to her, she told me the news by phone as if we had been life-long friends. No, it is not a great job. He is helping out in the kitchen in a small restaurant in Miami Beach. "I make sandwiches and gyros," he told me, "but you have to start somewhere, *hermano*."

I MET LÁZARO GARCÍA Cernuda in the municipality of Arroyo Naranjo in Havana. He was one of the opponents of Fidel Castro's dictatorship who dared to speak to the foreign press on the occasion of Pope John Paul II's visit in January 1998. I remember vividly the fear in his eyes, how his words trembled, his day-old beard, and the poor little house where he welcomed me. However, I also remember that Lázaro spoke with the conviction that if he did not speak out against the lack of democracy and freedom on the island—no one else would. "In Cuba there is no so-called freedom of religion; after the Pope left, all the promises of greater freedom were promises in vain," he told me. "It was a ruse by the government to make us believe that there was going to be a change, even though we knew it was a farce."

Those attacks against Castro's regime, ironically, prevented him from going to jail. "After we spoke with the foreign press," he said, "it was not a good idea for the Cuban government to throw us in jail, but there was constant repression." When Lázaro speaks of dissidence in Cuba, he always uses the plural. It is us against him. The "him" is always Fidel.

Ever since Lázaro decided to participate in the Pro Derechos Humanos Party in Cuba, he had been without work. "In order to find a job, they ask you for a letter from the CDR (Comité de Defensa de la Revolución)," he explained, "and obviously the CDR was not going to give me a letter because of my dissenting opinions." Lázaro was a pathology technician, but from 1992 until he left Cuba, he was prohibited from working. "Any citizen who confronts the Cuban government cannot lead a normal life," he told me. "They are deprived of the most basic rights, and they have no purchasing power."

As Lázaro's opposition activity increased, so did the pressure from state security agents for him to seek political asylum in the United States. "Starting in 1997, we led them to believe that we were in discussions with the U.S. Interest Section in Cuba," he recalled, "but they aren't fools. They have a massive intelligence system, and they forced me to make the decision."

WHEN LÁZARO SPEAKS OF "the decision," he is referring to his forced departure from Cuba and his arrival in Miami. Measuring his words carefully, he told me that "exile is the second Cuba, but it is also a prison of sorts because it's very hard to be far away from the land where you were born."

Lázaro received political asylum from the U.S. government, and as soon as he can, he will begin the necessary steps to obtain a U.S. passport. This does not make him uncomfortable: "The American passport does not take away the Cuban one . . . We are very grateful," he commented, "eternally grateful to the U.S. government." When I asked him about how he had adapted to life in Miami, I detected a hardness in his voice. "It has been a very abrupt change," he said, but then quickly added, "But once you are here, the future is great." The truth is that Lázaro had a very hard time when he first arrived in the United States. One week after he arrived, his mother in Cuba died, and he decided not to go back for her funeral. "Even though we were allowed to return, we wouldn't," he said, "until Castro's days are over."

His mother's death and not having a paying job were two factors that he had not considered when he decided to come to Miami. English was another. "What has really bothered me is the language," he told me. "I spent all my time fighting for human rights in Cuba, and I neglected myself, I never took the time to learn English." However, Lázaro is convinced that he is well prepared to face difficult situations. "Cuba prepares you to overcome anything," he pointed out, jokingly.

Lázaro is continuously defining himself; sometimes as an opponent living in exile and other times as a Christian, but never as a cook. His comments are full of religious references and appreciation for those who have lent him a hand in his most difficult times. During our conversation, he told me how a professor had lent him an apartment in Miami Beach and how many people from the exile community had helped him with clothing and shoes and getting adjusted. "We are not really alone," he admitted, "but we are missing the most important thing, our little piece of land."

Living in exile has not eroded Lázaro's political convictions. Besides learning English, Lázaro and his wife, a dissident who was unable to finish her degree in physics and astronomy, are trying to raise money for the members of the opposition they left behind in Cuba. They are eating wire, as Cuban exiles in Miami say, referring to those who barely have enough to eat, but even so, think first of helping those who need more help than they themselves.

Lázaro, the dissident living in exile, spends his mornings making plans to set his island free and his nights making sandwiches for hungry *miamenses*. His mission seems to be to end hunger. He no longer lives with the fear he did when I met him in Havana. "Cuba is a big jail," he said. "After that, nothing frightens you."

I said goodbye and we promised to keep in touch.

"Bye," I said. "Talk to you soon."

"Okay, *hermanito*," he replied, trying out one of the few words he knew in English. *"Que Dios te bendiga."*

19 CENTRAL AMERICANS: FROM WARS, LAWS, AND HURRICANES

Miami. Doña Carla was lucky. She obtained a tourist visa at the U.S. embassy in Tegucigalpa and made the jump from Mexico, landing smack in the middle of Miami. When an immigration agent asked her how long she planned to be in the United States, she said, "Just a few weeks." She showed the agent her hotel reservation in Miami Beach and he believed her, she didn't have to show him the wad of dollar bills she had bound with a rubber band in the event they asked her how she planned to support herself. They stamped her passport and she passed through customs with a suitcase so big and worn out that it took two people to pick it up.

Like thousands of immigrants who enter the United States illegally as tourists, Doña Carla plans to stay and work. She is not alone. Contrary to what many think, most undocumented immigrants do not cross the Mexican-U.S. border by foot; they come by plane and then they extend their stay beyond what their visas permit.

After the enormous damage of Hurricane Mitch in Honduras, Doña Carla only wanted to work in the United States long enough to save enough money so she could finish construction on her house in Tegucigalpa. "It's screwed up there," she said. "There are no jobs and if there are they pay very little, and the city is in ruins." She wanted to stay in the United States for a while and then return to Honduras. If she could not save enough money to finish the house, she would come back and do it all again, until the last curtain was hung.

"What is going to happen the next time you try and enter the United States as a tourist?" I asked her. "The stamps in your passport will show that you stayed longer than you were allowed."

"Ahhhh," she responded with a smile. "I know someone who will put the date that I want in the passport for two hundred dollars."

Doña Carla is a good example of the cyclical immigrant, who does not plan to remain in the United States but who instead comes only for a while to work, and then returns home. She knows what to do, and her complicated immigration ploy works; it hasn't failed her for more than ten years.

HONDURANS TO THE NORTH, BUT FIRST THERE IS MEXICO

Most Central Americans with whom I spoke have had to cross through Mexico in order to reach the United States. The consensus is unanimous: "The most difficult part is crossing through Mexico."

José Lagos, from the Unidad Hondureña in Miami, told me that for the Hondurans who make the journey from their country to the United States by land, it is much more dangerous to cross Mexico than Guatemala. When I asked what the Hondurans experienced in Mexico, he replied, "Unfortunately I have not heard anything good." He continued, "I have heard of people drowning in the rivers, rapes, and robberies in Mexico. Mexico is much more difficult than Guatemala: first you have to cross through it, then there is the problem of the accent—which gives us away as Hondurans—and later on there are the coyotes. Many things happen."

Then, in the United States, the complications are of another kind. Lagos was worried about the unequal treatment that Hondurans in the United States have received. Immigrants of other nationalities, like the Nicaraguans, for example, were included in an immigration program (Nacara) in order to avoid being deported. Hondurans were not. It all seemed so hopeless, until Hurricane Mitch arrived.

After the hurricane in late 1998, Hondurans were included in another immigration protection program known as TPS. In 1999, 102,026 Hondurans sought the protection offered by this program. However, the abuses continued. "We are described as hard workers; we put up with a lot, and we keep going," Lagos told me. "But we are also reserved; sometimes we are exploited and easy prey for unscrupulous lawyers."

The difficult experience of the 600,000 Honduran immigrants in the United States is not unique.

GUATEMALANS: DISCRIMINATED AGAINST THREE TIMES OVER

Julio Villaseñor, president of the Guatemalan Unity Information Agency (GUIA), calculated that one of every two Guatemalans in the United States is undocumented or has not permanently defined his immigration status. "Most come to the U.S. by land, and all sorts of things happen to them on their journey," Villaseñor told me. "Many Guatemalans have to live in Mexico for a while before continuing on to the United States, and there are rapes, murders, and abuses by the Mexican authorities, just like what happens with the Guatemalan authorities when those from the south come here."

During the decades of war in Guatemala, the flow of immigrants to the north was steady. Even now, in times of peace, the immigrants keep coming to the United States. "Even the people who said they were fleeing the war," Villaseñor admitted, "were also coming for economic reasons."

For many Guatemalans, the war is not over for them when they reach the United States. "Back in Guatemala sometimes jealousy is sparked when we send photos, and they get this false illusion that we came and just picked money up off the ground," said Villaseñor, who came to the United States in 1981. "That is why it is very hard to tell a Guatemalan not to come. But the way things are here in California, the chances for success are minimal."

Then he explained why. "There have been several stages: It used to be easy to get a Social Security number or a driver's license. Now it is very hard, very hard." Some Guatemalans have it worse than others. More than twenty languages other than Spanish are spoken in Guatemala, and the indigenous Guatemalans who decide to emigrate to the United States feel rejected more often. "These indigenous Guatemalans suffer double, even triple discrimination because they don't even speak Spanish," Villaseñor told me. "They speak Quiche or Kanjobal." In fact, in the Pico-Union area of Los Angeles, there is a community of about 4,000 indigenous Kanjobals who work primarily in the garment industry. When a relative arrives, they all lend a hand, support him, and find him a job. And they bring with them their old cultural practices.

Among the Kanjobals, it is usually the men, not the women, who learn Spanish, because they are the ones who have traditionally gone out to work. Many indigenous Guatemalan women who do not speak either English or Spanish will spend their days inside their apartments. "The indigenous Guatemalan women are discriminated against three times once they arrive in the U.S.," Villaseñor said. "By the Americans, by the Guatemalans who only speak Spanish, and by the men—their fathers, brothers, and husbands."

The language barrier is the reason many Guatemalans do not even find out that they qualify for permanent residency or for immigration programs allowing for temporary stays. "They do not know about the benefits of programs like Nacara or ABC, or anything," Villaseñor went on. "I don't speak Kanjobal, so even I can't help them."

"The Guatemalan is hardworking and honest, and we come with the intention to work," Villaseñor concluded. That will, though, has not turned into residency permits for all Guatemalans.

WHILE THE SALVADORANS ADAPT TO CALIFORNIA . . .

Not as many Salvadorans come to the United States today as they did while war tore their country apart. Nevertheless, Carlos Baquerano, president of SALED (the Salvadoran-American Fund for Leadership and Education), was surprised that an old friend of his in San Vicente had decided to try his luck in the United States. "He's coming because he wants to look for new opportunities," he told me. "He has struggled there and he can't take it anymore; everything is so expensive."

With the exception of Panama, the relationship between the United States and El Salvador seems tighter than the U.S. relationship with other Central American countries. There are several airlines that have flights coming and going to San Salvador every day from Los Angeles and Miami, and the American cultural influence in El Salvador is indisputable. Furthermore, there is the strength of the dollar. Salvadorans send one billion dollars a year back to their country. The question becomes trying to use that money not only to help Salvadoran families survive—one of every two benefits in some way—but also to channel those investments into long-term projects. Every Salvadoran in the United States contributes to improving the life of three or four in his country.

"I believe that we have a history of adapting faster," said Baquerano, who arrived in the United States into 1980. "We listened to the Beatles, groups from here, Fleetwood Mac, Bread; there has been a strong American influence for some time now." One only needs to look at the billions of dollars the United States sent the Salvadoran army in the 1980s to wipe out the guerrillas, and the constant military presence of the United States in that nation, to see this influence.

"We are less nationalistic than the Mexicans," Baquerano pointed out. That rapid adaptation to the United States has begun to set apart that 15 or 20 percent of all Salvadorans who decided to emigrate. "There [in El Salvador], they say we have become gringos; I swore that I still had a Salvadoran accent—I always used *vos*, I say things like *vaya pues, fijáte, te ves bien chivo*, you know, traditional words—but there they say no."

For the most part, "here" for Salvadorans abroad is California, and "there," without question, is El Salvador. The Salvadoran community here is one of the most organized. "I think that we are a community that fights, that takes action, that does not give up when we see something isn't right," Baquerano said. "Maybe we have developed a more advanced level of social and political consciousness than other groups because of all the wars." Nevertheless, to date, Salvadorans have only one state senator in California, Liz Figueroa, who was born in San Francisco but whose parents are Salvadoran.

The adaptation of Salvadorans to the American social and political panorama has not been free of complications, discrimination, and rejection. They have felt opposition not only from some Americans but from other members of the Hispanic community. To cite one example, there is no game between the Mexican and Salvadoran soccer teams in any stadium in southern California which does not end in violence or ugliness in the stands. The greatest tension occurs off the playing field. "Maybe the Mexicans feel threatened in the job market," speculated Baquerano, whose organization brings together almost all the Central American communities in California. He points out that the problem is not just with the Mexicans. "Ever since we started coming here, it has been hard for us to gain acceptance from other traditional groups, like Mexicans, who saw us as a threat to their labor force." The enmity between Salvadorans and Mexicans, on the other hand, has often been exaggerated. There are more and more families made up of both Salvadorans and Mexicans, and even Carlo Baquerano has a sister who is married to a Zacatecano.

Salvadorans in the United States clearly do not want more conflicts. They have more than enough problems with what forced them to leave the country where they were born than to take a stab at the American dream. Now the only thing missing is for the effort of thousands to be translated into U.S. residency permits.

. . . THE NICARAGUANS ARE BUILDING SOUTH FLORIDA

Mario Lovo is a Nicaraguan lawyer in Miami who despairs when he sees how his fellow countrymen are exploited. He is particularly bothered when a Nicaraguan is unable to legalize his status in the United States because he left everything until the last minute or, worse, because of bureaucratic obstacles.

When I spoke with him, he proudly mentioned how 45,623 Nicaraguans had applied under the Nacara law for permanent residency in the United States. Thousands more, though, will continue to live on the fringes of the law, in Miami, San Francisco, and the Northeast. "Since they don't have documentation or Social Security numbers," Lovo said, "we have no way to prove when they entered the U.S." So there is an army of Nicaraguans working under the threat of deportation.

"Half of all domestic employees and men who work in construction are Nicaraguan, and they are the ones who are building Miami," the lawyer assured me. "There isn't a more loyal domestic employee than one from my town, and I can bet that all the politicans, judges, and millionaires in south Florida have an illegal Nicaraguan employee working in their homes."

Since these people do not pay taxes for their employees, and there is no paper trail for them—nor are there people with the courage to testify for them—there is no way for them to legalize their status, even if they were here before the deadline established by Nacara. "How can I prove they entered the country legally and that they qualify?" Lovo wondered.

Many Nicaraguans found in Nacara their first chance in decades to legalize their residency in the United States. Those are not the ones that Lovo is worried about. He is worried about the others, those who are out of the game. "Those," Lovo said, "are the Nicaraguans of the catacombs, the silent ones; they can't go back to Nicaragua, but they aren't legal here either."

MARIO BRUNO'S TWO HEARTS
Mario Bruno Jiménez, first and foremost, is my friend, but his story has had a profound impact on me. We can say that he truly left one heart in his country of birth, Nicaragua, to take another one in the United States.

It is uncertain whether Mario's problem was due to the change in lifestyle, the stress, the meat, the rumba, the joy with which he lived his life, or a medical predisposition, but a few months after he arrived in Miami, his Nicaraguan heart stopped. He had a heart attack, then another, and then one more. But Mario Bruno had no plans to die. "My profound faith is what has kept me alive," he confessed. He is the greatest example I have of a man who knows how to open and close the fountain of life with his faith.

When Mario Bruno realized that his old heart could not stand much more, he had his name put on the list for a donor heart. The situation was extremely complicated. The normal wait is a year and a half. He is convinced, though, that it was the hand of God that enabled him to get a new heart in just four months.

His white professorial beard, his ear for music, and his strong, miraculous hands project the image of a man of physical and spiritual fortitude. It is hard to imagine him with a huge scar across his chest. It is hard to see, but I'm sure that when he stands in front of the mirror he says, "What a nice scar, how nice."

When the Sandinistas were eating away at his patience and his land, and they wanted to take his sons for the obligatory military service, he came to Miami with his wife, Leticia, and their six children, Mario Alberto, Máximo Antonio, Pablo Rafael, Carol Johanna, Iván Alfonso, and Karla Josefina. He literally began his life over again in the United States, but not only because he received a new heart; he also left behind, in his memories, the good job and better times he had had in Nicaragua, to begin his own business in the United States, and it is going very well. He has no boss and no set schedule. He enjoys a ceviche with his wife as well as early morning chats with his children. He surfs the Internet like a kid and eats sushi like a Japanese person. Mario Bruno is a celebration of life.

He travels regularly to Nicaragua. His native land and some small family problems beckon him. He has a U.S. passport, but he has never hesitated to say: "I am Nicaraguan."

When I see him every week, so full of energy, so happy, so helpful, so optimistic, so eager to move forward, I can't help but think that I would settle for just half, just a little piece, of his heart.

20 VIEQUES AND WHAT IT MEANS TO BE PUERTO RICAN

Independence is the only benefit we gained in return for everything else.

Simón Bolívar

San Juan, Puerto Rico. Vieques changed everything. Now people talk of a before and an after in Vieques. Never before have Puerto Ricans felt so Puerto Rican, even though they have American passports, even though many of them still want Puerto Rico to become the fifty-first state in the Union. Vieques roused Puerto Rican consciousness. "No, I am not American. I am Puerto Rican. . . . I have a U.S. passport, but that does not make me any less Puerto Rican." That is what I have heard lately inside and outside of Puerto Rico, loud and clear, without any ambiguity.

Vieques has also caused Puerto Ricans to intensify their permanent search for identity and their roots. Today, they have no doubt that being Puerto Rican is something unique. Aside from this certainty, however, everything else seems to be up in the air.

The most basic question still has no concrete answer: What is Puerto Rico—a country (like in the Olympics), a colony (like in wars), or an undetermined territory (between involuntary independence and becoming the fifty-first U.S. state)? The lack of definition for more than a century of the relationship between the United States and Puerto Rico is the historical cause of this and other questions. There is no resolution; it is neither independent nor is it a state, and the free, associated state has created a balance that is easily upset. The deeper question is if in the future Puerto Rico will cease to be Puerto Rico and become part of a much larger nation.

Many Latin Americans cannot understand why so many Puerto Ricans are willing to hand over their island and subordinate their culture to another country. Millions of Latin Americans died fighting for independence in Latin America, so it is difficult to understand why statist Puerto Ricans want to be part of a nation different from their own.

In the meantime, a Puerto Rican's daily reality is full of ambiguities and a lack of definition. Puerto Rico's lack of political definition and the consequences this has in the lives of its inhabitants, is a question that does not promise a resolution any time soon. It is this lack of definition that explains why many Puerto Ricans in the United States are in the strange situation of being immigrants with American passports.

POLITICAL TALK

Elections in Puerto Rico come and go, but none ever seems to be definitive. Even if they were definitive for Puerto Ricans, the U.S. Senate has never showed much interest in considering the results, and even less so in an election year like 2000. Now, despite the enormous political differences that exist among Puerto Ricans, with the free statists and the statists sharing almost all of the pie, the most significant fact in recent years in Puerto Rico is the consensus reached regarding the island of Vieques.

Puerto Ricans from all political spectrums were in agreement that the U.S. Navy should not continue to carry out military excercises on the island of Nena. Despite Governor Pedro Roselló having had his arm twisted in negotiations with Bill Clinton's government to reach a solution, many Puerto Ricans saw the agreement as a betrayal. Roselló was seen by many Puerto Ricans with whom I spoke as a hypocrite for having said in Washington that he would not allow a single bullet more in Vieques, only to change his position later.

The clash on the island of Vieques made one thing perfectly clear: for the first time in many years, Puerto Ricans were identifying themselves as something other than Americans. Identity, as psychologists well know, is formed when we confront what is unlike us. So, in the matter of Vieques, Puerto Ricans told Americans: We are not the same.

I think I heard correctly, and what I heard at the end of the twentieth century were calls, often cries, for autonomy for Puerto Rico. This was noteworthy on an island where the independent vote had not even reached 5 percent in recent elections. The cries were louder and louder, and they were unwavering, and in the end, they could well change the future relationship between the United States and Puerto Rico. Congresswoman Nydia Velázquez, to cite one example, said that it was "time to free the people of Vieques from the military occupation of their land." If Puerto Ricans wanted to kick the Americans out of Vieques, could it be that they also wanted them out of all the Puerto Rican islands?

In a note that President Clinton sent to his national security advisor, Samuel Berger, in the fall of 1999, Clinton addressed the Vieques situation, saying, "They [the Puerto Ricans] do not want us there; that is the main question." The United States, in other words, was well aware that there were parts of Puerto Rico where they were not welcome.

The matter of Vieques is like having someone sleeping in your house for years, and then saying to him, "You know what? I want you to remove all of your things from the room where you have been sleeping and don't ever come back again." Anyone with a little bit of common sense would say, "I agree, but not only will I leave the room but I'll leave your house and, whatsmore, don't expect any more economic aid like before, or think that one day you'll come and live with me." The situation is much more complicated, of course, but the message with respect to Vieques was clear: Puerto Ricans did not want the United States there. Regardless of whether or not the

United States Navy leaves Vieques or limits its military excercises or
if there are elections on the island of Nena, the damage to the relationship has been done.

Despite Governor Pedro Roselló's dream that Puerto Rico become
a state in late 1999, the idea that was taking hold was that of involuntary independence for the island. The distance between both territories was so great that, put into practice, it could end up
strengthening Puerto Rico's autonomy and its distance from the
United States without either party really wanting that.

The daily lives of Puerto Ricans living in the United States have
already felt the repercussions from the political confrontation over
Vieques. How can Puerto Ricans completely feel part of a country
that is clashing on such a key matter with an island where they were
born or where their parents and grandparents grew up? How?

I recently received a letter from a Puerto Rican who clearly
revealed this ambivalence. He said, "I am not in favor of independence for my island, but I don't feel like an American either."

THOSE WHO LEFT FOR NEW YORK
New York. The number of Puerto Ricans in the United States has
been growing steadily for the last sixty years. It is estimated that in
early 2000, there were about 3.3 million Puerto Ricans living in the
United States. (In Puerto Rico the figure was closer to 4 million.)

Historically, the greatest concentration of Puerto Ricans has been
in New York City. According to a *New York Times* report published in
late February 2000, in 1998 there were roughly 800,000 Puerto
Ricans in the city. However, though they continue to be the largest
Hispanic group, they have lost ground to the Dominican and Mexican communities. While Puerto Ricans made up 79 percent of the
Latino population in New York in 1950, they now make up only 37
percent.

The same report indicates that in 1999, four of every ten Puerto
Ricans in New York were living below the poverty level due, in part,
to the loss of jobs in the manufacturing industry. (On the national
level, 35 percent of Puerto Ricans live in poverty, compared to 27
percent, on average, of all Hispanics.) This shows that U.S. citizenship does not guarantee well-being. There are many other factors
that hinder the socioeconomic growth of Puerto Ricans in the United
States.

When I spoke with Juan Figueroa, president and advisor of the Puerto Rican Legal Defense and Educational Fund (PRLDEF), he was still angry about the *New York Times* article. He believed that the report was incomplete since, just like previous reports, it brought out the negative aspects of the Puerto Rican community in New York and not its virtues. "The article does not say that in New York City almost 95 percent of elected Latino officials are Puerto Rican," Figueroa pointed out to me. "Nor does it say that Puerto Ricans hold very important positions in the business world, in politics, and in entertainment; for example, Jennifer López and Marc Anthony." For Figueroa, the socioeconomic problems of Puerto Ricans in New York are rooted in a "combination of discrimination, a lack of resources in urban areas, and a terrible educational system; the problem with public education for all Hispanics, not just Puerto Ricans, is serious."

This lawyer, who is responsible for one of the most respected organizations of Puerto Ricans in the United States, also complains about the unfair treatment his fellow countrymen receive with respect to other U.S. citizens. "When they deal with us here, they treat us just like other Hispanics—for example, the police—and it's not surprising that some Puerto Ricans feel as if they just crossed the border yesterday," Figueroa said.

"Do Puerto Ricans feel like immigrants with an American passport?" I asked him.

"They treat us like that just because we are Puerto Rican," he responded. "They treat us differently and we feel different, even though we are, like most people in this country, U.S. citizens."

Figueroa believes that the conflict between Puerto Ricans and the U.S. Navy over Vieques has generated an unusual degree of consciousness among all islanders, and that's not all. It has emphasized what it means to be Puerto Rican, something many had forgotten. "It is unprecedented in the history of Puerto Rico that the three parties and all the political leaders, inside and outside of the island, have spoken with a single voice," he explained.

"This is one of the first moments for us as a nation, as a people," Figueroa pointed out. "We have recognized that our association with the United States has disadvantages and that our power is very limited; our desires have not been heard."

The coming months and years will not be free of conflict. "After

Vieques," Figueroa reflected, "we will be ready to question our relationship with the United States, inside and outside the island, and we will not take positions that we have adopted blindly, like a religion."

IN MY CONVERSATIONS WITH Figueroa and dozens of other Puerto Ricans—statists, free-statists, independents, and those who are apolitical—I have reached the inevitable conclusion that Puerto Ricans today feel more Puerto Rican than ever, and it is because of Vieques. Something that would be so ordinary in any town in the United States, is momumental in the life of Puerto Ricans.

Suddenly, the Puerto Rican in New York, who has always been treated differently despite holding a U.S. passport, knows that he or she is not alone in feeling that the American is different from him, and has different interests. The Puerto Rican on the island, regardless of whether he supports statehood or a free associated state, also knows that he will never be able to renounce his Puerto Rican identity or his *puertorriqueñidad*.

It is difficult to know how the Vieques dispute will end, or what the permanent political status of the island will be, but the recent conflict with the United States has already had a positive impact on how Puerto Ricans identify themselves.

"I am Puerto Rican and nothing else." That is what I am hearing.

21 PUERTO DOMINICANS AND NEW DOMINICANS

Miami. The television screen had shown all it could; it was about to explode. Once again, a badly built boat filled with dozens of Dominican immigrants had sunk in the Mona Passage. It had almost reached its destination—almost. It sunk 100 yards off the coast. That doesn't count, though. Seventeen survivors, each one of whom had paid $170 for the seventy-five-mile trip, were arrested by the Puerto Rican Border Patrol. Others disappeared into the Isabella mountains. Ten bodies were found. The rest were taken by the sea.

The images showed the swollen, purple body of a man whose skin was so taut from the effects of the salt water and the sun that it looked like he was about to explode. One reporter pulled back the sheet that covered him but quickly replaced it. He couldn't bear it. Nor could I. I turned off the TV.

San Juan. "I am not prejudiced against Domincans," a Puerto Rican businessman said to me. I believed him. I know him to be a magnanimous person. "But lately I see them everywhere and they do not appreciate the opportunity they have being here in Puerto Rico." Then he explained to me that on some occasions, like at baseball games in the Caribbean series, he had felt strange being surrounded by Dominicans on his own island.

It doesn't take a genius to understand why the Dominicans keep coming to Puerto Rico. One professional couple summed it up for me in the following way: "The housekeeper who worked for us earned one hundred dollars a month at most in Santo Domingo. Here in Puerto Rico she can earn one thousand dollars or more."

For many Dominicans, however, being in Puerto Rico means facing problems of discrimination, racism, and xenophobia. This matter is so troublesome that two teachers, Carmen Sara García and Ivette Maisonet Quiñones, warned their students at the Universidad del Sagrado Corazón about the dangers of reflecting these prejudices in their journalistic work. In their style manual, *Periodismo sin Gazapos (Journalism without Blunders)*, they wrote:

> In Puerto Rico, the denial of the existence of racism against blacks is a generalized social position. Nevertheless, human behavior as well as language demonstrate its presence. Racism exists in Puerto Rico, along with xenophobia against some of the country's inhabitants. These two prejudices are revealed in discriminatory practices when offering services, in access to good education, in getting a job, in access to purchasing power, in the restriction of residential areas, and in the limited public presence (or absence) in political and social positions of power of Puerto Rican blacks.

The discrimination that some Puerto Ricans feel on their own island is suffered on a larger scale by entire groups of Dominicans. Dominicans in Puerto Rico do the work that the Puerto Ricans themselves don't want to do, just as in the United States with other immigrants. The Puerto Dominicans, as I will call them for the purpose of identification, are subject to abuse, exploitation, discrimination, and rejection. It is estimated that there are approximately 150,000 Dominicans living in Puerto Rico today.

In the mornings, in the more elegant neighborhoods that surround the Puerto Rican capital, you can see small armies of Dominican women getting off buses and heading off to Puerto Rican households to clean, sweep, mop, polish, wax, tidy, iron, wash, mind the children, and anything else that might occur to the *señora*.

Dominicans and Puerto Ricans need each other, but that is something immigration authorities do not want to understand. I know Puerto Rican families that have practically adopted Dominicans so that they can later bring their families over legally from the Dominican Republic. However, I also know many cases of Dominicans who live with the fear of being deported and who, therefore, accept wages that are far below what a Puerto Rican would earn in the same circumstance.

Dominicans are able to give a name (and sometimes a surname) to the reasons they left Quisqueya. The endless Balaguer government and his populist obsession for grandiose projects were unable to pull most people out of poverty. In September 1998, Hurricane George closed in on the Mona Passage, and many lost the little they had. Hopes for real change during Leonel Fernández's regime quickly vanished.

"Do you know what they call the group that was in power with Fernández?" one Dominican whom I respect a lot asked me. "The *comesolos*." He would later explain that other governments at least had the decency to divide up the budegtary pie among a wide pool of collaborators and businessmen. But the past government, he explained, only handed out favors to a reduced circle of *amiguitos*. "*Comen solos,*" he said—"they eat alone."

People generally leave a place if they cannot fill their stomachs. Dominicans leave their island for Puerto Rico and New York.

NOT LONG AGO, AN indignant Dominican businessman contacted me after he had heard me say that the Dominican Republic was one of the poorest countries in the continent.

"Please don't say that," he asked me.

"What do you want me to say then?" I answered back. "It's information I got from the United Nations."

"It gives us a terrible image."

I am convinced that good publicity is not going to rescue most

Dominicans from poverty. For that, jobs and a good governmental plan free from corruption are needed, along with generations of effort. However, every day there are Dominicans who are not willing to wait for that moment to come, and crossing the mountain into Haiti is not an option; in Haiti the people are much poorer than they are.

The poorest of the poor do not even have the opportunity to emigrate, for they cannot cover the most basic transportation costs. Other Dominicans, those who have a little money—those who can get a loan from an aunt or a grandfather, those who are able to save up a few dollars—look beyond the sea.

"The Mona Passage is to Dominicans what the southern border of the U.S. is to Mexicans," I was told by a young Puerto Rican girl who was intimately familiar with the deaths attributed to the stormy straight between the Dominican Republic and Puerto Rico. While Puerto Rico is often the last hope for Dominican immigrants, other times it is merely the springboard for reaching New York. To be Puerto Dominican is hardly a condemnation, but to be New Dominican is for many the real chance to make it big.

New York. When Víctor Morisete and his brother arrived in this city in 1982, they were carrying luck with them in their suitcase. The day after they arrived, Víctor's brother found a job. It took him one day, just one day, to find his way, and Víctor, who was just eighteen years old at the time, entered school shortly after that.

Today the story of Víctor and his brother would be hard to duplicate. Half of the 40,000 Dominicans who come to New York each year do so without immigration papers. At present, at least one of every five Dominicans in the United States is undocumented. What are the main problems that hinder the advancement of Dominicans in the United States? "First, what a Dominican needs when he arrives in the U.S. is a job; that is fundamental," Víctor Morisete, who is the director of the Asociación de Dominicanos Progresistas (ADP) in New York, explained to me. "To have a job that pays more than eight dollars an hour."

According to the ADP, the average income of a Dominican in New York is only $6,600 per year. "And that is well below the poverty level in the United States," Morisete pointed out. "It is a result of immigration laws; the lack of eligibility to take advantage of immigration laws has had a very negative effect on Dominicans."

The second most important problem for New Dominicans is education, and in this they are not alone. "The entire Hispanic community is suffering due to the lack of quality education," Morisete said, "and the Dominican children who come here need a quality education."

The third problem is not being able to live in a safe place, not just free of crime but of toxic substances too. That is to say, in apartments and housing not at risk for lead poisoning or substances that can cause asthma and other illnesses.

In order to confront these three problems political power is needed, the power to decide. Unfortunately, the numerical force of the Dominicans in New York does not have an equivalent political representation. In early 2000, there were only three judges and one state assemblyman, city councilman Guillermo Linares, in New York City, who were of Dominican origin.

Like the Mexican community, the Dominicans have an immigration barrier. Any non-Cuban or non–Puerto Rican Latino in New York who aspires to an elected office needs, first and foremost, time; time first, to become a U.S. citizen.

In comparison with the Puerto Ricans, Dominicans are relative newcomers to New York. In the final years of Trujillo's dictatorship, in the early 1960s, many Dominicans emigrated to New York. After the revolution, the numbers began to grow. There are currently one million Dominicans living in the United States, 200,000 of whom are undocumented.

As the percentage of Puerto Ricans in New York decreases, that of the Dominicans and Mexicans—two communities that share many things—has increased. Among the many things they share is the difficulty in legalizing their immigration status and the fact they take the most difficult and lowest paying jobs. Despite this and the extremely low per capita income, Dominicans abroad provide one of the main sources of capital for the Dominican Republic; one of every four Dominican families depends on the transfer of funds from their fellow countrymen in the United States. In the new millennium, newly arrived Dominicans were not as lucky as Víctor Morisete's brother in finding a job in one day. Even so, they continue to come, convinced that the opportunity for work and to help their families from afar is better than being condemned to life on an island with little or no social mobility.

I TURNED THE TELEVISION back on. The images of the dead Dominicans were still overwhelming the screen. I knew that sooner or later
that footage would reach the homes of thousands of Dominicans
who were considering emigrating, but that would not stop them.
Hunger is stronger than fear. So the hope was that the next boat
loaded with undocumented Dominicans would be sturdier and
wouldn't capsize in the Mona Passage, 100 yards from the Puerto
Rican coastline.

22 THE NEW COLOMBIAN EXODUS

I am one more. Like the intellectual, like the reporter, like
the human rights activist, like the displaced person, like
(the comedian) Pacheco. No more, no less. It is my turn to
relinquish my homeland, my life, my soul, my country.

Francisco Santos
Journalist for El Tiempo de Bogotá
Founder of the anti-abduction association, País Libre,
and of the anti-violence movement, No Más.
He left Colombia in March 2000.

Miami. It must be terrible if every time you arrive at an international
airport, customs and immigration officials question you and subject
you to a strip search because you hold a Colombian passport. Sometimes it would seem that they do it just to humiliate you and not

because they expect to find drugs in your belongings or documents that would reveal your intention to remain in the country permanently. It must be terrible if when every time someone mentions your country, the words abductions, murders, death threats, guerrilla, and violence come up, as if there were nothing else. Perhaps that is why Colombians frequently ask: What do you think of us?

It is now a kind of ritual. Every so often one of my Colombian friends asks me: "What do they think about us here? Do we have a bad reputation? What do you think about what is going on in Colombia? Do you think the United States wants to get involved?" Colombians have the habit, as so few do, of asking others what they think about them. It is as if they do not believe what they see and they need someone else to tell them how things are, and things do not look good.

Here, from far away, it seems like the situation in Colombia is getting worse before it gets better. We are accustomed to receiving despairing images of Colombia thanks to the international media: a car bomb that killed ten in Medellín, other explosions in Cali; a guerrilla group that hijacked a group of airline passengers and parishioners who were attending mass; the other rebel group that controls a third of the country; the economy taking a dive; the country, in 1999, experiencing the worst economic depression since the 1930s; the killing of humorist Jamie Garzón along with 125 journalists since 1977; the fact that there are more murders in Colombia than in China (which has a population forty times greater); the fact that in the last twelve months more than 850 civilians have been killed by guerrilla and paramilitary groups—no, more than that. I could keep going, but these examples more than illustrate my point.

Maybe for Colombians this is all old news and they have become hardened to such violence. After every act of terrorism, or abduction, or particularly gruesome murder, I hear: "No more, we will not allow this to keep happening in Colombia," only to hear later about yet another act of terrorism, another abduction, or another brutal murder.

Here, from afar, it seemed obvious that the Colombian army could not win the war against the rebels and drug traffickers, and that the government, with fewer and fewer resources, was wasting away to the bone. The voids in power that have been left by one government after the other have been occupied by guerrillas, drug traffickers, and members of the paramilitary. Neither the army nor the government of Colombia could win the battle.

I know all too well that the media, television in particular, tend

to exaggerate and to present only one part of the story as if it were the whole truth. Naturally, there is another side of Colombia—the one that is strong, united, hardworking, successful, peaceful, export-producing—but that is not the one depicted outside the country. Only the bad news, the explosions, the murders (like that of Garzón), and the abductions reach us.

Since only the bad news is broadcast, the United States has become alarmed. The United States, as we all know, has had a cyclical interest in Latin America. For long periods of time it forgets all about entire countries, only to later get deeply involved in their matters. Well, these days, the United States is looking very closely—with a magnifying glass—at Colombia.

The signs are everywhere. There is the offer of $1.6 billion in U.S. aid so that, as stated by the White House, the United States can help "the Colombian government push into the coca-growing regions of southern Colombia, which are now dominated by insurgent guerrillas." There are other signs as well. For instance, when you see one of the anchors of a major television news program in the United States travel to a country, you had better fasten your seat belt, for there will almost surely be trouble. Those people do not travel for pleasure, and they are expensive.

In the summer of 1999, Dan Rather of CBS was in Colombia because something had popped up on the radar screen in Washington. Rather's trip came after a reconnaissance plane carrying five U.S. soldiers was shot down. At that time there were between two hundred and three hundred U.S. soldiers and agents working in Colombia, and the fear of the Pentagon was that the United States would be brought into a complicated conflict.

When U.S. politicians talk about Colombia, the comparison is not with Kosovo but rather with Vietnam, where U.S. participation grew gradually. In fact, it is very difficult to think that the United States could intervene militarily in Colombia in a large-scale way, or that Americans would want to, or that President Andréas Pastrana would allow it. It would mean his political death. There is no doubt, however, that the highest officials in the U.S. military have been studying how to lend Pastrana a hand for months.

Then-secretary of state Madeleine Albright wrote a long essay in which she pointed out that Colombian drug traffickers produce more than 80 percent of the world's cocaine. She also noted that both the guerrillas and the paramilitary used drug trafficking to finance their operations. Her conclusion was that Colombia's problems have spread beyond its borders, thus causing serious implications for the security and stability of the region. In other words, Colombia had become a national security problem for the United States, and there were some in the United States who were dying to use force to resolve the matter. Colombia is not Kosovo, though, and a little war of seventy-nine days, like the one in the Balkans, would not put an end to the drug trafficking or the guerrilla warfare. So what can be done?

From afar, the only viable choice seems to be a dialogue for peace. President Andrés Pastrana knows—although he doesn't like it—that he could never win and that his army is not as strong or as clean or as well trained as he would like. He also knows that he could never support a large-scale military intervention by the United States. Negotiation was the only choice left. Besides, Pastrana's word was still good, unlike that of Ernesto Samper. Having been a journalist, Pastrana knows that all he really has is his credibility. I am aware that Pastrana's popularity is at rock bottom and that he is criticized for having handed over a part of the country to the guerrillas. This is not a popularity contest, however, and his strategy clearly has risks. It is a question, quite simply, of achieving peace. Those who have a better idea may raise their hands.

Is negotiation difficult? Of course; but if the Salvadoran and Guatemalan rebels were able to negotiate a peace with their respective governments and integrate into civil society, why won't the Colombians be able to do so as well?

POOR, BUT IN MIAMI

While this was occurring in late 1998 and early 1999, there was talk of the new Colombian exodus. Authorities assured everyone that this was not true; that the massive number of Colombians leaving their country was solely in response to a well-known practice of Colombians taking trips abroad for vacation or business. The difference this time was that many of those who were leaving Colombia were doing everything possible to not go back. Better undocumented than dead, some thought. Without papers but without fear, concluded a few more. Poor but in Miami, joked others.

An article in the *Miami Herald* calculated that on February 2000, there were approximately 50,000 undocumented immigrants who had come from Colombia to the Miami-Dade area of south Florida alone. This number does not include the thousands more all along the east coast of the United States, especially in New York. Under the headline, THE UNSTOPPABLE FLIGHT OF COLOMBIANS TO THE UNITED STATES, the same newspaper, citing figures from the Colombian government, later reported that between 1996 and 2000, 800,000 Colombians had left their country for the United States "People leave their country for economic problems which have their origin in violence," said Jesús Ramos, ambassador from Colombia to the OAS, to a reporter from *El Nuevo Herald* (March 14, 2000.)

Lines at the U.S. embassy in Bogotá were enormous and the obstacles, gigantic; but everyone who got a visa, after his life had been analyzed as if in a confessional, felt like a child at a carnival. Most, it is true, come and go; but those who stay are increasing in number.

Today, in the United States, many of these Colombian immigrants, legal and illegal, are experiencing a new battle; their country is falling to pieces in a warlike conflict. However, the United States is not giving them any special immigration consideration (like that which refugees and political exiles from other war zones have received).

Colombians today can be characterized as always fighting against adversity. They fled Colombia because of war and a lack of opportunities, and in the United States all they want is to live in peace, without the threat of deportation. It is not a lot to ask; it is what has been given to other groups in similar circumstances. That is why thousands of Colombians are trying to pressure the U.S. government through protests and signatures, so that they grant them TPS, a special immigration condition requested by the president himself, in order to temporarily prevent the risk of being deported.

It is hard to determine how many Colombians have come to the United States in the last twenty-four months, but I have my own personal tally. I know a Colombian architect who wanted to work as a reporter in the United States, a young mother who feared for the safety of her two children and was looking for a way to stay in Miami, and a news director whose wife was living in fear that someone in the family would be kidnapped and who demanded that her husband leave Colombia as soon as possible or else.

MAKING THE MOST OF THE WORST

Violence, ironically, has forced Colombians to make the best of it. One Colombian politican told me that Colombians live in the present and make few plans, for history has shown that we are only in the world five minutes. Colombia has experienced long periods of violence, and merely surviving is a feat in itself.

I know few people that are as happy as the Colombian people. A party with Colombians turns into a festival and a celebration of life. To the rhythm of merengue, salsa, and *vallenato*, every party in Colombia is a negation of the death that has plagued them for decades, and this spirit spills over onto other things.

Despite the enormous problem of drug trafficking, the drawn-out guerrilla conflict, the distrust of corrupt leaders, and the economic stagnation, Colombia has not come to a standstill. This is important to point out, for few nations facing a similar crisis would have kept their essence intact like Colombia. *This too shall pass.*

Colombians wait anxiously for the day when they can tour their own country without fear of being killed, the day when people mention the name of their country and don't think of violence, the day when they can arrive at an airport and be treated with genuine courtesy and respect, the day when they will be welcomed, wherever they go, and the day when there is peace in their land. Until that happens, the exodus, whether drop by drop or in floods, will force Colombia to continue to dig deep within to bring out the best of itself.

23 THE MUDDY SHOES OF VENEZUELA

San Bernardino, Caracas. After Hugo Chávez's first year in office, the economy had contracted by 7 percent, half a million workers joined the unemployment lines, and the skyrocketing oil prices could not do much to get 80 percent of Venezuelans out of poverty. In other words, many Venezuelans were not seeing the butter on their bread. However, if the populist, popular, authoritarian, and centrist style of President Hugo Chávez was not the reason many Venezuelans decided to emigrate, then the terrible rain of December 1999 became the sign to leave that some had been waiting for.

THE SHOES MUST HAVE belonged to a four- or five-year-old boy. They were white with blue stripes. The soles were slightly worn, the laces gone. I found them amidst the mud, branches, and rocks that came down the hill from Ávila in a torrent. Did the boy who was wearing these shoes survive? I don't know. What I do know is that I have always noticed—maybe because there is no logical explanation for it—that the first thing that victims of disasters and accidents lose is their shoes.

The last estimate I heard, from the Civil Defense of Venezuela, was that the number of deaths due to the rain and flooding surpassed 20,000. Many people with whom I spoke, though, believe that President Hugo Chávez's government is hiding the real figures. Why? There is suspicion among some Venezuelans that President Chávez downplayed the danger of the torrential rains and downpours so that people would go out to vote in the election on December 15 and approve the new constitution that he wanted so much. This new Venezuelan magna carta included, of course, the reelection of the president, which would allow Chávez to remain in office for twelve more years.

Why did the government not declare a state of emergency before the election and after two weeks of uninterrupted rain? Why did it not cancel or postpone the election when it found out about the first deaths in the state of Vargas? Why did it not inform the people, on national radio and television, to prepare for possible mudslides and flooding? Why were the most vulnerable areas not evacuated on time? Could politics and the interest in being reelected have taken priority over the well-being of ordinary Venezuelans? These are just questions.

Chávez, emboldened by the results of the election—seven of every ten voters voted for him—appeared at a press conference on election night downplaying the bad weather. Naively he said, "San Isidro Labrador, get rid of the water and bring back the sun, might be the slogan for this moment; or Bolívar's: If nature opposes us we will fight against her, and we will make her obey us."

Bolívar's words in Chávez's mouth sounded arrogant, and nature clearly did not obey the president. When one of the flood victims, who had been walking for five days, heard Chávez's comments, he responded to him on television: "He said that he was going to change everything, that he was fighting against nature; let him come fight now, let him see what has happened to us." After one year in office, that was the first crisis that Chávez had had to confront which he could not resolve with words, publicity, or bullets. His enormous popularity was beginning to erode—falling from 90 percent to 70 percent—after several unfortunate decisions, like the one to open

Maiquetia international airport to flood victims and to isolate Venezuela from the rest of the world. The victims could easily have been given shelter in a less strategically important place, like a hangar. Populism, however, won out over pragmatism. When the *chavistas* realized their mistake, it was too late; Venezuela was cut off from the world. Because of this, neither help nor investments could reach Venezuela.

Shortly before Christmas in 1999, I flew from Miami to Caracas, literally on top of the cargo of a Venezuelan Air Force C-130. I spent the four-and-a-half-hour flight on top of a container filled with food, medicine, and wheelchairs for the flood victims. All commercial flights in and out of Caracas had been cancelled. Thousands were stuck in Venezuela and others couldn't get back in. The scenes I witnessed in the Miami airport, with passengers who had been sleeping in the terminal for days, was chilling, but naturally it was nothing compared to what I found in Venezuela. I saw a country that could not see beyond its borders, like the ill who are in great pain. Venezuela was looking inside. I toured the most devastated areas during Christmas, and I didn't see a single Santa Claus or Christmas tree. It was clear that in this country, unlike the rest of the world, no one was worried about the so-called Y2K crisis and possible terrorist attacks. Venezuela was undergoing something much worse.

I can still see the eyes of Esmérida, who spent thirty of her fifty-three years in a little house that the river, which runs through the neighborhood of San Bernardino, swept away in one fell swoop. I can also see the persistence of Alejandro, the policeman who refused to leave what remained of his half-destroyed, mud-filled home in Catia La Mar; the desperation of Mariela when she realized that the new course of the torrent coming down the hillside ran right by her kitchen; and the crazed, shirtless father who was crying on TV as he recounted how he lost his five children in the flood.

The story that had the most profound impact on me, however, was that of an eleven-year-old girl who tried to save her little cousin who was only three months old. They were both being swept away by a strong current that was flowing toward the ocean. The man who told me the story said that after a great deal of struggling, the girl ran out of energy and let the baby go. The baby drowned, but the older girl was able to grab onto a plastic container, and she was later rescued at sea. I cannot even begin to imagine what that girl-heroine must be dreaming each night. That is the first time in my life that I did not identify the color green with life. From the air, Venezuela was completely green; the rain had left it that way, but it was the green of death.

After this disaster, Venezuela was in danger of being stuck in the twentieth century; it would take years to get back to where it had been; and where it had been . . . was not very good. There are now more poor than when Chávez came into power, more homeless than before, more unemployed than before, and after one year in power, the economy had shrunk. Only the sudden increase in oil prices averted the financial collapse of the nation. The dream of a change for the better, which Chávez had offered to the hungriest, was waterlogged, and it could take years to dry.

Furthermore, this tragedy allowed the de facto militarization of Venezuela. The government capitalized on the chaos caused by the flooding: soldiers were everywhere, congress was dissolved on December 22, 1999, and political opponents and independent journalists began to feel the stomping of the boots.

I was not surprised, therefore, by the perception of a new exodus to the United States. In fact, wealthier Venezuelans were already leaving, in small planes, via Aruba, Curaçao, San Juan, and Santo Domingo. Just as Central Americans began to arrive in Miami after Hurricane Mitch and Colombians after the intensification of war, there was now a trail of Venezuelans leaving their country. The footprints were fresh:

1. A Venezuelan actress told me she was going to sell the property she had acquired during her lifetime in Venezuela because she had lost faith in Chávez.
2. Because of the high levels of crime and unemployment, a couple of Venezuelans mentioned they had put their apartment in Caraças up for sale and they were going to try their luck in Miami, without visas and without jobs. "At least," he said, "my children will be able to breathe clean air and play in a park without the danger of being kidnapped or killed."
3. The drain of talent has already occurred. One of the best-known journalists in Venezuela called me the other day and began to fish

around to see if he could get a job in the United States. "Things are impossible here now," he said.

That is how many Venezuelans are—with their shoes muddy and looking for a shinier, brighter present.

LIFE IN THE UNITED STATES

24 NOSTALGIA, AROMAS, AND TACOS

I left Mexico for the United States almost two decades ago, but every time I return for a visit I religiously perform the same ritual. First, I eat some *taquitos al pastor,* with onion, cilantro, salsa verde, and a few drops of lemon, and then I try to catch up on the recent changes

I am convinced that nostalgia begins with the mouth and continues with the nose. The aromas that bring me back to Mexico are very specific and, at times, with a bit of effort, I can evoke them: the rain-soaked lawn and then the sun coming out again, the lotion my father used, the steam from the kitchen of my cynical aunts, the skin of my first girlfriend and the interior of my Volkswagen.

As fate would have it, I have broken my nose three times. Little by little, after each operation, I have lost my sense of smell. I can only pick up very strong odors. Maybe that is why the few aromas that I have, so closely guarded in my memory, carry me instantly through time and space. Always to the past.

Always to Mexico.

Always.

25 THE CALL

It is the call we all dread, particularly those of us who live abroad. It is that ring that wakes us up so abruptly in the early morning and sets our hearts pounding. There is never good news when that call comes. On the other end of the line, there is always an illness or an accident, and, without fail, it happens to those we love most. When the call comes we have to leave at once, and there is always the doubt over whether we'll get there in time, if we'll be able to help, in the best case scenario, or say goodbye, in the worst. Anguish takes over.

My father had a third heart attack, and he had to have an emergency operation in Mexico City. I listened to everything in the darkness. Before I hung up, I said, "I'm coming." I turned on the lamp, and the light cut through the room like a knife. My eyes were not bothered, though. I felt numb. In that semiconscious state, I made a couple of phone calls and then headed for the airport.

The flight to Mexico was completely full, and the next flight wasn't for two days. I put my name on the waiting list anyway. I felt like I was having one of those nightmares, where you want to run but you can't. I think I finally got a seat on the plane out of sheer persistence. I bought the ticket for close to double the regular price, which was the first time in my life I was thankful for paying the highest fare on a flight. I don't really remember passing through customs and immigration in Mexico City; the next thing I remember was being at the hospital. When I arrived, the operation had just ended. "He's in serious but stable condition," they told me. "He had a triple bypass." Just like that, plain and simple, no euphemisms.

My family and I spent the next few days practically living in the claustrophobic waiting room in the intensive care unit. Only a couple of glass doors separated us from him. I had never pictured him as a sick person, only as a survivor, fighting furiously for his life. We were all afraid to leave the waiting room.

My father survived, but the memory of that phone call marked me forever. For years I had waited for it. Often they were wrong numbers in the middle of the night for which I berated the caller for the scare and for waking me up, and a sigh of relief before hitting the pillow again. Other times they were scatterbrained friends who live in other time zones or who have schedules like vampires calling just to say hello. For those of us who have chosen to live far from where we were born, however, the call comes sooner or later. Every one of us who packed our bags one day and left share that anxiety.

Mexico City, June 1994

26 THE REDISCOVERY OF HISPANICS

Finally. CNN has discovered us. We exist. I saw a report in February 1998 on the Cable News Network (CNN) about the extraordinary growth of Spanish language media in the United States. The phenomenon has been taking place for decades, but CNN, along with millions of Americans, barely noticed. The tone of the report was one of astonishment. CNN is the discoverer that spreads news around the world, as if it were a modern-day Christopher Columbus. What had it discovered? The presence and the power of the Hispanic in the United States.

The CNN report forms part of one of those cycles of interest and disinterest which we Latinos are used to. The interesting thing, however, is that those cycles are disappearing little by little—or they are no longer as pronounced as before—thanks to an obvious reality: There are more and more Hispanics in the United States, and our growing political and economic power is being felt in every corner of the country. It isn't so easy to overlook us anymore. The reasons, which are many, have to do with numbers, political power, and money.

NUMBERS

There are more than 35 million Hispanics in the United States today, more than 12 percent of the total population. It is likely that the real figure is much higher, since undocumented immigrants have more important things to do than answer the questions of the pollster from the Census Bureau. Latinos in the United States also have, on average, more children than African Americans or whites. One study carried out by the National Center for Health Statistics indicates that in 1995, Hispanics were responsible for eighteen of every one hundred births in the United States. That figure is increasing by almost 1 percent each year, and counting the uncounted undocumented immigrants, Hispanics are already the largest minority in the United States. Moreover, we must add to the population growth of Hispanics in the United States the thousands of undocumented immigrants who cross the border from Mexico in order to find work.

With high reproductive rates among Hispanics, and the constant influx of immigrants, there is no danger, either in the short run or the long run, that assimilation to mainstream United States society will dilute the power of Hispanics. The power is in the numbers. The future of the growing, but still very limited, political power of Latinos depends on how to use this demographic phenomenon.

POLITICAL POWER

If all Hispanics voted like the Cuban Americans in south Florida, the history of Latinos in the United States would be quite different. Voters of Cuban descent represent more than 50 percent of the population in the county and city of Miami. When there are elections, they vote for their own. That is why the main political offices in south Florida are held by Hispanics, and their concerns are always a priority for the candidates, regardless of their race or color.

The political power of Cuban Americans is unquestionable and is felt as far away as Washington. Suffice it to say that U.S. policy toward Cuba, centered around the strengthening of the embargo against the island, is strongly influenced by the Cuban exile community. Even President George W. Bush admitted in an interview that the Cuban-American vote in Florida had been very important in the past presidential elections held on November 2, 2000.

Miami is the best example of what could and should happen in other cities where Hispanics are becoming a majority, but there is still a long way to go. Almost 40 percent of the residents in metropolitan Los Angeles are Latino, and therefore four of every ten important local government offices should be in the hands of Hispanics. Even the mayor of Los Angeles should be Latino. However, the reality is very far from that ideal.

For immigration and historical questions, the Mexican-American community has still not achieved the same level of political representation that the Cuban-American community has. Part of the problem is that there are millions of undocumented Mexicans and as many more who have resisted becoming U.S. citizens. But with the new Mexican law that allows dual nationality, the apprehension created by anti-immigrant laws such as proposition 187, the fear of being deported, and the anxiety over the possibility of losing the right to certain social services, applications for U.S. citizenship have hit new records.

There is still, however, a long way to go for cities like San Antonio, Chicago, New York, and San Francisco, among others with high concentrations of Latinos, in order to resemble Miami. Why should they resemble Miami? Well, as one of the pioneers of Spanish media said to me, Miami is the only U.S. city that treats Hispanics like first-class citizens, in schools and restaurants as well as in government offices and movie theaters.

The success Hispanics have achieved in Miami has still not had an impact on the national level. If Hispanics are 12 percent of the U.S. population, logic would indicate that twelve of the one hundred Senate seats should be filled by Latinos. But there is not a single senator today with the last name of Pérez, Suarez, Rodríguez, or Hernandez. That too will change—soon.

MONEY

It is true that the power of numbers has not translated instantaneously into political power for Hispanics. Nevertheless, the demographic growth of Hispanics is having a very important impact on world business. As an advertisement for used cars (or was it mattresses?) says, "What matters here is cash."

According to a study by the Asociación Hispana de Responsabili-
dad Corporativa (HACR), the purchasing power of Latinos, rose
from $211 billion in 1990 to $348 billion in 1997, reaching almost
$400 billion in 2000. That last figure is higher than the gross domes-
tic product of Mexico. The consequences of this growing economic
power are seen and heard everywhere.

The radio stations in Los Angeles with the largest audiences are
broadcast in Spanish, despite frequent tantrums from their English
language competitors. The most watched television news broadcast
among 18- to 49-year-olds is also in Spanish. Hispanic radio and television stations dominate the market. However, commercials in English continue to sell at higher prices than those in Spanish. Why?

Unfortunately, the high audience numbers of Spanish stations do
not necessarily mean a proportional increase in revenue. There is still
a great deal of reticence among large American companies to invest
in Spanish advertising. There have been great advances, however.
AT&T, for example, spent $1.4 billion in 1997 on advertising for His-
panics, according to the *New York Times*. That represents an increase
of 14 percent over the previous year. Other companies are following
in the footsteps of AT&T. They are baby steps, but they are welcome.

Hispanics not only determine what is seen on television in many
cities but they also influence the type of merchandise carried in
stores. In the United States, more tortillas are sold than bagels, and
more hot salsa than ketchup. What's more, large companies like
Sears have been forced to adapt their stores to the Latino taste,
which has meant more black brassieres and fewer checked pants.

This is not the result of a cultural invasion but of the greater purchasing power among Latinos. One study by the University of Southern California indicated that the annual wages of Latino men rose
over ten years from $14,900 to $18,900. The same report points out
that immigrants in California are learning English and escaping from
poverty at an unprecedented rate. That matters.

The enormous contributions of immigrants coming from south of
the border to the country's economy also matter. In the most extensive study carried out to date, the National Academy of Sciences concluded that immigrants, primarily composed of Latin Americans,
contribute $10 billion annually to the economy of the United States.
Immigrants are a tremendous business.

Also, there are entire industries, like the textile industry, the agricultural industry, and the service industry—restaurants, hotels, and clean-ing—that depend on Hispanic immigrants and undocumented workers. If we add to that the fact that thousands of American families are put-ting the care of their children in the hands of immigrant women, we can conclude that the contribution of Hispanics to U.S. culture and society have reached unanticipated levels in just a few years.

THE DISCOVERY AND REDISCOVERY of Hispanics will continue in the United States, particularly in places where there has not been a strong Hispanic presence. As we grow in numbers, in political influ-ence, and in purchasing power, no one will need CNN to realize that we are here and that we count. It is just a matter of time. It will be, I fear, an uphill journey filled with obstacles. The anti-immigrant, anti-Latino current, which flared up during the approval of propositions 187 and 209 in California, is far from disappearing.

This country is undergoing an identity crisis and still does not dare to see itself as a multiracial, multicultural society. There are still many who have not realized that the United States stopped being predominantly white long ago. That is why some continue to discover us and are surprised when they see us. Hispanics today, though, are making strides, and the footprints are there for all to see.

POSTSCRIPT: In March 2001, I was invited to participate on the ABC program *Nightline* to talk about a subject that surprised several of its American producers. They had apparently just discovered that there are many areas in the United States where only Spanish is spoken: Miami, Pilsen in Chicago, the Bronx in New York, Santa Ana in Cal-ifornia, San Antonio in Texas, and the Salvadoran section of Wash-ington, D.C.

For those of us who live here, who speak Spanish, and who form part of the more than 35 million Latinos in the United States, that type of information may not be surprising. After all, it is part of our daily lives. For instance, when I get up in the morning I listen to the radio, watch TV, read the newspaper, and check the Internet, all in Spanish. I speak with my children, my wife, my friends, and my colleagues at work, and I conduct business in Spanish. I go to the supermarket, the barbershop, the gas station, the dry cleaner, and restaurants, and I need only Spanish. This has been true in all aspects of my life. There are millions of Latinos just like me who use only Spanish, and that's just fine, thank you.

This is not to say that we do not speak English. Of course, we do, and it is essential for getting ahead in this country. Far from the commonly held stereotypes and prejudices, most Hispanics are bilingual and can communicate in English as well as Spanish. What is new, however, is the impressive growth in the population that prefers to express itself, amuse itself, and listen to news in Spanish.

The debate twenty years ago was over the assimilation of Hispanics to American society. Sociologists assumed that Latinos—just as the Italians, Irish, and Polish had done before them—would integrate into the United States without great resistance, and gradually forget their language, their culture, and their roots. They were mistaken. The melting pot dried up.

Spanish is more present than ever in the United States. Some of the most watched news programs in Miami, Los Angeles, Houston, Chicago, and New York are in Spanish. The most listened-to radio stations in states such as Florida and California are in Spanish. Never before have there been so many newspapers and magazines in Spanish in this country, and millions of people prefer to receive their e-mails and to surf the Internet in Spanish (and Spanglish). Ten years ago, only 25 percent of Latinos listened to and watched news programs in Spanish. Today, that figure has increased to almost 50 percent. Neither the Italian nor the Polish immigrants ever had radio and television networks in their own language. Hispanics do.

This immigration is different. First, because of the proximity of the countries of origin. It is not the same to cross from Tijuana to San Diego or from Havana to Miami as it is to travel from Naples to New York. Second, technological advances—faster and safer airplanes, cellular telephones, and the Internet—keep us in constant contact with what we left behind. Third, Hispanic families have more children than other groups; and finally, there is an impressive flow of new Latino immigrants into this country and nothing has stopped it—not more guards on the border or higher fences or the danger of the cold, the rivers, the smugglers, or coyotes. Each year, a million new legal immigrants enter the United States, and each day a thousand undocumented immigrants slip across the border. It is not surprising, then, that we are the most vibrant and powerful minority in the United States.

What surprised the producers of *Nightline*, as well as millions of Americans, was that immigrants who speak Spanish are quickly and dramatically changing the face of the United States. It is not a pure white country anymore; it is a mixed nation that by 2059 will be made up purely of minorities. That is the process that is already under way.

You need not be a wizard or Walter Mercado to see the future; there will be more and more Hispanics, our still-precarious political power will eventually increase, and the Spanish language will be more widespread. What seems like a rarity today to many Americans—entire communities communicating only in Spanish—is just a prelude of what's to come, a little piece of the future of the United States.

27 CALIFORNIA IS THE FUTURE

"California is an island on earth."
—*Carey McWilliams*

Los Angeles. I love coming to this city; it's like stepping into a time machine and travelling into the future. You don't need to look into a magic ball or read *The Third Wave* by Alvin Toffler to picture tomorrow. You only need to take a quick look at the streets of California. California reinvents itself everyday, and as California goes, so goes the rest of the United States. California is probably the most dynamic state in the country. New ideas do not scare Californians; they are part of its culture. California is also where we can get a glimpse of how the United States will look in the twenty-first century.

California recently became the first U.S. state where non-Hispanic whites are no longer the majority. Today, California is a state made up of minorities, and this has enormous repercussions, particularly in the way that such diverse groups as whites, blacks, Latinos, and Asians will have to coexist and share power.

The numbers tell the story. According to the Census Bureau, in California in the year 2000, no race or ethnic group was a majority. Of the 33,871,648 total inhabitants, 46 percent (15,816,790) are white, 32 percent (10,966,551) are Hispanic, 11 percent (3,752,596) are Asian, and 6 percent (2,181,926) are black. The rest of the population is made up of native Alaskans, native Americans, and those who are considered multiracial.

The change is dramatic. In 1970, eight of every ten Californians were white. Today they are another minority. As the number of whites decreases, the number of Hispanics increases. It is no surprise, then, that whites are complaining so much, and that from time to time they try to resist the inevitable by passing laws against and unleashing unfair criticism of the Latino population. For instance, if the ominous Proposition 187 had become law, thousands or perhaps millions of immigrants would not have access to medical services, and their children would not be able to go to public schools.

There are two fundamental reasons for the change occurring in California: First, the continuous immigration from south of the border; and second, Hispanic families tend to have more children than other ethnic groups. Some whites, blacks, and Asians may not like this situation, but there is nothing they can do about it, except to adapt and to learn to live together. (For some, this was not an appealing option, so they went to other states, particularly during the recession in the early 1990s.)

It is easier to speak about tolerance, of course, than it is to live it. Violence and ethnic tension are everyday occurrences in California— just look at the bloody gang wars. It is also difficult to go one day without hearing someone reporting a case of discrimination. You hear it all: whites discriminating against Hispanics, African Americans, and Asians, and cases where whites feel pushed aside.

Violence, however, is not a constant. California is an experiment underway, and tensions arise because of the differences and contrasts. There are more Mexicans in California than anywhere else outside of Mexico City. There are more Salvadorans than anywhere else outside of San Salvador. There are more Guatemalans than anywhere else outside of Guatemala City. This is true of many other groups.

There are times when I am driving, and in less than two minutes I pass a taqueria, a Korean restaurant, a chicken restaurant, and then a sushi place, to finally smell the unmistakeable aroma of grilled hamburgers filtering through my open car window. Los Angeles smells like the world. It is the multicultural society par excellence. It has a mixture of all Latin Americans as in Miami, Chicago, and San Antonio, but it also benefits from an enormous Asian influence for obvious geographic reasons; it is the first point of entry for immigrants coming from countries such as Japan, Thailand, South Korea, China, and Taiwan. The social tapestry of California is multicolored. From a distance it is beautiful; but close up, the challenge lies in preventing the threads from coming loose and having one color be more predominant than another.

In a short conversation I had with the Mexican poet and writer Octavio Paz before his death, he said, "The United States is a multiracial, multicultural country," and that is precisely "the great historical challenge of the United States." As put forth in his argument, the idea of the melting pot, in which all ethnic groups would end up assimilating, failed because it excluded minorities, like blacks and Mexicans.

Today, rather than speaking about the United States as a society that looks like a great big bowl of soup, without clear differences between its elements, the trend is to compare the nation to a salad in which each group maintains its characteristics, despite sharing the same space. I recently had the opportunity to visit an elementary school, and I noticed a drawing of an enormous salad on the blackboard. It was a social science class, and the name of the salad was the United States. American students already understand, because they live it every day in the classroom, but many American adults still do not understand that their country is no longer white. They do not understand that if they took a good look around them, with their minds open, they would find features of mixed races and not ethnic purity. In other words, to be American is to be multicultural, multiethnic, and multiracial.

California is the future of the United States. In this new millennium, the United States will become a nation of minorities; it will become like California is today. To get used to the future, take a short walk, with your mind and eyes wide open, down any one of the streets of this city.

POSTSCRIPT: Early in the twenty-first century, the Hispanic population was beginning to outnumber the black population in the United States. Why? There are two principal reasons.

First, immigration to the United States, both legal and illegal, remains constant, and the largest groups of those who have recently arrived come from Latin America. Second, the birthrate among Hispanics continues to increase. According to the National Center for Health Statistics, the number of babies born to Hispanic mothers in the United States rose from 14 percent of the total in 1989 to 18 percent in 1995. So, for every one hundred children born in the United States, eighteen are Latino, despite the fact that the Hispanic population made up only 10.3 percent of the population at that time. In 1995, 679,767 babies of Hispanic origin were born, compared to 532,249 born in 1989. A report from the same organization indicates that mothers of Mexican origin have an average of 3.32 children in their lifetime, Puerto Ricans 2.2, and Cubans 1.7. (Blacks and non-Hispanic whites have an average of slightly more than two children.)

Of the 2.7 million new Hispanics in California registered by the 2000 census, most were the result of more births in Latino families, not immigration.

Because of these factors and the constant flow of immigration from the south, we are experiencing the Latinization of the United States. Census figures show that Hispanics were only 5 percent of the population in 1970. That figure rose to 9 percent in 1990, and slightly more than 12 percent in 2000. In 2030, Hispanics will make up 18 percent of the total U.S. population, and in 2050, that number will reach 22 percent.

28 LORETTA AND THE VOTERS' REVENGE

Many radio and television news broadcasts in the United States did not even mention this piece of news in early 1998. They didn't have time: The Bill Clinton and Monica Lewinsky scandal was at its height, and Boris Yeltsin was warning about the danger of a world war. In newspapers it appeared, if at all, buried in the inside pages. The news had to do with a democratic congresswoman from California, Loretta Sánchez. Who? It's true, outside of Orange County, almost no one knew who she was, but she is the protagonist of one of the most important electoral victories for Hispanics in the United States.

The story goes like this. In the November 1996 elections, Loretta Sánchez, an amateur politician, beat Congressman Bob Dornan, who had held the seat for almost twenty years. Her lead was only 979 votes, but she won. Dornan simply couldn't believe it. He had won the last ten elections for U.S. Congress, and he found himself beaten by a candidate whose name he couldn't even pronounce.

Dornan, one of the most conservative politicians in the United States—he is anti-immigrant, anti-abortion, anti-homosexual, and anti-Communist—believed that his rhetoric would guarantee his seat forever; but he was wrong. Without realizing it, his electoral district (46) changed, and Hispanics were moving in. So when many of those Latinos went out to vote in 1996, they decided to choose someone who was like them, someone who would have more concern for their daily problems than for the politics of Washington. That is why Dornan lost, and he proved to be a very bad loser.

THE MILLION-DOLLAR TANTRUM

Instead of admitting that he had lost touch with the people and accepting his mistakes as a politician, Dornan claimed that a tremendous electoral fraud had robbed him of victory, and as the Republican U.S. congressman was controlled by people in his party, they began an investigation. A committee of the U.S. House of Representatives carried out an investigation, and after a year of searching through documents, they reached the conclusion that Loretta Sánchez had, in fact, beaten Bob Dornan. They discovered 748 illegal votes in the November election (although they never said if they were in Sánchez's or Dornan's favor). They then solemnly declared that there was no evidence to prove that the number of illegal votes would be enough to overturn the election. Case closed.

In short, Robert Dornan's tantrum cost approximately $1 million. That is what the committee spent on the fruitless investigation. It was all for nothing. Unfortunately, the Republicans who made up the investigatory committee preferred to believe the white man from the start, and not the Hispanic woman. Because of their prejudices, we all wound up paying the bill.

Loretta's victory was not a fluke. In 1998, Dornan challenged Loretta again, and again he lost. Loretta, whose parents were born in Mexicali and Nogales, understood better than Dornan that the United States is becoming a multiethnic and multicultural society, and that not even Pat Buchanan or the Ku Klux Klan can prevent that from happening. That is why Loretta won. Now the "Dornan syndrome," symbolized by the ostrich burying its head, was threatening to sabotage the careers of other distinguished politicians in California, as well as in New York, Texas, Arizona, New Mexico, and Illinois.

The news of Loretta Sánchez's double victory was buried in the avalanche of the Clinton scandal and the possibility of a new military confrontation with Iraq. It was even drowned out by El Niño, which was aggravating the world climate. Nevertheless, it is worthwhile to rescue it, for the future of Latinos in the United States will be filled with stories like Loretta's.

POSTSCRIPT: What in the world could Bob Dornan have been thinking when he believed that he could win the election in a district, in a state, and in a country that he no longer knew? According to a study by the United States Hispanic Leadership Institute in 1996, the first year Dornan lost, the number of Hispanics registered to vote in the United States rose 25.3 percent since 1992. The number of Latino voters rose 14.1 percent. It was with these votes that Loretta won.

Every time elections are held in the United States, the same thing occurs: There are more Latinos of voting age, more Hispanics registering to vote, and more people of Latino origin who have decided to exercise that vote. In 2000, roughly 9 million Hispanics were registered to vote (2.2 million in California alone), and it was estimated that 7 million Latinos would exercise their vote in the presidential elections. As time passes, those figures will multiply. The Census Bureau estimates that in fifty years, the Latino population in this country will triple. The 30 million Latinos there are today will become 98 million by 2050, and they will jump from 12 percent to 24 percent of the population. By 2100, one of every three people in the United States (33 percent) will be Latino. Non-Hispanic whites will make up 48 percent of the population, and the remainder will be composed of African Americans (13 percent), and Asians. In 2100, there will be 570 million people living in the United States.

We don't have to wait that long, however, to see the changes taking place. The number of elected Hispanic politicians in the United States—from the district level to the state level—increased from 4,704 in 1987 to 5,864 in 1992, according to census figures. That tendency continues today.

What all this means is that candidates like Dornan or Buchanan, with an anti-immigrant policy of exclusion, will have fewer chances of winning in a society that will be composed of ethnic minorities. The Lorettas of California hold the future in their hands. The first Hispanic president in the history of the United States, in fact, has probably already been born.

29 ACCOMPLICES OF THE UNDOCUMENTED

We are all accomplices of the undocumented immigrants—all of us, in Mexico as well as in the United States. These undocumented immigrants are able to live and prosper in the United States because all of us, in some way, support what they do. That's all there is to it.

There are approximately 6 million undocumented immigrants in the United States, most of Mexican descent. They are able to obtain jobs because there are U.S. companies that are willing to employ them, despite the punishments immigration laws impose. For many companies, it is simply worth the risk to hire undocumented workers rather than pay the higher wages that U.S. workers or foreigners with green cards demand. This occurs every day in California, Texas, Florida, Illinois, and New York. Although it may be hard to believe, even in the most unsuspecting places, there are undocumented workers.

I read somewhere that thirty-eight Mexicans were arrested in an

INS raid in Cincinnati, Ohio. In Ohio! They were working for none other than the company that was constructing the building of one of the largest corporations in the world, Procter and Gamble. Even though this corporation obviously did not hire them directly, the construction company was indeed an accomplice of those undocumented Mexicans, since they hired them in order to keep the costs of the new building down.

On other, more mundane levels, there is also evidence of this complicity. We are accomplices of the undocumented immigrants when we hire them to take care of our children and clean our houses, when we eat the fruit and vegetables they pick, when we go to restaurants where they serve us, when we stay in a hotel where they are employed, when we live in homes that they built, when we conduct business in offices where they work, when we drive on roads that they paved, and when we buy what they sell. In short, undocumented immigrants in the United States participate in practically everything we do. We are their accomplices, whether we know it or not.

The idea of a strike by undocumented workers to show Americans their true economic value to society has been circulating for some time. I think the idea is naïve and not very practical. How many immigrants could bear a couple of days, a week, or even a month without working? As a mental exercise, though, it sounds interesting. If all the undocumented immigrants went on strike for a month, hundreds or perhaps thousands of businesses in the United States would fail, work in the fields would come to a halt, the service industry would be seriously affected, and inflation would shoot up to third-world levels.

The economic, cultural, and social contributions of immigrants, both with and without papers, is more than documented. That is why the behavior of many U.S. politicians who criticize the undocumented—but at the same time benefit from their work—seems so hypocritical. Could it be that former California governor Pete Wilson and former presidential candidate Pat Buchanan, two of the main critics of immigrants in the United States, do not consume the products and services that the undocumented provide? Of course they do. If Wilson and Buchanan practiced what they preached, they would avoid any contact, direct or indirect, with the undocumented; and if that were so, they would have to go live on Mars. Not even the president of the United States can avoid contact with products or services provided by undocumented workers.

The government of Mexico, naturally, is also an accomplice. Since Mexico does not have work for the undocumented, due to its long history of government corruption and waste, it suits the current administration to come to their defense. It is not an act of generosity but of self-interest. Mexicans in the United States send billions of dollars a year back to Mexico, and it would not benefit the Mexican government if the undocumented returned; it wouldn't know what to do with them, and they would cause the manipulated unemployment figures to skyrocket.

In Mexico as well as in the United States, we are all accomplices of the undocumented immigrants, voluntarily or involuntarily. The only way to end the hypocritical and opportunistic way in which the undocumented in the United States are treated is by giving them amnesty, just like in 1986. The Mexican government is afraid to propose that to the United States, and it terrifies U.S. politicians, but someone is going to have to make a stand. The undocumented workers benefit from our complicity; now, all that's missing is that this complicity be recognized legally, on both sides of the border.

POSTSCRIPT: Where do the undocumented workers come from? From heaven. That answer is not in jest. They come from heaven in the allegorical sense, due to the enormous boost they give to the economy of the United States and that of the countries they come from, by sending dollars back home. They also come from heaven in the literal sense because, contrary to popular belief, most undocumented immigrants came to the United States by plane and did not cross the border on foot.

A study by the National Immigration Forum (Autumn 1994) states: "Most undocumented immigrants don't come to the U.S. by crossing the border illegally. Six out of ten enter the United States legally with student, tourist or business visas, and become 'illegal' when they stay in the United States after their visas expire." This same group also reports that every year, more than one million immigrants enter the United States. Of these, close to 300,000 are undocumented.

The INS points out that the ten countries in early 2000 that sent more undocumented immigrants to the United States were, in descending order: Mexico, El Salvador, Guatemala, Canada, Haiti, the Philippines, Honduras, the Dominican Republic, Nicaragua, and Poland (*Foreign Affairs*, March/April 2000).

Also contrary to the perception of many Americans, more legal residents enter the United States each year than do undocumented workers. In 1993, for instance, approximately 700,000 people with permanent residency entered the United States; this is more than double the number of undocumented immigrants who entered that year.

Where do the legal residents come from? According to the National Immigration Forum, in 1993 most legal immigrants came from these ten countries:

COUNTRY	NUMBER OF IMMIGRANTS
Mexico	109,027
China	65,552
The Philippines	63,189
Vietnam	59,613
Former Soviet Union	58,568
The Dominican Republic	44,886
India	40,021
Poland	27,729
El Salvador	25,517
England	18,543

In early 2000, the list of the ten countries that sent the most legal immigrants to the United States had changed slightly: Mexico, the Philippines, India, Vietnam, China, the Dominican Republic, Cuba, Ukraine, Russia, and Jamaica (*Foreign Affairs*, March/April 2000).

30 THE LABYRINTH

Miami. Being an immigrant in the United States is a drag. Really. Not only do we have to face unfair attacks, prejudices, and discrimination, but we then have to be scholars of immigration law—to avoid being deported. The effort, of course, is worthwhile: Millions of immigrants in the United States have found the freedom and opportunities that did not exist in their countries. The process to legalize our immigration status, however, is a minefield.

I am not exaggerating. After the 1986 amnesty, when more than three million people became legal residents of the United States, immigration laws became a veritable labyrinth. Who could possibly understand what was going on? Nacara, TPS, HP–36, 245–I, CCS, and lately, amnesty—these are all immigration programs whose details are so complicated that only a few obsessive lawyers and finicky public officials can understand them. Without getting bogged down in detail, suffice it to say that in the eyes of the U.S. government, a Nicaraguan or Salvadoran immigrant is not the same as one from Honduras or Guatemala, and a Cuban boat person who sets foot on U.S. soil has many more advantages than a Mexican wetback who swam across the border. Why do these differences exist? Why are people not treated equally? There are many answers, although none is satisfactory.

Some groups, like the Cubans and Nicaraguans, have been better defended and represented in the U.S. Congress than the Hondurans, for instance, despite the latter having been devastated in a much greater way by Hurricane Mitch. Fleeing more than four decades of Fidel Castro's dictatorship is better, from an immigration standpoint, than fleeing the more than seven decades of corruption and authoritarianism of the PRI in Mexico. Escaping political violence in El Salvador is looked upon more favorably than escaping death squads in Guatemala or poverty in Haiti or the Dominican Republic.

If you come to the United States as an investor, immigration doors are open; if you come howling with hunger and fear, as a political refugee, you have to convince some bureauocrat that if they deport you, you will be killed. In other words, immigration regulations in this country are like a pile of jumbled, incongruous, and arbitrary little laws with no logical order. When no one understands anything, it is the lawyers who end up winning. Even the simplest immigration procedures require legal advice. I know many people who have shown up at INS offices to ask a question or have a document legalized, and they have wound up being arrested and deported, with no chance of returning for years.

In this atmosphere of confusion and fear, millions of immigrants prefer to save a few cents and consult a lawyer, which is another problem in itself. In my case, I was lucky to have found very good, efficient, and responsible lawyers, but I also know a few unpresentable crooks too. A few days ago, a Mexican friend, a mother of four of modest means, asked me to try and locate her lawyer. He had disappeared after receiving a payment of $250 and she had not seen him for two years. Instead of doing the simple procedure for which he had been hired, he vanished. After much effort and many phone calls, I finally located him. He promised to resolve my friend's case or return the money to her. The next time I tried to find him, he had already changed his address as well as his telephone and beeper numbers. He is a crook.

I mention this story in an attempt to make understandable the true dimension of the problem. Immigration laws in the United States are so tangled and arbitrary that no one, without help, can understand them or apply them. Even the immigration officials interpret identical cases in different ways. What can be done? What is the alternative? What is the solution? A general amnesty, like that of 1986.

In the United States, there are close to 10 million Latin American immigrants who have immigration problems; more than half are undocumented, and the other half have temporary permits, suspended deportations, requests not yet resolved, the hope of remaining, and the fear of being deported at any time, without explanation. These 10 million human beings are not even second-class citizens.

In addition to having to live with the prejudices against them, Hispanics are easier to exploit in their jobs because they live in fear that if they complain they will be deported, and their children would not benefit from all the educational and health benefits that the rest of the population receives. It is a subclass of 10 million poor, discriminated against, exploited people who for now have no legal recourse to legalize their immigration status.

The first step in helping them emerge from that hidden and fearful existence is to grant them amnesty. When an immigrant knows he will not be deported, chances are greater that he will find a respectable job and better schools and doctors for his family. An immigration amnesty is not new. It would mean that all Latin Americans who are currently living in the United States would have immigration rights similar to those of the Cubans. When Cubans set foot on U.S. soil, they are protected. Of course, they have the special, unfortunate situation of fleeing the only dictatorship on the continent. Nevertheless, other Spanish Americans should not be treated so unequally.

A general amnesty—that is the quickest, most direct way to untangle the immigration labyrinth in which more than 10 million people in the United States are trapped.

POSTSCRIPT: With the 1986 immigration amnesty, close to 3 million foreigners were able to legalize their status. Of these 3 million, 1.6 million were living in California, with 800,000 in Los Angeles alone.

31 THE *METEDÓLARES*

On the occasion of then-president Bill Clinton's visit to Central America, it was fitting to take a look at who, from afar, were sustaining the economies of their native countries: the *metedólares*— immigrants who send money back to their homelands. On March 8, 1999, Clinton set off on a three-day mission to distribute almost a billion dollars for victims of Hurricane Mitch in Honduras, Nicaragua, El Salvador, and Guatemala. Although it was a lot of money, it barely helped cover the most basic needs and only shored up foreign debt payments.

It would have been much more useful had Clinton promoted a permanent amnesty for the millions of undocumented immigrants who were living in the United States. Because of the Monica Lewinsky scandal, Clinton's credibility had suffered a serious blow, but he still had enough influence left to push for an immigration agreement that would legalize the status of millions of people. In the end, he never did, but there were many strong arguments for granting a definitive amnesty to the undocumented immigrants (aside from the fact that it would be in the interest of the United States not to have to send help south of the border so often).

These immigrants—the so-called *metedólares*—are one of the main sources of income in their respective countries, in Mexico as well as in Central America. They provide direct, continuous, and tangible aid. The funds they send are free from internal conflicts and, therefore, much more reliable than the promises of local politicians, which generally go up in smoke.

There are entire towns in Latin America that live off the money sent to them from the north. There are no longer any young men— and increasingly fewer women—in these towns, as they have risked it all and gone to the United States. Without the transfers of dollars, these places would become ghost towns, and they would disappear from the economic map.

The figures generated by these dollars are impressive. Although Mexico was not seriously affected by Hurricane Mitch, it has the largest army of *metedólares* in the continent. There are more than 7 million Mexicans born in Mexico and living in the United States. From these immigrants, in the last decade, Mexico has received an average of $4 billion a year in transferred funds. However, in 1999, the income sent back to Mexico from the United States could have been as high as $8 billion—$6 billion via electronic transfers and $2 billion via family and friends—according to Rodolfo Tuirán, secretary general of the Consejo Nacional de Población (*Reformal,* March 20, 2000).

Ironically, those remittances are categorized by Mexican bureaucrats as "unidentified income." Whatever you call it, the remittances compete with tourism and oil on the list of the principal sources of foreign currency in Mexico. They are equal to 50 percent of the direct investment in the country, and to 60 percent of oil exports.

In Central America, the scenario is much the same. The million and a half Salvadorans who live in the United States—primarily in Los Angeles, Washington, New York, Houston, and Atlanta—sent $1.285 billion back to their country in 1998, according to Banco Central figures. Salvadorans, just like Guatemalans, have benefited from a U.S. law that protects immigrants involved in the war against

Communism. Many, however, either are still ignorant of the law, do not qualify for it, or fear being deported.

Guatemalans are the oldest Central American population in the United States. There are Guatemalan immigration records in Chicago that date back half a century. Presently 1.5 million Guatemalans live in the United States, and they send at least $500 million a year back to Guatemala.

Honduras and Nicaragua, the two countries most affected by Hurricane Mitch, now depend more than ever on the dollars that are sent from the United States. The 600,000 Hondurans who live primarily in cities, such as New Orleans, New York, and Miami, send an average of $600 million a year to Honduras.

The 350,000 Nicaraguans living in the United States are also helping to sustain their country. Concentrated mainly in Miami, they contribute $250 million a year to the Nicaraguan economy, if we believe the figures of the Banco Central de Nicaragua. (The figure could be as high as $400 million if we rely on extraofficial reports.)

As we can see, the money sent by Mexican and Central American immigrants back to the nations where they were born becomes an extremely important financial contribution. In fact, Central American countries receive much more money every year from fellow countrymen abroad than the generous assistance offered by Clinton. That is not to say that what Clinton offered Central Americans was peanuts, but Central Americans could have helped themselves even more if they had been given a permanent amnesty so they would not have to live day to day with the insecurity and the specter of deportation. Every Central American in the United States sends an average of $667 a year to their family members in their native countries.

Let's add it all up. The $1.285 billion sent by Salvadorans, plus the $500 million by Guatemalans, plus the $600 million by Hondurans, plus the $250 million by Nicaraguans equals $2.635 billion in transferred funds every year. That is almost triple Clinton's offer.

Therefore, when Central American presidents met with the U.S. president in March 1999, they should have said to him: Thank you for the money, but we prefer amnesty for our *metedólares*.

POSTSCRIPT: The Tomás Rivera Policy Institute reported that "the percentage of an immigrant family's income that is sent to his home country annually has increased dramatically in the last decade. In

1989, immigrants sent between 6 and 16 percent of their incomes to their home countries. For some nations, the increase in remittances was greater than the increase in immigrants' income" (March 3, 1997).

At the same time, it is perfectly clear that the families that receive that money depend on it to survive. Remittances make up 40 percent of the budgets of families in the Dominican Republic who receive money from their relatives in the United States, and 51 percent of the budget of Salvadoran families in the same situation.

The interesting thing here is that the money transfers also wind up helping U.S. companies and the U.S. economy; much of the money that is sent to Latin American countries is used to buy imported products that generally come from the United States. In other words, the immigrant who sends money back to his country of origin is basically helping two entities: first, his family, and then, U.S. companies that export their products. Not a bad deal.

32 WHAT IMMIGRANTS CONTRIBUTE TO THE UNITED STATES

Whether immigrants contribute more to the United States than they take from it is a question of much debate. In the early 1990s, many believed that immigrants were costing the government billions of dollars. A study commissioned in 1994 by the federal government reported that the seven states with the greatest number of immigrants—Texas, California, Arizona, Florida, New Jersey, New York, and Illinois—spent $3.1 billion on educating undocumented immigrants, almost $500 million to encarcerate immigrants convicted of crimes, and $422 million on medical expenses. These figures are probably correct. Nevertheless, this study, and others like it, did not take into consideration the enormous contributions that immigrants make—not until the National Academy of Sciences got involved.

A panel of the best-known scientists in the country found that after everything was accounted for, legal and undocumented immigrants contributed close to $10 billion a year to the U.S. economy.

While it is true that they are an additional expense to the government, they also contribute revenue, consume products, create jobs, invest, pay taxes directly and indirectly, and take jobs that many Americans don't want. What the study hints at, but does not say directly, is that the presence of immigrants is very positive for the United States, not only in the economic sense but in the cultural sense as well. The face of the United States has been transformed by immigrants.

The Urban Institute went beyond these findings in a study they conducted in 1994. It calculated that immigrants contributed between $25 billion and $30 billion a year to the U.S. economy. The study recognized that those who just arrive tend to be poor and young and have little work experience. After ten years of living in the United States, however, immigrant families tend to earn higher wages than native-born Americans.

According to the Alexis de Tocqueville Institute, inhabitants of cities with the greatest number of immigrants have less poverty and less crime than those with very few immigrants. In the early 1990s, for instance, 38 percent of those residing in Los Angeles were immigrants, compared to only 2.5 percent in St. Louis. However, Los Angeles had a higher per capita income ($16,188) and fewer families living in poverty (14.9 percent) than St. Louis, whose per capita income was $10,798, and where 20.6 percent of the population was living in poverty. Likewise, in Los Angeles there was less crime (9.7 percent for every hundred inhabitants) than in St. Louis (16 percent). Also, in New York, where immigrants made up 28 percent of the population, the economic levels were higher and crime lower than in Cincinnati, where immigrants made up only 2.8 percent of the population. Similarly, San Francisco was doing better than Birmingham, Alabama; and Santa Ana, California, outshone Shreveport, Louisiana.

Finally, in a study carried out by UCLA and the University of California, Berkeley (*Immigration Issues and Policy in California*), Dr. Leo Estrada and Marcelo Cruz established that "during times of economic recession, there is resentment for the 'other,' the 'outsider.' " The two professors summarized five commonly held misperceptions:

- Immigration leads to overpopulation.
- Immigrants take jobs away from native-born workers.

- Immigrant workers depress wages.
- Immigrants use too much government assistance.
- Recent immigrants are not assimilating into American society quickly enough.

These five perceptions, according to the two researchers, are mistaken. Estrada and Cruz concluded that "instead of 'taking' jobs from native-born minorities, immigrants play a very significant role in the labor market by holding jobs that have been hard to fill by native-born workers. Immigrants also contribute to the creation of new jobs by circulating their wages in the local economy and adding to the regional and federal tax base. Studies that attempt to measure the 'cost and benefits' of immigrants have generally concluded that benefits exceed costs."

What more can we say? The facts are there for all to see.

POSTSCRIPT: The 2000 census counted 281,421,906 people in the United States. This total can be broken down as follows:

RACE		
White	211,460.626	(75.1%)
Black or African American	34,658,190	(12.3%)
American Indian and Alaska Native	2,475,956	(0.9%)
Asian	10,242,998	(3.6%)
Native Hawaiian and Other Pacific Islander	398,835	(0.1%)
Some other race	15,359,073	(5.5%)
Two or more races	6,826,228	(2.4%)
HISPANICS OR LATINOS		
Hispanic or Latino	35,305,818	(12.5%)
Not Hispanic or Latino	246,116,088	(87.5%)

The percentage of Latinos with respect to the total population in the United States has increased every year, as can be seen in the following table.

PERCENTAGE OF HISPANICS (OF THE TOTAL POPULATION)	
1995	10.3%
1996	10.6%
1997	10.9%
1998	11.2%
1999	11.6%
2000	12.5%

According to census figures obtained in March 1997, the Hispanic population broke down along the following ethnic lines:

Mexicans	64%
Puerto Ricans	10%
Cubans	4%
Central and South Americans	14%
Other	8%

The 2000 census recorded 35.5 million Hispanics, and that figure breaks down as follows:

Mexicans	58%	(20.6 million)
Puerto Ricans	9%	(3.4 million)
Cubans	3%	(1.2 million)
Central and South Americans and Others	30%	(10.1 million)

Latinos are a very young population. According to the 2000 census, of Hispanics living in the United States, 35 percent are eighteen years old or younger, compared to only 26 percent of the general U.S. population.

RACISM

33 JULIAN SAMORA AND THE DOGS

When Julian Samora was a young boy, he went to a public park in Colorado, but he was not allowed in. There was a sign that read: NO MEXICANS, NO INDIANS, NO DOGS. That experience marked him for the rest of his life. Sadly, I found out who Juan Samora was too late. He died at the age of seventy-five. I now know that thanks to this Mexican-American sociologist, there are more Hispanic students in U.S. universities today. As he himself used to say, his life was defined by the need to prove that he was just like everyone else. In fact, when he died on February 2, 1996, Julian had proved that he was much better than everyone else.

Julian Samora was born in the small town of Pagosa Springs, Colorado, on March 1, 1920. Thanks to a scholarship, he was able to finish college, and three more scholarships allowed him to keep moving forward. Julian Samora eventually received master's and doctorate degrees and went on to become one of the most important professors at the prestigious University of Notre Dame. There, he did all he could to attract Hispanic students, and little by little, Notre Dame, besides having a good football team, became a magnet for the most intelligent Latino students in the United States.

At Michigan State University, where he began his teaching career, he formed the Julian Samora Research Institute, dedicated to the study of Latino issues. Samora was truly a pioneer in the rescue of the "forgotten Americans," that is, the Hispanics who make up such an important part of the United States and who had received so little credit.

Julian Samora paved the way, not only for himself but for thousands of Latinos who proved over and over again that they can be equal to or better than their American colleagues. Julian saved these Hispanics from oblivion. We no longer see the kind of sign today that Julian Samora saw in Colorado when he was a boy—signs which prohibit Mexicans, Indians, and dogs from entering public parks. We don't see these signs, thanks to people like him. There are still many signs and barriers to knock down, but that is now up to us. Julian Samora did his job.

POSTSCRIPT: Retirement for Julian Samora never meant not working. When he retired from Notre Dame in 1985, he began work on the historical account of four families that had been living in the southeast United States since the sixteenth century.

Among the many well-known books written by Samora, cofounder of the Concilio Nacional de la Raza, are *Los Mojados: The Wetback Story* (1971) and *La Raza: Forgotten Americans* (1966).

34 JOHN ROCKER—FACE-TO-FACE WITH A RACIST

Miami. Some people are always sticking their foot in their mouths. That is the case with John Rocker, the pitcher for the Atlanta Braves. I had the opportunity to meet him in February 2000, and it was truly an unpleasant experience. Before I describe that conversation, however, let me explain why the comments of an arrogant twenty-five-year-old boy made news all around the United States.

In an interview with *Sports Illustrated* (December 1999), Rocker made racist comments that cost him a temporary suspension from professional baseball as well as a small fine. In that interview, Rocker said the following: "I am not a big fan of foreigners. You can walk an entire block in Times Square in New York and not hear anybody speaking English. Asians and Koreans and Vietnamese and Indians and Russians and Spanish people and everything up there. How the hell did they get into this country?" The short answer, Mr. Rocker, is that most foreigners in the United States came by plane. The United States accepts more than a million legal immigrants each year. More than half the undocumented immigrants also come by plane; six of every ten illegally extend their tourist, business, or work visas once they are in the United States.

I don't think that John Rocker was really interested in an academic answer when he asked, "How the hell did they get in?" John Rocker is not an intellectual. He says that he made those comments because he was bothered by the way people treat him every time he plays in New York, and it was easy for him—just as it is for many Americans—to blame his misfortune on foreigners. Rocker may think that foreigners are to blame for the country's problems, but that is simply not the case. Only ten of every hundred inhabitants in this country were born in a different country. (In 1910, on the other hand, fourteen of every hundred inhabitants in the United States were foreigners.) Those immigrants that bothered Rocker so much contribute billions of dollars a year to the U.S. economy, but I don't think Rocker is a person who has much talent for numbers. His talent consists of grabbing hold of a baseball and throwing it very fast, at ninety-five miles an hour. That's it.

Might Rocker have said those things out of fear of being replaced by the extremely talented foreign athletes that are playing Major League Baseball in the United States? Rocker was born in Macon, Georgia, and it is not likely that in that little corner of the United States there were many foreigners. On the baseball diamond there are, however, and very talented ones. There is Liván and el Duque Hernandez, Sammy Sosa, and Igor Gonzalez—who, by the way, earns $27,000 for each at-bat—to name a few. If Rocker wants to play on an all-white team, I'm afraid he'll have to go back to Macon, and it might not even be possible there.

Here's what Rocker had to say to *Sports Illustrated* about New York:

It is the most hectic, nerve-wracking city. Imagine having to take the number 7 train to the ballpark, looking like you're riding through Beirut, next to some kid with purple hair, next to some queer with AIDS, right next to some dude who just got out of jail for the fourth time, next to some twenty-year-old mom with four kids. It's depressing.

It must be very difficult for John Rocker, knowing that not everyone in the world earns $217,000 a year as he does for throwing little balls into a catcher's glove. Unfortunately, 99 of 100 young Americans will not have the chance to become a millionaire playing baseball, nor do ill homosexuals, ex-convicts, or single mothers.

During our conversation in a television studio in Miami, I asked Rocker about all of this. The conversation went like this:

> "Are you a racist?"
>
> "No, absolutely not."
>
> "Why did you make such a remark?"
>
> "It was just a case of, you know, having a really tough time in New York this year," he responded. "People spitting on me and dumping beer on me, and I was just a little upset about that, about some of the situations up there; and I was a little frustrated, and I was just, simply, venting one day."
>
> "Do you think it was a stupid remark?"
>
> "Oh, definitely. It was a mere case of me blowing out some steam and it came out the wrong way. It totally misrepresents the kind of person I am."
>
> "Would you want to apologize directly to Hispanics?"
>
> "It was just a misguided remark in a time of frustration. If anybody took those comments the wrong way, I apologize. By no means those comments represent the kind of person I am."

I was never quite sure if what Rocker told me was true or if it was all part of a public relations campaign to clear his name. I found it odd, for example, that he showed up for our interview with the Venezuelan baseball player, Andrés Galarrage, as if saying, "See, I have Latino friends."

The Braves were completely outplayed by the New York Yankees in the 1999 World Series. Rocker's problems, however, had already begun in the play-offs of the National League East against the New York Mets. Rocker's pitching at key moments in the series eventually enabled the Atlanta Braves to beat the Mets and move on to the finals. Rocker could handle the pressure from the batters but not from the fanatic New York fans, who booed him and really got to him. It was in that atmosphere that Rocker gave it all he had: He began to pitch amazingly well, and he let out all his racial prejudices. Once the bottle was opened, he didn't know how to close it.

It would be easy if racists had an "R" painted on their foreheads. Then we would be able to walk down the street and say, "Hey, look, there's a racist" and head the other way. Conversely, we'd see someone who did not have an "R" on his forehead and talk to him, approach him for a job, or anything else. Things are not that easy, though. In the United States some racists—and I have known many—seem like good people; they have children, pay taxes, and know the national anthem by heart. Deep down, however, they feel superior to you simply because they are white and you are Hispanic, black, foreign, speak another language, speak English with an accent, or just because you look different. When I met Rocker before the interview, for example, he greeted me with a smile, exposing his perfectly even teeth, and he seemed like a typical, brawny athlete. He is over six feet tall, pale, 225 pounds of pure muscle, has extremely long arms, very short hair full of gel, is a lively conversationalist, and is also good-looking, judging by the girls who go wild when they see him. He also throws baseballs like a magician. In other words, he did not have an "R" painted on his forehead. While I was talking to him, however, I could not stop thinking about the comments he had made to *Sports Illustrated.*

When my friends from other countries ask what the best and the worst things are about the United States, I have a pat answer. I tell them that the best thing is that the United States has given immigrants the opportunities and the freedom that our own countries denied us—and the worst is racism. It is not blatant racism, like the kind that kept Professor Julian Samora out of parks in Colorado. That kind of racism, I believe, is disappearing. The racism that inflicts pain now is that of people like John Rocker. It is a more subtle racism, but it also shows the worst side of the United States. It is the racism of Pat Buchanan, who calls all Hispanics

"José" and who would like to put an end to immigration to the United States. It is the racism of American parents who do not want their children to have Latino friends or their daughters to marry African Americans. It is the racism of factories that fire their employees simply for speaking Spanish, and the racism of those that mistakenly believe that foreigners are taking jobs away from Americans. It is also the racism of those who want to deny educational and medical benefits to children of immigrant workers, of the police who stop you because you are not like them, or those who don't wait on you in a restaurant or a bar just because you are mestizo or brown. It is the racism of those who hang up on you because they say they can't understand your English, and of those who do not look you in the eye and who treat you as if you were invisible. It is the racism of those who say, "But you don't look Hispanic," and of the 10,000 fans that gave John Rocker a standing ovation at his first spring training game in northern Florida in 2000.

Rocker believes that he is cured—as if racism were transmitted by a mosquito bite—because he underwent several sessions with a psychologist to deal with sensitivity issues. Unfortunately, Mr. Rocker, racism is not cured that way; racism is nursed at home.

Rocker agreed to speak with me and even apologized for his racist comments. Deep down, though, his ambivalent eyes shed doubt. I still do not know if to him I am one of those foreigners "who are everywhere," not knowing where the hell I came from.

POSTSCRIPT: "Have you ever been discriminated against, Jorge?" is a question I have been asked more than once. My answer, up until then, was always the same—never. In part, it is luck. Whenever I have felt mistreated or a discriminatory intention, I jump into action, I complain, I counterattack. I do not let myself be discriminated against.

I understand that as a journalist, I am in a privileged position. Moreover, most Americans I know are open and fully accept that their society is composed of many different racial groups. Nevertheless, every day there are many immigrants who refuse to denounce acts of discrimination because they fear losing their jobs, their houses, and their money, or simply because they do not trust the weight of the law. It is frustrating, it seriously affects the well-being of many families, and it creates problems of self-esteem.

The battle, I believe, is one by one, case by case, cry by cry. Only in this way are the Rockers, Buchanans, Dornans, and Wilsons of the world going to understand that the pure white world they imagined in their prejudiced minds no longer exists.

35 HOW TO KILL AN IMMIGRANT AND GET AWAY WITH IT

In the early-morning hours of February 4, 1999, the African immigrant, Amadou Diallo, was stopped in the entranceway of the apartment building where he lived in the Bronx, New York, by four police officers in civilian clothing. Diallo, a twenty-two-year-old immigrant from Guinea, was a traveling salesman, and according to his family, he worked twelve hours a day, most days of the week. He had never been in trouble with the law. When the police stopped him, he was unarmed, and he tried to take his wallet out of his back pocket. It was possible he was trying to provide identification. The four officers said that they felt threatened by the African immigrant's movements, and they thought that he might be about to pull out a gun. So they shot him forty-one times. Nineteen bullets hit Diallo's body. He died immediately.

Could something like this have happened in one of the elegant apartment buildings across from Central Park in New York? Would these four police officers have fired at a blond-haired white man in the same way? Probably not. What should Amadou have done to avoid being killed? Sing the national anthem out loud? Say the rosary? Stand on his head? I don't know. Amadou did what any innocent person should do when he is stopped by the police: Try to identify himself.

Amadou's death makes it clear that because of the racism that is ingrained in the minds of so many Americans, every African and every immigrant in the United States is dangerous. It shows that every one of us who does not live in the right area is in question, and every one of us who does not look like the false stereotype of an American is also in doubt.

Former senator and onetime candidate for the presidential nomination of the Democratic Party Bill Bradley was right when, referring to this case, he said, "I think it shows that when racial profiling seeps so deeply into somebody's mind, a wallet in the hand of a white man looks like a wallet, but a wallet in the hand of a black man looks like a gun."

The four officers who, ironically, formed part of an anti-crime unit, thought that Amadou might be a rapist or a thief or a gang member, just because of the color of his skin, just because he lived in the Bronx, just because his movements outside the building where he lived looked suspicious. Just because of that, they killed him. Not even a dog gets shot at forty-one times. To the four New York City police officers, however, Amadou's life was never worth much.

New York police, like police in many other places in the United States, stop blacks and Hispanics more often than whites. New York State Attorney General Eliot Spitzer released a study in December 1999 that corroborated this fact: For every one hundred whites that the police stopped to question, they stopped 123 blacks and 139 Hispanics. So, regardless of the fact that there are many more whites than minority groups in New York, blacks and Latinos are seen as criminals and stopped more often by the police, just because of the way they look.

After Diallo's death, the most reasonable outcome would have been for an impartial jury to find the four officers guilty of at least involuntary homicide or use of excessive force. However, after a series of legal maneuvers, such as the trial being moved from New York City to Albany, the state capital, a jury of eight whites and four blacks found, on February 25, 2000, that the four officers were not guilty of anything.

When Amadou's father, Saikou Diallo, was informed of the decision, he called the verdict a second crime. The four officers, Sean Carroll, Kenneth Boss, Richard Murphy, and Edward McMellon, remained free. These officers shamelessly blamed Amadou publicly for his own death. He never should have moved, they said, or stuck his hand in his pocket.

These officers, who now say that it was all an accident, shot forty-one times at an innocent, unarmed immigrant whose only sin was to be poor and black and live in the Bronx. The four officers remain free, with no charges against them. They have shown us how you can kill an immigrant and get away with it. Police officers and civilians alike have learned a lesson. Amadou, I fear, will not be the last innocent immigrant to die at the hands of the police, or for racist reasons, in the United States.

36 VIDEO JUSTICE

> They beat me worse than they would an animal.
> —*Alicia Sotero, immigrant attacked by the police*

Los Angeles. There is no doubt about it: If the brutal beating of two Mexican immigrants in Riverside, California, in 1996 had not been caught on film by television cameras, the police officers responsible for it it would still be doing as they please, smiling from ear to ear. The general perception is that if these crimes had not been caught on videotape, there would be no chance to point the finger at the culprits. Is that how we get justice? It is very difficult in a country that has consciously and collectively decided to turn its back on immigrants, but it's better than nothing.

Enrique Funes, who put up no resistance, took at least six blows from an officer's club before falling to the ground. Alicia Sotero, previously known as Leticia González, was struck once, pulled by the hair, thrown to the ground, kicked, and finished off with two more blows. When we saw how those two officers beat Enrique and Alicia without any provocation, it makes us think that there are two kinds of justice in the United States: one for the whites, the rich, and the famous, and another for all the rest.

I wonder if those police officers would have beat a couple of blond university students with Boston accents with the same excessive force and enthusiasm of a baseball player. They probably wouldn't even have stopped them. Officers Kurtis Franklin and Tracy Watson knew perfectly well what they were doing. They were not rookies; when the incident took place, Franklin had been with the Riverside police department twenty years, and Watson, five years.

When the chase ended and the rickety van which was carrying Enrique, Alicia, and nearly twenty other immigrants came to a stop, the officers assumed that they were all undocumented and that they could abuse them with impunity. This time, however, they were mistaken. They were being watched by television cameras.

Kurtis Franklin and Tracy Watson—don't ever forget their names—felt invincible in their impeccable khaki-colored uniforms, protected by their clubs and their guns. As soon as they saw two easy, vulnerable victims, they began to dish out blows and insults. What they did does not require courage, and their enthusiasm to hurt an unarmed couple showed extremely limited intelligence. I still don't understand how they weren't aware they were being filmed from the two helicopters. What were they thinking? That the helicopters from the media were there to applaud their caveman-like behavior? Or worse, maybe they actually did realize they were being filmed and didn't care.

In the United States, one's word is not always enough to get justice. We live in an era of video justice. Images control everything. Videos bring us closer to the possibility of punishing those who break the law, and sometimes a videotape is the only recourse that exists to denounce police brutality. This is how the police officers in Los Angeles who beat Rodney King, in March 1991, lost their jobs. A patrolman in South Carolina who, with a gun in his hand, forced a woman out of her car, threw her to the ground, and threatened to make her undress, was also fired because the incident was caught on videotape. Is it a coincidence that Rodney King, Enrique Funes,

Alicia Sotero, and the woman in South Carolina were all members of a minority group in the United States?

In other countries, the idea of video justice has many drawbacks and flaws. A videotape cannot always solve the crime; for that, political will is also necessary. It was successful in identifying and putting Yigal Amir behind bars, the man who murdered Israeli Prime Minister Yitzhak Rabin. In Mexico, however, in the case of Luis Donaldo Colosio, it did not have the same success. The murder of the PRI presidential candidate in March 1994 in Tijuana was caught on film, but most Mexicans believe that those responsible for Colosio's murder are still free.

Here in the United States, the videotapes that have emerged recently show the police as protagonists, and they are filled with hate. This racial, ethnic, and sexual hatred does not appear in a vacuum, it is fed by demagogy and fascist speech, and by a public eager to blame immigrants for the problems in their nation. Therefore, incredible as it seems, some were quick to blame the beating on the Mexican immigrants themselves, for having entered the country illegally, and not the Riverside police.

What happened in California is not an isolated incident. From 1987 to 1996, at least twenty-six Mexicans have died at the hands of state police. Most crimes committed by police, however, still go unnoticed and unreported, and penalties are much less severe. In this digital, postindustrial age, high technology—hidden in a lightweight and easy-to-use video camera—is increasing the statistical probability that those crimes will be filmed and penalized.

Prejudice and racial attitudes are not going to disappear just because of images on TV, like those of Franklin and Watson beating Enrique and Alicia. Perhaps in the future, though, the police will think twice before beating an immigrant, a woman, a black, or a Hispanic. That is the power of the videotape. Big Brother is watching, but the roles have changed. In this case, Big Brother is not the state or the police; Big Brother is every one of us with a video camera.

SPANGLISH

37 LONG LIVE SPANGLISH!

I have been *wacheando* the recent debates of the wise men of Spanish letters on the future of the language with great interest. I have heard very little, though, about Spanglish, the mix of English and Spanish heard more and more frequently in America, the United States, or Gringoland, as you wish. I am convinced that, like it or not, Spanglish will have a great deal of influence in the way that Spanish is heard and written this century.

During the first international congress of the Spanish language, held in Zacatecas in the spring of 1997, there was a great deal of support for the idea of Spanish as a dynamic, ever-changing language. I was particularly drawn to a quote by the Spanish Nobel Prize winner Camilo José Cela. He said, "Language is a fiercely boiling torrent, quite the opposite of a lake of stagnant water." All right. So, without having to *bulchetear* anybody, Cela got right to the point. It would have been *superinteresting* to pick his brain on the subject of Spanglish, but I couldn't attend the *mitin*. I am sure we would have enjoyed it a great deal.

For those of us who crossed *el borde* to come work in the north, the proposal of novelist Gabriel García Márquez to simplify grammar, before grammar winds up simplifying us, is also very helpful. If after crossing the border, you spend a lot of time in front of the *tubo* watching English-language programs, the first thing you *forguetas* is grammar and spelling. For instance, let's take the matter of the "b." If "b" and "v" are pronounced the same in Spanish, then why the differentiation? In Spanish-language magazines in the United States, I often find the word *governador*, spelled like that, with a "v," as if from the English *governor*. It looks funny, but it sounds the same. Maybe we should get rid of one of the two "b's" and retire spelling altogether, as the Colombian Nobel Prize winner proposed. Which one would we keep? The "b" or the "v"? *Vida* or *bida*? *Burro* or *Vurro*? For now we can leave it pending.

Some people find the very notion of Spanglish and the obliteration of spelling and grammar annoying and shocking. One day I asked the Mexican writer Octavio Paz if using Spanglish was correct and he replied, "I do not think it is correct or incorrect; it is awful. These mixed forms are transitory forms of communication among men." Paz clearly did not like Spanglish, but at least he understood its origin and necessity.

The assistant director of the Royal Academy of the Spanish Language, however, sounded horrified. In Zacatecas, Miguel Martín Municio said that Spanglish was an affront to the Spanish language, that it revealed a lack of education and that people should not be allowed to speak however they want. Who does he think he is? A guardian angel? The word police?

I'm sorry that Mr. Angel is so narrow-minded. It seems that he doesn't really know what he is talking about, or maybe he was afraid of losing his job. He has probably never been in Santa Ana, Hialeah, Pilsen, or Queens. He can keep his useless dictionaries. Language is formed and developed at home, at work, between friends, in front of the *tivi*, and listening to *la radio, man*. Not in dictionaries. Just look what happened with Latin. Classical Latin ended up in the tomb, while vulgar Latin was still alive and kicking.

These are just some of the words in Spanglish that more than

35 million Hispanics in the United States use every day and which cause such *jorror* to the guardian angels of Castillian: *trocka* (truck), *yarda* (yard), *estorage* (warehouse), *liquear* (to leak, but can also be a synonym for going to the bathroom), *carpeta roja* (red carpet treatment), *llamar para atrás* (to call someone back), *faxear*, (to send a fax), *taipear* or *typear* (to type on a typewriter or computer), *frizar* (to freeze), *lobbyista* (lobbyist), *rufero* (roofer), *ganga* (gang), *hacer sexo* (take a guess), *sexista* (chauvinist), *tener química* (to have chemistry with someone), *grincar* (greencard), *medicare* and *medicaid* (Medicare and Medicaid), *welfare* (welfare), *social security* (Social Security), *billions* (instead of thousands of millions), *modem* (modem), *mouse* (computer mouse), *cliquear* (to click the mouse), *weder* (the weather), *show* (television show), *bilingual* (instead of *bilingüe*), and a *bonche* more one can find on any website.

Spanglish is OK. There is no shame in Spanglish. Spanish, likewise, has nothing to fear. Spanish can handle everything: technical terms, anglicisms, and even the elimination of accents. There are 400 million people around the world who speak it, which is why it should be a language that reflects reality, not the whims of academics. I prefer to say *aseguranza* instead of *seguro*, and *computadora* instead of *ordenador*, and to be understood in Los Angeles, Miami, Chicago, and New York.

Spanish is "a language that is bursting with richness," as García Márquez said. Therefore, Spanish should not fear Spanglish. On the contrary, Spanglish is a cousin of Spanish. The point is not to make Spanglish a new language, like some tried to do with ebonics, the variation of English spoken by some African Americans. The point is that Spanish must be completely open to the contributions of Spanglish. Don't forget, Don Angel, Spanish is as much ours as it is yours. Take it easy—*agárralo suave*. This language can be used in many ways. You just have to *darle un chance*.

We must forget about the academics and the *tichers* of the Royal Academy of the Spanish Language—those who in their ivory towers make rules and conventions that no one follows. We must listen to the people, and make Spanish, with the gifts of Spanglish, an even richer and more flexible language. Spanish speakers in the United States are in the strange position of being able to contribute more than those from any other country in the world to the development of Spanish. Long live Spanglish!

POSTSCRIPT: The Internet is the vehicle that has contributed most to Spanglishization. This is because the United States, the lone superpower, has the lead in the Internet world. Most services on the Internet are in English, the majority of Internet companies are American, and no country has as many computer users as the United States.

Currently, there are more than 100 million people with access to the Internet in the United States, a figure that increases daily, since libraries and schools are now enabling more and more Americans to access the World Wide Web. In 1999, thirty-two out of every one hundred people in the United States had a computer or access to one. This percentage shot up in 2000. In Mexico, on the other hand, only three out of every one hundred people have a computer or access to one. The number of users in Mexico barely surpasses one million.

Mexico is not an isolated case. Latin America, in general, is far behind in cyber matters. According to the International Data Corporation, in 1999 there were only 7 million people in the entire region with Internet access. This figure, nevertheless, will double in two or three years. (Like a computer virus, Spanglish will continue to spread with every new user.)

Americans, moreover, spend more time surfing the Net than people in any other nation. PriceWaterhouse Coopers reported that Americans spend more than five hours a week online, twice as long as the French, Germans, and English. It is not surprising, then, that they also spend much more money purchasing items online. How much? In 1999, Americans spent approximately $18 billion on Internet transactions (without paying a single cent in taxes). Latin Americans, on the other hand, spent only $160 million (according to the Santiago Chamber of Commerce). Forecasts, nevertheless, are for e-commerce to increase several times over in a very short time, in both the United States and Latin America.

Unfortunately, the digital gap between the United States and Latin America is growing. This is understandable, for an American needs to save two or three weeks of his salary to buy a computer, while a Latin American would need to save for months or even years to buy one. It is increasingly difficult to thrive, cut off from the new technology. Whoever stays behind misses out on his piece of the pie, and whoever refuses to use Anglicisms, Spanglish, or cyber-Spanish will have a difficult time communicating efficiently on the Internet.

38 THE FUTURE OF SPANISH IN THE UNITED STATES

The other day, I called the *rufero* to come and have a look at my house because there was a *liqueo*. The entire *carpeta* was soaked. He came in his *troca* to *wachear* the problem, and he wanted to know if I was going to pay him or if it was covered by the *aseguranza*. After counting how many *tiles* he would have to replace, he gave me an *estimado*. I told him to leave me the number of his *celfon* or *biper*. If no one answers, he said, leave a message after the *bip* and *te hablo p'atrás*.

The first suggestion I have for those who are horrified by language like this—and who have a legitimate interest in knowing what it is that Latinos in the U.S. speak—is to put aside the opinions of the serious academics with long beards and big waistlines and listen to the people in the street. In cities like Hialeah, Florida; Santa Ana, California; Queens; Manhattan; Pilsen; Chicago; and the West Side in San Antonio, whoever does not speak Spanish or something similar may feel discriminated against. The Spanish spoken in these places, however, is a Spanish that Cervantes or even the pragmatic Sancho Panza would not understand.

Here, in the United States, the word *greencard* is better understood than *tarjeta de residencia*, or residency card. (A Chilean professor even proposed that it be written *grincar*, the way it is pronounced.) For those who use the benefits of *welfare, medicaid,* or *unemployment*, it is easier to refer to a word than to a long and incomprehensible explanation.

Then, of course, there are those pseudo-translations of Spanglish that have taken hold of the language. *Ganga* means bargain, but on the streets of east Los Angeles, no one would confuse a gang with the opportunity to obtain a bargain. Everyone also knows that *el bordo* or *el borde* is to the south, even though they have never had to cross the border illegally. *Tener sexo* is frequently used in place of *hacer el amor* (to make love), even though whoever is doing it almost never complains about the wording. *Hacer lobby* (to lobby) is used just as often as the Spanish word *cabildear. Surfear* (to surf the Net) is easier than saying *correr tabla. Ambientalista* (environmentalist) is shorter than saying *defensor del medio ambiente. Sexista* is not found in the dictionary, but it is a word with a broader meaning than *machista*, and *soccer* is now replacing *futbol.*

Things become complicated when the same word in Spanish means different things for those groups that make up the hybrid group called "Hispanics." *Darse un palo* in Puerto Rico means to take a drink. *Darse un palo* in Mexico—well, let's just say it's something quite different. Even the simplest tasks are challenging. Chileans say *corchetera* (stapler) for what the Cubans call *presilladora*, the Mexicans *engrapadora*, and some Puerto Ricans *clipeadora.*

These examples support a very simple hypothesis: The Spanish that is spoken in the United States is a living, changing, dynamic language that is subject to the influences of the media, and it is futile to try and resist or reject it. The United States can contribute more to the growth of the Spanish language today than any other Spanish-speaking country in the world. No, I do not support poorly spoken or written Spanish, but I do believe that we have to be much more open-minded in accepting the continuously evolving new words and expressions provided to us by our experience in this country. New concepts enrich our culture, they do not denigrate it.

The most realistic goal is to speak English and Spanish well and to have children that are *bilinguales*, as a well-known politician from Los Angeles would say. We are now having the same discussion in the United States about Spanish and Spanglish that the Romans had about classical and vulgar Latin, and we know how that turned out: Vulgar Latin prevailed, just as in the United States a very impure Spanish, combined with a Spanglish unrecognizable in Madrid, will prevail.

Any mother or father who wants to maintain Spanish as the language spoken at home knows what I am talking about. Usually, both English and Spanish are used in the same conversation. No matter how hard they try, English tends to prevail among the new generations. The need to speak English in order to succeed in this country, the influence of schools, and the bombardment of English from TV and the Internet are winning the war against Spanish, word by word. At the same time, Spanglish has become a bridge of sorts: a generational, linguistic, technological, digital, and cultural bridge.

What will Hispanics of the future speak? Responding to that question is of vital importance for the development of the Spanish-language media in the United States. Radio and television executives would like to have a magic ball in order to find out if in two or three decades Hispanics will speak more English than Spanish, if they will adapt or if they will remain more independent than other ethnic groups in their cultural customs, like the Italians or the Poles. There are more than 35 million Latinos in the United States today, half of whom prefer to communicate in Spanish, 35 percent in English, and 15 percent of whom are bilingual.

How will Latinos communiciate with each other in the future? For the time being there is no need to worry. The continuous immigration to the United States (estimated at 1.3 million per year by the Census Bureau), as well as the high birthrate among Latinos, assures a captive audience that will speak—or at least understand—Spanish for years to come.

Many purists are shocked to see that Spanglish, word by word, is gaining ground in Spanish dictionaries. The truth of the matter is that it's not worth the aggravation. Just listen to the radio, the television, or people on the street, or speak with the new generations of

Hispanics, and you will easily be able to confirm for yourself what the future holds. In the future, there will be no pure Spanish for Hispanics.

POSTSCRIPT: On February 4, 2000, a carpenter named Casillas became the first member of a U.S. jury who did not speak English. Casillas, forty-three years old at the time, used a translator in a drug-trafficking trial in Doña Ana County.

39 THE SPANGLISH PROFESSOR

His enemies call him "the destroyer of the Spanish language," but far from destroying the language, Ilan Stavans, professor at Amherst College in Massachusetts, has spent the last three years compiling a dictionary of Spanglish that contains more than six thousand words. "To speak about the purity of the Spanish language in the United States is utopian," Stavans told me in a telephone conversation. "Purists want to keep Spanish frozen in time, as if languages do not change."

The fact is that more than 35 million people in the United States are of Hispanic origin—58 percent from Mexico, 9 percent from Puerto Rico, 3 percent from Cuba, and 30 percent from Central and South America—and very few of them speak Castilian Spanish as dictated by the Royal Academy of the Spanish Language. They speak a mixture of Spanish and English with lots of localisms, anglicisms, and unique expressions brought from their native countries. What they speak, in many cases, is Spanglish.

"What is Spanglish?" I asked the thirty-eight-year-old Mexican-born professor.

"Spanglish is not a language," he replied. "Nor is it a dialect, even though it is on its way to becoming a dialect. It is jargon, or slang."

Ilan Stavans is convinced that "we are witnessing an extremely creative verbal phenomenon that is making us rethink the way that Spanish itself developed throughout the centuries. Spanglish dates back to 1848 (the Treaty of Guadalupe Hidalgo), when Mexico lost more than half of its territory to the United States. At that time, groups of Mexicans suddenly found themselves living on land controlled by Americans, and they had to confront a language and a culture that were not theirs. According to Stavans, the phenomenon of Spanglish intensified during the Spanish-American war, when Spain lost Cuba and Puerto Rico to the Americans.

With the withdrawal of Spain from the American continent, Spanish, in its purest form, came under attack. "It is not a phenomenon that is limited to the United States," Stavans told me. "Spanglish includes many Colombian words and Venezuelan words . . . and, in fact, Spanglish is not the same for Mexicans or Cubans or New Yorkers." Despite the many variations—which depend on the different ethnic groups and where it is spoken—it wasn't until the second half of the twentieth century that an awareness of Spanglish as something unique, something that was neither English nor Spanish, arose.

There is no doubt that Spanglish is here to stay. "In the very core of the nation, we speak Spanglish," the professor noted. "And educated people as well as the less educated speak it." It is true. I have heard lawyers and doctors speak Spanglish with their servants and cleaning people, and politicians and government officials in Texas, California, and Arizona often use Spanglish in order to communicate with the poorest voters. Spanglish has infiltrated all layers of the Latino population in the United States, and as a journalist who has lived here for almost two decades, I admit it is often easier to use a word that is from neither English nor Spanish in order to communicate and report in the quickest and most efficient manner.

Despite its extensive use in the United States, Spanglish comes under frequent attack. As we saw in the previous chapter, the Mexican poet Octavio Paz told me that Spanglish was awful. Intellectuals, especially in Spain and among the members of the Royal Academy of the Spanish Language in particular, do not tire of branding those who defend and use Spanglish as ignorant and aberrant. This bothers Stavans a great deal. "There are now more Hispanics in the United States than the entire population of Spain," he pointed out. "It seems ridiculous that the people from the Academy believe that the only thing they need to do is ignore what we are speaking and try to impose a different language on us. For decades, academic circles have viewed Spanglish as a deformation and a prostitution of the language," he went on. "What I propose is that it is no longer possible to view it so negatively."

In recent years, the technological revolution, fostered by the Internet, has given rise to an explosion of words in Spanglish. Some now even call it cyber-Spanish. Examples of such words are *faxear, cliquear, downlodear, webear,* and *webon.* This cyber-Spanish uses no accents and does not have the letter "ñ" or the upside-down question mark and exclamation point, since most computers in the United States do not have Spanish-language capability.

Members of the Royal Academy, logically, want to maintain their illusory control over the language and its honorary seats. Their centralism and arrogance speak to other centuries when Spain was Spain—that is, a true empire. They have not yet realized that they cannot determine what is spoken, and how more than 400 million Spanish speakers express themselves. Today, they move at a turtle's pace, and they still refuse to accept Spanglish words in their dictionaries. It is quite clear, however, that reality has overtaken them, and they risk being seen as even more obsolete and senile.

Let us leave the past and jump to the future. Professor Stavans has two children: Joshua, who is eight, and Isaiah, three. He is teaching them both Spanish and English, and he does not discourage them in the least from experimenting with and communicating in Spanglish. What's more, far from believing, as Paz does, that Spanglish is a transitory form of communication, Ilan believes that it is being developed and strengthened. "I am not a prophet, but I do not think that Spanglish is disappearing," he told me before his busy schedule forced him to leave. "Neither Spanish nor English will survive in their current forms." After the announcement of his *Dictionary of Spanglish*, or *Diccionario del Espanglish*, he gave more than fifty interviews to the press. "I don't think it's at all improbable," he concluded, "that in two hundred or three hundred years there will be great works written in Spanglish."

43 WORDS FROM THE DICTIONARY OF SPANGLISH
(Published with authorization from Professor Ilan Stavans.)

SPANGLISH	ENGLISH	SPANISH
antibaby	birth control pill	píldora anticonceptiva
ancorman	anchorman	presentador de noticias
babay	bye-bye	adiós
beseler	best-seller	éxito de librería de Ventas
brainstormear	to brainstorm	considerar ideas
brode	pal, buddy	hermano, amigo
cibernauta	web navigator	usuario de la internet
databasis	database	base de datos
drinquear	to drink	beber
estufiar	to sniff drugs	inhalar drogas
fletera	a female flirt	coqueta
guacheur	to watch out	observar con cuidado
gufear	to goof around/joke	bromear
hood/hud	hood/neighborhood	barrio
imail	e-mail	correo electrónico
imailiar	to send e-mail	enviar correo electrónico
jaina	honey, sweetheart	cariño
kenedito	traitor (from J. F. Kennedy)	traitor
lis	lease	renta
lobi	lobby	cabildear
lonchear/lonche	to eat lunch	almuerzo
llegue	hit, punch	golpe
maicrogüey	microwave oven	horno de microondas
maus	computer mouse	elemento de computadora
mopa	mop	trapear

SPANGLISH	ENGLISH	SPANISH
mula	money	dinero
nerdio	nerd	estudioso/tímido
parisear	to go to parties	festejar/ir a fiestas
pimpo	pimp	padrote
printear	to print	imprimir
queki/queque	cake	pastel
ringuear	to ring/call someone	llamar por teléfono
sochal	Social Security number	numero de seguridad social
taipear	to type	teclar
tiquetero	ticket seller	vendedor de boletos
troka	truck	camión
ufo	UFO	ovni
víbora	penis	pene
vate	water	agua
wachear	to watch	ver/observar
yanitor	janitor	empleado de limpieza
yoguear	to jog	trotar
yuca	young urban Cuban-American	cubanoamericano

SOURCE: *Hopscotch 1:1*, Duke University Press.

THE AMERICAN DREAM

40 WHY MARTA WANTS TO LEAVE MEXICO

When I spoke with Marta on the phone, she had already made up her mind. She would travel by bus with her three daughters from Lerda, in the state of Durango, to Tijuana. Once in Tijuana, she would board a plane with the hope of reaching the United States, maybe Dallas, Texas.

It was a complicated matter, because neither Marta nor her three girls—Marcela, ten, Martita, eight, and María, six—had visas to enter the United States. "They ask for a lot of things," she said. The only thing they had were their Mexican passports, just off the press.

"How do you expect to enter the U.S. without a visa," I asked Marta.

"Well," she replied, "my husband is there and has a contact, and if we pay that person $1,000 per girl, he will make sure they get in without any problems."

"A thousand dollars per girl!" I remarked. "Isn't that a lot?"

"Well, yes," she said. "But what can I do? It's worth it."

Marta is twenty-nine years old. She began to study nursing but was unable to finish. The girls, the rent, and the poverty she had inherited forced her out into the street. Her husband, Juan, went to California a year ago, and although he sends money from time to time, it's not enough. He is now saving money to pay the $4,000 he needs to bring his wife and three daughters to the United States.

"It's very hard," Marta said. "There are jobs, but they pay so little; a lot of jobs in the assembly plants making denim." Instead of going to a factory, Marta decided to make *gorditas* with beans and cheese, chilis, and roast meat and sell them on the street. She sells them for the equivalent of two dollars a piece, and she earns $150 a week. It is not enough, though, for her and for her daughters' school.

"Here, even though my daughters go to a public school, it isn't free," she explained. "Supposedly, it's free, but they ask for a lot of money for uniforms, fees for the exams, and to pay the custodian."

Marta is obsessed with her daughters' education. If they succeed in reaching the United States, Marta wants Marcela, Martita, and María to take advantage of the educational system as much as possible. The immigration status can come later. "I want them to study, and there, every child studies," she said. "If they can get legal status, fine."

"What if they can't?" I asked her.

"Well," she said, "first I would like my daughters to go to school. Then we can save money and return to Mexico. That's the plan."

"Why don't you just stay in Mexico, then?"

"Here the government is useless," she said. Then she went on to tell about a television program where she saw the unpleasant display of politicians criticizing each other and "airing each other's dirty laundry." "You can't trust anyone."

Marta doesn't lose sleep over the matter of discrimination against immigrants in the United States. "I'm afraid of discrimination," she said, "but not all people are bad." Besides, Marta "has many family members spread out across the United States who come and go as if they owned the place." So the road for Marta had already been paved.

"No matter how poor immigrants are in the U.S., no matter how bad their situation, they live better than we do," Marta concluded. "I am convinced that I must go. Here in Mexico you can't study or work; there you can."

Before our conversation ended, I knew that Marta was going to leave Mexico with her three girls and go to the United States to join Juan. "Why not?" she said, almost defiantly. "No one owns my life."

41 SOCCER CHILDREN

Miami. Nicolás David is a child of the World Cup. I'm convinced that he made his first soccer kicks to escape from his mother's womb, after the goal that Mexico scored, defeating South Korea in the 1998 World Cup game in France. The shouting in front of the television screen was so great that he couldn't stay calm inside. He had to get out to see what was going on. He was born the next day, the second Sunday of June, after the referee blew the final whistle of the third World Cup game of the day. What a day!

Now that Mister Nick—as his sister Paola would say—is alive and kicking, I hope to be able to instill in him the same enthusiasm for soccer that I had when I was a boy. I didn't care where or how I played; I would play in the streets or the parks, the bathroom or the kitchen, with a leather ball or a rolled up piece of paper, alone against the wall, or in a chaotic mob in which the whole school would participate. I was a boy who grew up with soccer. I hope my boy is as lucky.

My friends here in the United States cannot fully understand that in the rest of the world, soccer is much more than just a sport. Not only is it a piece of culture, but it is also an extremely important part of our first experiences as part of a group. It is an odd pairing; competition and unity at the same time. Some of the best moments of my childhood are tied to a soccer ball. Other not-so-good moments are also linked to a ball. Let me explain.

During the 1978 World Cup in Argentina, I had to have my nose operated on because of an injury that had occurred years before which had never been attended to. To my surprise, when I woke up in the middle of the operation—apparently the anesthesia was losing its effect—I found the Mexican doctors watching a World Cup game on a portable television as they were operating on me. Naturally, my first reaction was to ask them what the score was, but instead of an answer, they gave me more anesthesia.

The operation did not help at all. A few months after the surgery, my nose was just as crooked as before. Maybe if the doctors had paid more attention to my nose and less to the World Cup . . . No, that would be impossible. It was my mistake, I admit it. I should never have had the operation in the middle of a World Cup.

With the 1998 World Cup in France, I revisited the passion that motivates the childish attempt of twenty-two players to kick a ball inside a rectangle. It is a cyclical passion that explodes for one month every four years and which can be misinterpreted by those who do not carry it in their blood as temporary insanity.

WHEN MY WONDERFUL SON Nicolás was born, my wife Lisa's parents and siblings came to visit us. They are Cuban and live in Puerto Rico—two nations that have no real soccer tradition. So, I was afraid that when they saw me shouting like a lunatic at the television every time Mexico, Chile, Spain, Colombia, Paraguay, Argentina, or Brazil would play, they would think that Lisa had made a huge mistake marrying a Mexican soccer fan. Oh, well!

Naturally, my son first began to nurse, cooed by the cries of *gooooooooool* by Andrés Cantor and Norberto Longo, the Univision sportscasters who did the Spanish-language commentary in the United States for the World Cup in France. Missing a goal in the World Cup is a sin, so I would steal satellite signals from Mexico from Televisa or Televisión Azteca in order to watch the games. If I was in my car, there was nothing like hearing a Colombian or an Uruguayan describing a game, play by play, in the greatest display of how to fit a thousand words into a minute.

It never occurred to me to listen to the games in English on ABC or ESPN. How boring! In English, they continuously explain to the viewers how soccer is played only with the feet and that the winner is not necessarily the one who is ahead, mentioning absurd statistics like shots at goal or corners. Besides, compared to the emotional commentators in Spanish, those broadcasts seem more like a funeral mass. They would only have made the baby fall asleep.

I wanted Nicolás, in his first days of life, to eat, drink, and sleep soccer (just as a television commercial had so appropriately suggested). So, that's how it was. Nicolás does not know it yet, but he spent the first few days of his life watching and listening to soccer. Subliminal education, without a doubt.

I do not consider myself a crazed soccer fanatic, but I do feel differently from most Americans during the days when the World Cup is being played. (And I have lived through four in the United States.) Soccer is a secondary sport here, and maybe even tertiary; it does not generate the enthusiasm that basketball star Michael Jordan did, or the batting of the New York Yankees, or a touchdown by the Denver Broncos or the Dallas Cowboys. So, I am not the least bit surprised by a Harris poll that found that three out of four Americans did not know that the World Cup was being played in France, and that only two out of ten had seen part of a match.

What a waste! The World Cup is equivalent to thirty consecutive Super Bowls, and they missed an extraordinary show; there have never been so many goals in a World Cup, ever. Nevertheless, nothing ruined the World Cup final for me in France that Sunday, July 12, 1998. I was next to my son, celebrating his fourth week of life, and in front of the television, listening to the cry of *goooooooool*.

When all is said and done, he is just as much a child of soccer as I am.

POSTSCRIPT: I had an informal conversation with then–vice president Al Gore, during which I told him how difficult it was to define my son's ethnic origin. He had to fill out forms for the 2000 census, and there was no category that covered all of Nicolás's multiracial roots.

"Look," I said to the vice president, "my son was born in Miami, but I am Mexican, his mother is Puerto Rican, and his maternal grandparents are Cuban. How do we define him? As Puerto-Cuban-Mexican-American?"

"It's easy. He's an American."

He's right.

On the census forms, there was not a single category that included all the history that Nicolás carried in him and of which we, his parents and grandparents, are so proud. So I put an "x" by "Hispanic" and then three more "x" 's in the little boxes whose descriptions read "Mexican or Mexican-American," "Puerto Rican" and "Cuban or Cuban-American."

I made the people at the Census Bureau work overtime, but this was the only way to accurately reflect the emerging face of America.

42 LA VIDA LOCA

Miami. Before I begin, I want to make two things perfectly clear: first, I know nothing about music; and second, I don't know Ricky Martin. I point this out because lately I have heard a lot of criticism of Ricky: He can't sing or dance, he's a product of marketing, and his CD *Livin la vida loca* is not very creative. You know what? None of that really matters. What matters is that Ricky Martin has become one of the most visible Latino faces in the United States and in the world, and whether we like it or not, he is paving the way.

I don't know Carlos Santana, nor do I know Jennifer López, although I did run into her one night at a party. In this age, when celebrities have replaced heroes, and entertainment news hard news, Ricky Martin, Santana, Jennifer López, and Christina Aguilera form part of a group of Hispanic performers that are helping to eliminate prejudices and do away with the negative perceptions that millions of Americans have with respect to Latinos.

Although I may never have heard one of his CDs, Ricky Martin has managed to present himself as an intelligent bilingual young man, with an image that is full of energy; someone who knows how to promote his career, knows the movers and shakers of the recording industry, and who is a multimillionaire in his own right.

How many Latinos like him can appear on the cover of *Time* magazine, sing at the World Cup in France, record a duet with Madonna and Luciano Pavaroti, and sell two million CDs in less than three weeks? Ricky Martin, along with others like Gloria Estefan, Enrique Iglesias, Elvis Crespo, Jennifer López, Marc Anthony, and Christina Aguilera, are in many ways ambassadors of what is Latino in the United States, regardless of where they come from. They are ambassadors not only because of the music they sing and the language they speak, but because, by integrating into the mainstream, all Latinos are integrating, little by little.

Naturally, it helps the image of Hispanics when Julio Iglesias can walk into the White House as if it were his, when Carlos Vives helps out at a telethon, and when Shakira appears on one of the most watched television programs in the United States. The gossip also helps, such as Luis Miguel going out with Mariah Carey, and Thalía marrying recording executive Tommy Mottola. If Hispanics are integrating into the show business world in the United States with greater success, it is inevitable that they are then included in its affairs, parties, bashes, and gossip. Frivolous? Yes. But the message is clear: Hispanics are part of this country too.

Of course, we should not promote the stereotype that all Latinos dance salsa and sing with mariachis; the Hispanic community also includes doctors, lawyers, engineers, diplomats, and writers. We should recognize, however, that nowadays, entertainment personalities, to the beat of the conga, are the springboard for the entire community. For one thing, they are better known and more entertaining than the nineteen members of Congress who represent us in Washington. (I know a couple of congressmen who live faithfully by former President Richard Nixon's saying that the greatest sin in politics is to be boring, but I'll leave that for another occasion.)

When people like Glorita or Luismi or Julio or Arjona or Vives or Maná appear on MTV and open an American ear, they also open a mind. It is easier to talk to Al Gore, Hillary or Bill Clinton, or Bill Gates, for instance, if they have first listened to Celia Cruz, Tito

Puente, or Armando Manzanero. It is also easier to speak with a senator or an American businessman about the problems in Latin America if they understand Spanish and have read Fuentes, García Márquez, and Vargas Llosa, and they have a point of reference, even if it is musical.

What this group of singers, performers, and entertainment personalities of Latin American origin are doing is representing an increasingly larger and stronger community in the United States. The following are statistics provided by the Association of Corporate Responsibility in Washington:

1. In 1999, the more than 30 million Hispanics in the United States spent roughly $400 billion; this is more than the gross national product of Mexico, a nation of 100 million people. (In 1997, the purchasing power of Hispanics was $211 billion, and in 1998 it was $348 billion.)
2. In the year 2005, there will be more Hispanics than blacks in the United States; the birthrate of Latinos today is double that of African Americans.
3. Contrary to the thinking that all Hispanics are undocumented immigrants, single mothers, gang members, and opportunists, most Latinos belong to the American middle class.

There are other, lesser-known facts that are equally significant. The most watched television station in Miami broadcasts in Spanish, not English, and the most listened-to radio station in Los Angeles broadcasts in Spanish, not English. In other cities with high percentages of Hispanic inhabitants—like San Antonio, Houston, New York, and Chicago—radio and television programs in Spanish compete successfully with those broadcast in English. The Hispanic population is not only growing in strength and economic power, but it is also dominating the media in certain cities. Unfortunately, this phenomenon still has no political equivalent. That is the next step.

For now, what is significant is that the presence of Hispanics in the United States is being felt—because of its growing economic power—and it is being heard, thanks to our performers. It is unimportant whether critics prefer Francisco Céspedes's *La vida loca* to Ricky Martin's *Livin la vida loca*. (I too like the former better, though I prefer the video of the latter.) What is important is that our Latino voices are heard, in English and in Spanish, so that American society may someday see itself for what it is: mulitcultural, multiethnic, and mulitracial.

POSTSCRIPT: Hispanics are in fashion in the United States. Christina Aguilera, Enrique Iglesias, and Edward James Olmos were key figures in the half-time show at Super Bowl XXXIV. Billions of people saw them perform. Soon after that, on February 23, 2000, Carlos Santana cleaned up with eight Grammy Awards, and drummer Tito Puente also took home a Grammy. What is missing, then? That the power of music be transformed into political power. Besides obtaining seats in the most exclusive club in the United States—the U.S. Senate—we must find our way into the Supreme Court, where not one of the nine justices has a Latino last name. We know where we need to go; we just need to make the leap.

43 CHEF CRISTINO

Captiva Island, Florida. "I began as a dishwasher. What do you think?" said the chef of one of the most elegant restaurants on the exclusive island of Captiva off the central coast of Florida. He was wearing his immaculate white chef's hat with noticeable pride. It was impossible not to notice, and it's no wonder—after all, how many successful people from Oaxaca are there in the United States?

That night, looking out at the Gulf of Mexico, Cristino Ramírez had much to celebrate. The day before he had become a U.S. citizen, and months before that, he had been named executive chef of the very restaurant where he had started as dishwasher. He appeared with an expensive bottle of California wine, and we became immersed in friendly conversation.

"Do you feel that you betrayed Mexico by becoming a U.S. citizen?" I had to ask him. He almost jumped out of his seat. "Of course not," he said. "I didn't betray Mexico; what you carry inside is forever." Then, more calmly, he explained that he made the decision to become a U.S. citizen when the Mexican government made dual nationality possible.

Cristino, in fact, has spent almost as much time in the United States as he has in Mexico. When he was sixteen years old, he realized that his future was limited, and after trying his luck for a while in Mexico City, he continued north to Texas, and then later to Florida. He had a rough time. He can still recall the two and a half months he spent without work because the drought had destroyed the tomato crops. "But I didn't give up," he said. "Anyone else would have thought about going back, but I didn't." He made the right choice.

He qualified for the 1986 amnesty by a matter of days. Finally, his papers were in order. The rest would not be so difficult. With the rain came better times, and he went from the hard work in the fields to the kitchen. He worked seventy hours a week in two restaurants, cleaning floors and washing pots and pans to survive. Cristino's eyes, however, were never still. He learned from all the cooks and waiters with whom he worked, and ten years later, he was offered the most important job: chef. Today, you might find him preparing lobster thermidor or a filet mignon. He does not make hot sauces with chile chipotle, however, "because people can't take it."

Ironically, this succesful Oaxacan chef cannot eat what he likes most—Mexican *tortas*, or sandwiches. "They don't have *teleras* or *bolillos*," he said with some resignation. "You can make *tortas* with French bread, but it's not the same." Another thing Cristino misses is soccer. "This place is full of Americans," he said. "Sometimes I go to the beach by myself to play."

I saw his business card, which read "Christino Ramírez, Executive Sous Chef." "You spell Christino with an 'h'?" I asked. "I don't," he responded. "But everyone else does."

It doesn't really matter how you spell his name. Everyone who eats in this sophisticated little corner of the world takes a piece of Chef Cristino's hard work and dreams with him—from Oaxaca to the world.

44 THE AMERICAN DREAM — MEXICAN STYLE (OR MARÍA AMPARO'S *SANTITOS*)

María Amparo is not seeing things. Rather, she has an internal life that is rich, and an imagination that is reality-proofed. That is why she can write that a woman saw an apparition of St. Judas Tadeo on her oven, telling her that her daughter wasn't dead and that she was just out having a good time.

Ever since I met her in 1983, María Amparo has imagined things. Her magic, however, consists of making things that she thinks up materialize. So, first María Amparo imagined that she could leave Mexico empty-handed and make a decent living in the United States, and she did more than that. Her first bed was on the ground of a dilapidated dive, the Fiesta Theater in Los Angeles. She now lives in a two-story house. Then, she imagined that she could start an advertising agency, and not long after that, she became an executive and owner of an agency along with her husband, Benito. María Amparo also imagined that she would be a mother, and even though Mother

Nature was telling her no, she said yes; she took some strange con-coctions and beat Mother Nature. She now has two wonderful chil-dren: Marinés and Iñaki.

This woman who built herself up from head to toe—from her pure white feet to her magnificent dark hair—had a calling: to be a writer and to invent the worlds in which she wanted to live. Her first stories in Spanish—which she calls *micruentes* because they are short and *cruento*, or gory—were published in several maga-zines in Mexico, like *Plural*, *La Brújula en el Bolsillo*, and *Adrede*. As if that were not enough, after only a few years in the United States, María Amparo took a courageous leap, and she began to write in English. She told herself, "If I am in the United States, I am going to write in English; just like that." She recalls, however, that her determination didn't last long. "After writing forty pages in English, I thought: I'm crazy." The Spanish-English dictionary became a necessity, and the inevitable happened. "I learned a lot of English, and my vocabulary grew." Since María Amparo imagined the universe in Spanish, I am sure that many doubted whether she would be able to translate her imagination into English. These were people who did not know her.

Her first stories in English were written without great difficulty. In the first story, which she wrote for a class she was taking at UCLA, she misunderstood the teacher's instructions, and instead of writing about something haunting, she wrote about the experience of a little girl on a hunting trip. In the story, a girl ends up carrying the hand that the tour guide cut off with a machete after a snake bite. The story was so good that María Amparo went from student to teacher in just a short time.

Besides taking that leap, María Amparo also tried to jump through hoops. She wrote her first novel in English, not in Span-ish. When she finished the novel, she thought that she "had to do things like they do here [in the United States]." She got an agent, sent twelve copies of the original manuscript (complete with cards of the saints, rosaries, and crucifixes) to the leading U.S. publish-ing companies, and in a week she had received four offers. The trick had worked.

Her novel, *Santitos* (or *Esperanza's Box of Saints*), quickly became a literary success in the United States—both the English version and the Spanish translation—and one of the best-selling books in

Switzerland, Spain, Holland, Italy, and France. "I think that roughly three hundred thousand books were sold in thirteen languages," she told me.

In 1999, her publicist mind still intact, she traveled to sixty-seven cities to promote *Santitos*. It was the perfect formula: an amazing novel accompanied by a marketing barrage carried out by a curious and tireless traveler. That is the story of her first novel. The story of the movie, however, was quite different.

At the same time María Amparo was writing her novel, she was also writing a film script in order to make her dialogues sound more natural. At the end of this experiment, Esperanza, the protagonist, was speaking like a true native of Vera Cruz. To top it off, María Amparo had another book in hand and the possibility to make a film in the other.

By way of the Sundance Institute, her script reached the hands of the young Mexican director Alejandro Springall. Why did she decide to make the movie with Springall if he had never directed a movie? Like almost everything she had done, it was out of instinct. "And because Alejandro is as foolish as I am," María Amparo said. The movie was filmed in Tlacotalpan, Tijuana, Los Angeles, and Mexico City. It was released in Mexico in October 1999 to favorable reviews, and in February 2000 it was released in the United States.

Why attempt something so risky, something at which many others had already failed? María Amparo's reasoning was sound. "I believe, in part, that Hispanics are in fashion," she said, lapsing into Spanglish and speaking about the 33 million Latinos in the United States that understand Spanish. "Just look, there are at least two Spanish language networks on TV. On the radio, the stations that dominate in certain cities, like Los Angeles, Chicago, and Miami, are in Spanish. In the press, magazines, and record industry, it's the same story. The only thing missing is that at your neighborhood multiplex two of the ten movies that are showing are in Spanish. That, I bet, is the next step."

THAT WAS NOT María Amparo's first important bet. She placed her first one on Benito Martínez, the tall, thin, eccentric boy she had met in Mexico when they were both working in the government office of ISSSTE. "We didn't see any future in Mexico," María Amparo told me, "and we said: Let's go," and they left. Their university pals, Chu-

cho and Marco, had already gone to Los Angeles, and they offered
Benito and María Amparo work helping out with publicity for Mexican movies.

They formed an agency called United Spanish Advertising, which
later became Acento Advertising. But this wasn't what they really
wanted to do. Benito preferred painting, and María Amparo wanted
to write. "After three years in the U.S., we had had it," she recalls,
and in 1986 they sought refuge on a ranch in the Mexican state of
Hidalgo; but they got tired of that too.

In 1989, they were on their way back to Los Angeles, with a six-
month-old baby and another on the way. It would be their final
return. "For many months, I felt like a tourist in the U.S.," María
Amparo recalled. "I never imagined that I would stay. I went to Disneyland and to Venice Beach, and I did everything tourists do, but
one day I realized that I had already been to Disneyland several times
and I said, gosh, I think I'm really an immigrant." Then, without hes-
itation, she said, "I think I can live here for the rest of my life."
Period.

Those of us who knew them believed that in the end, Benito
would end up an artist and María Amparo the administrator, but
Benito focused on making the agency a success, and to do this he
had to put aside his painting and sculpture for a while. Suddenly, the
tables had turned. "I was writing at night while Benito watched Seinfeld," she recalled. Besides watching Seinfeld, Benito pursued new
clients, made presentations, kept track of the money, and did a jug-
gling act in order to keep his family afloat. The first indication that
Benito, the businessman, was doing well was when they installed a
jacuzzi in the yard, and building the second floor of the house was
proof that the effort, born years ago in a dive in central L.A., had
finally paid off.

The agency was only a parenthesis in Benito's life. The last time I
spoke with him—we had breakfast one morning like two old-timers
remembering when we would share popcorn and chocolate bars—he
told me about an exhibit of his work shown in the Northeast, just him
alone, like the good old days. Benito has a special sensitivity, and his
art is infused with a sharp sense of humor. I still have one of Benito's
wonderful paintings, which comes with me whenever and wherever
I move.

Getting back to María Amparo, she is convinced that if she had stayed in Mexico, she would not have received the recognition for her creativity that has come to her so naturally in the United States. "A funny thing happened to me," she said. "In Mexico, I lived life, I didn't analyze it. In the U.S., I was able to look at Mexico from a distance, see the details, and understand many things about my country. I could not have written like this in Mexico."

"Like what?" I asked her. "Like, for example, the saints," she replied. "In Mexico, saints are everywhere in people's daily lives: They are in their wallets, in taxis, everywhere, but the people don't even notice them anymore. When I left Mexico, I was able to see this and reflect on it." In addition, there were the difficulties of everyday life. "In Mexico it's one obstacle after another; everything is a struggle," she recalled without much emotion. "Life is very hard. On the other hand, here you have an infrastructure to achieve what you want."

"What does an immigrant need to be successful in the U.S., María Amparo?"

"You have to keep plodding along," she said. "You have to work hard and make the right decisions. The opportunities are there. The trick is to see them and not to stop until you get them."

María Amparo, ironically, does not consider herself a successful writer. "Until I write my third novel, I won't know," she said, laughing. She describes herself as a very simple person. "I feel like a Mexican living in the U.S.," she said. "I am not a Latin author. I can't say that I am like Sandra Cisneros or Oscar Hijuelos. It's not my culture."

For many others, however, there is no doubt that this young Mexican, who for so long felt like a tourist in the United States and who fought off rats and cockroaches at night in the Fiesta Theater, could be one of the most convincing examples of the American Dream—Mexican style.

"If I hadn't become an immigrant," María Amparo concluded, "I would probably be in Mexico, and I'd be a mother just like any other."

OUR FUTURE

45 AM I AN IMMIGRANT, *PAPÁ*?

I was talking on the phone the other day with my daughter, Paola, who lives in Madrid with her mother. Suddenly, the subject of the Moroccan immigrants who were being chased and beaten by Spanish citizens came up.

"Ay, *papá*," she said. "They're blaming those immigrants for everything. They say they even killed a girl."

"Yes," I responded. "Just like they blame all of us, the immigrants in the U.S., for everything when things aren't going well."

"No, *papá*, you aren't an immigrant," exploded the voice of my wonderful thirteen-year-old daughter, who was probably remembering the negative words she had seen in newspapers and on TV about immigrants in Europe.

"Yes, Paolí, I am," I replied. "Immigrants are people who were born in a place other than where they are living, and you know that I was born in Mexico and I live in the United States."

"Am I an immigrant, *papá*?" she asked me, somewhat nervously.

"Well, you were born in Miami, but you live in Spain," I said, thinking hard about what I was saying to her. "So, yes, Paolí, in Spain you too are an immigrant. In the United States you aren't an immigrant, but in Spain you are."

"Ahhh!," she said. There was a pause, and then she added, "Well, it's not so bad being an immigrant. The only thing I don't like about it is that I have to get on a plane for eight hours in order to see you in Miami."

46 AMNESTY

In 1986, the United States granted amnesty to 3 million undocumented immigrants. Upon its approval, the U.S. Congress authorized a series of sanctions against employers who hired undocumented immigrants, with the hope of preventing more illegal immigration. It didn't work.

Undocumented immigration to the United States continued, and in 2000, there were more than 6 million people living in the United States illegally. It was then that the most powerful group of labor unions in the United States proposed a new amnesty. Its objective was to transform amnesty for undocumented immigrants into a central theme of the presidential campaign. That was the most serious proposal for temporarily solving the immigration status of millions of families since 1986. The Mexican government, however, obviously did not know how to capitalize on the opportunity to push for the amnesty for millions of people in the United States when they raised oil prices. What do undocumented immigrants from Mexico have to do with the increase in oil prices? A lot.

OIL AND THE WASTED CHANCE

When Mexico and the United States began to negotiate the Free Trade Agreement, they set two very clear conditions. The Mexicans said that the price of oil was not negotiable and that it was a very delicate and historically significant matter. OK, the Americans said. We won't ask for anything with respect to oil, but you can't pressure us to open our borders to more immigrants. You can forget about another amnesty! Fine, the Mexicans replied.

So, ever since January 1, 1994, this nonwritten agreement between the Mexicans and the Americans was respected. Everything was cool, until oil prices went through the roof. In the first three months of 2000, oil prices surpassed $34 a barrel, and the Americans, shocked, found themselves paying a small fortune to fill the gas tanks of their cars and SUVs. The more Americans paid, the more oil-producing nations like Mexico, Venezuela, and Saudi Arabia earned. For these latter countries, the strategy planned months earlier had worked. The world consumes roughly 77 million barrels of oil a day, but the Organization of Petroleum Exporting Countries (OPEC), and others like Mexico who are not members of OPEC, managed to reduce world production to only 75 million barrels. With that imbalance, the market and the dollar began to flow from north to south. Bad economic news for the Americans became excellent news for the Mexicans, Venezuelans, and Saudi Arabians. The United States, however, was not going to sit back idly, twiddling its thumbs.

Bill Richardson, U.S. secretary of energy, was soon appointed to put out the fire. He was chosen because he was a diplomat and had emerged from complicated situations with flying colors, and because he spoke Spanish, a basic element for dealing with the Mexicans on an equal footing. The problem was that if Richardson asked the Mexicans to increase their oil production, he would be breaking the nonwritten agreement between the two nations. That would leave the United States vulnerable in terms of immigration issues.

However, Richardson had orders from President Clinton to negotiate the price of oil with Mexico, any way he could. For months, the hard bargaining between the United States and the oil-producing countries, to try to stabilize the price of gasoline, would continue.

The American request, however, to increase Mexican oil production left the door open for Mexico to talk about the taboo subject in the United States: undocumented immigrants. The United States had lost its moral authority to avoid negotiating on this matter.

Now, the only thing missing was for someone in Mexico to ask for an amnesty for Mexican undocumented immigrants in the United States and, at least, for informal discussions on the free movement of Mexican workers in the United States to begin. This issue was completely avoided in the Free Trade Agreement negotiations. Although it may seem hard to believe, no one talked about it. Mexico was in the middle of an electoral campaign. Mexican president Ernesto Zedillo, with his characteristic ostrich tactics, did not want to get involved in any more trouble with just a few months left in Los Pinos, and none of the other presidential candidates in Mexico had any authority to push for an amnesty for their fellow countrymen.

So, Mexico lost an historic opportunity to influence, in a determining and effective way, the future of millions of Mexicans who live, vulnerable, in the United States.

THE AFL-CIO TO THE RESCUE

Ironically, the most important labor union organization in the United States did what the Mexican government did not want to or could not do. I say ironically because this group of labor unions has always been opposed to undocumented immigrants in the United States receiving amnesty. For labor unions, these immigrants were potential competitors.

The AFL-CIO, nevertheless, fully understood that the undocumented immigrants do not take jobs away from Americans and that, to the contrary, they create new economic and cultural opportunities for all who live in the United States. Instead of seeing them as enemies, the labor unions opted for trying to integrate those immigrants into their unions. So on February 16, 2000, in an announcement that surprised many, the AFL-CIO proposed granting an amnesty to the 6 million undocumented immigrants in the United States.

THE CANDIDATES AND THE NEW YORK TIMES

When the announcement was made, John Wilhelm, head of immigration matters for the AFL-CIO, stated emphatically that "the present system doesn't work and is used as a weapon against workers."

Then, explaining why this organization had changed its point of view with respect to an amnesty, he added, "The only reason a lot of employers want to hire a large number of illegal aliens is so they can exploit them." Bingo. The debate had begun.

Republican presidential candidate George W. Bush stood by his position against the amnesty. The following excerpt is taken from my interview with Mr. Bush in late 1999:

J. R.: Would you favor an amnesty for the 5 million undocumented immigrants in the United States?
G. W. B.: Not at this time. Not at this time, I would not.
J. R.: Why not?
G. W. B.: Because I think I need to know more of the facts and I wanna make sure I understand what the total consequences are, but I don't favor the amnesty right now. What I do favor is making sure that we put a program in place that recognizes there are people looking for work and there are people looking for workers, so they can combine the two. I hear this not just in the South but I hear this in the Midwest. You know, there are people who've got plants and are looking for workers, and we've got to make sure that we combine the two in a way that is not disruptive. I'll listen, but I need to be persuaded on the amnesty.

In the final stages of his campaign, no one had been able to convince Bush of the benefits of an amnesty.

The position of Democratic presidential candidate Al Gore was less offensive. Like Bush, however, he did not want to promise to push for an amnesty. This was our conversation in early March 2000:

J. R.: You have said in the past that you will support an amnesty and I'm here quoting "depending on the circumstances and depending upon the way it was described." Now, could you be more specific? What kind of circumstances are you expecting or how would you describe this amnesty?
A. G.: Well, I voted for the amnesty the last time it came up.
J. R.: Yes, in 1986.
A. G.: . . . And I was concerned that there were inadequate provisions made for job training and for opportunities to allevi-

ate poverty to fully integrate those receiving amnesty into the economy and into the American way of life to give them opportunities. And I think that any proposal to go and do this again should be accompanied by policies that would deal with the long-term effects. And we don't want to send the signal that just every year or so there will be another, because that's not fair to those who are playing by the rules, the majority who immigrate legally.

J. R.: But, in general, would you favor an amnesty?

A. G.: It depends on the circumstances. I think that it should be considered carefully. But I think that it should be looked at in the context of what the other provisions are and what the time limits are. What do you do about someone who immigrates illegally the day after the effective date? How do you prevent sending the signal that this is going to be a regular occurrence, and then you have open borders, which is not fair to those who have gone about it the right way and have immigrated legally. But I think we need to treat all people within our borders with respect.

Of course, many other people have voiced opinions on this matter. It is worth pointing out something else, though, that has no face but a great deal of influence. the *New York Times* has no vote, but it does have an important voice in American politics. So, when it published an editorial on February 22, 2000, opposing an amnesty, the idea was practically dead in the water. According the the *New York Times*:

> . . . the principal problem with amnesties is that they beget more illegal immigration. Demographers trace the doubling of the number of Mexican immigrants since 1990 in part to the amnesty of the 1980s. Amnesties signal foreign workers that American citizenship can be had by sneaking across the border, or staying beyond the term of one's visa, and hiding out until Congress passes the next amnesty.

SIX MILLION PEOPLE WANT TO LIVE WITHOUT FEAR AND WITHOUT BEING EXPLOITED

The journalists from the *New York Times* were right, in part. The last amnesty did not succeed in stopping undocumented immigration, because the sanctions on employers did not have the results they had hoped for, and, in some cases, it was truly laughable. In fact, nothing will stop illegal immigration until people understand that it is the supply and demand of jobs and not immigration laws that control it. So undocumented immigration to the United States will continue, uninterrupted, at an average rate of 300,000 people per year, unless, of course, some drastic measure is taken, like positioning soldiers on the border.

It is important to emphasize that the amnesty is fair and necessary for those people who are already in the United States. It is completely disingenuous to think that these immigrants are going to return to their native countries just because they don't have the proper documentation. Besides, it is absurd to imagine that—just like that—6 million people are going to vanish, and a massive deportation of millions or hundreds of thousands of people is impractical and impossible. The immigrants are here for themselves, yes, but even more so for their families.

I know an undocumented mother, for instance, who has been living in California for almost twenty years. She didn't qualify for the 1986 amnesty, but she stayed anyway, with the hope that her children, sooner or later, would obtain residency or citizenship. She was right. Her oldest daughter is about to become a resident. For her, the effort was worth it.

These kinds of stories are repeated, time and again. Of the thousands of undocumented immigrants I have met while living in the United States, I have only heard of one family—the family of the little girl whose letter I included in an earlier chapter—that decided to return to their native Mexico because they could not legalize their immigration status. All the others are still here. I admit that this is neither a scientific method nor a statistically correct way to determine how many immigrants stay, but it seems to say a lot.

Amnesty will not solve the thorny matter of continuous undocumented immigration to the United States; we must also seriously study the possibility of the free circulation of workers between Mexico and the United States. An amnesty, however, would allow millions of people, who through their efforts and hard work have made this country a better place, to live with dignity and freedom and without the fear of being exploited. Living with fear and hiding should not be part of the American dream.

POSTSCRIPT: With the election of George W. Bush in the United States and Vicente Fox in Mexico, the subject of undocumented immigration ceased to be taboo. Both presidents discussed the matter publicly in early 2001 in Guanajuato, Mexico. At that point, they designated a binational committee at the highest level to look for concrete solutions to a problem that is not going to disappear.

Vicente Fox's government wisely avoided using the word "amnesty"; his officials chose other words, such as the "regularization" of the immigration situation of Mexicans in the United States. That "regularization" would consist of granting Mexican immigrants in the United States access to Social Security numbers and driver's licenses, among other advantages. Likewise, it seeks to expand a new program for visiting workers. The reality, however, is that without an amnesty there will continue to be people in the United States who are discriminated against for three reasons: being immigrants, being Hispanic, and being poor.

47 JULY 1, 2059

Laguna Niguel @ New California. The president of the United States, Peter Martínez, announced today that for the first time in the nation's history, the white population is no longer the majority. In a ceremony in the cactus garden at the presidential ranch in Laguna Nigel, Dr. Martínez said that as of today, whites are only 49.9 percent (or 214 million people) of the population. Speaking in the two official languages, Spanish and English, Martínez added that Latinos continue to gain ground and that they now make up more than 26 percent of the population, with more than 114 million people. (The African-American population is 57 million (13 percent), and the Asian population is 42 million (10 percent). What this means is that as of today, all ethnic groups in the United States are minorities.

"We are a nation of many cultures," said Martínez, who was accompanied in the ceremony by his vice president, Eliana King-Chávez. "Our *fuerza* depends on *nuestra* diversity." Stressing his on-line campaign slogan—One Nación—Martínez used the occasion to calm the anxieties of the now white minority who fear losing more jobs in Michikansas. "My mother is New Puerto Rican, my father was born in Tijuana, and my *broder* is from Los Angeles," he said in his extremely long speech of three minutes and fifty-two seconds. "However, my soul is American and I am going to *gobernar* for everybody."

Seven million workers from Michikansas are worried about Beijing Incorporated's plans to move their video telephone factories to two assembly plants: one in Guatexpress and the other in Tegus City. Next week, Martínez has a teleconference with the Chinese prime minister to discuss that matter, as well as the binational project aimed at sending a manned space ship to Mars. The ship would be launched from the Independent Republic of Cuba-Rico.

A MICROCHIP OF HISTORY

Two decades ago, the president's official residence was established in New California. This was due to the lack of security at the White House, after a series of attacks by anarchist gangs. It has now been converted to a museum dedicated to the preservation of the Salvadoran culture in Guachintón.

The ultra state of New California extends from Sandiego in the south to Seattlegon in the north and Las Tres Vegas to the east. The largest concentration of Hispanics in the country live there. This is also Martínez's main block of supporters.

According to the Association of Cyber Reporters, people are satisfied with the performance of the first Latino president of the United States. Last week, polls indicated that Martínez would be reelected for a second term of two years in the Unity House @ Laguna Niguel. The next virtual elections will be held on November 2, 2060, from 10:00 A.M. to 11:00 A.M. In the past on-line elections in 2058, Martínez won with a margin of only 0.03294% of the digital votes over his opponent, the incumbent, from Old York, José Buchanan.

Buchanan's two-year term was characterized by racial disturbances and isolation from global issues. "I don't care about the world," Buchanan grumbled. What's more, he had proposed taking away American citizenship and the chance to vote on-line from the grandchildren of undocumented immigrants. His intention was to strengthen the white vote in the face of the emerging mixed vote, but it was a bad move.

The proposal lost by two votes in the one House, Congress, of 751 technocrats in Texazona. In addition, Hispanics voted in record numbers through Votenet, and they removed both Buchanan and his chief advisor Mickey Dornan from office. Today both spend their time playing microgolf.

THE INTERVIEW AND THE SOCCER GAME

After this morning's announcement, broadcast live to the screens of the beeper satellites of the more than 432 million inhabitants in the country, President Martínez put the historical date in context in a TV chat.

"This July 1, 2059, must signify the definitive end of racism and discrimination in the entire country," he told video journalist Barbara Aguas, from Espanglish TV-Times. "It took us 283 years to reach *verdadera* equality, but *llegamos*; here we are." Then, after taking a sip of *agua de jamaica*, he concluded, "In the United States of America, there is no majority and, as my grandfather used to say, we are all God's children; now we are all equal."

To celebrate the occasion, the national soccer team played a friendly match in the mega stadium in Santa Anna, which holds 354,000 people. The United States, three-time world champion, defeated the Puerto Brazil team 4–1. Six of the eleven members of the American team were women.

EPILOGUE   WHERE ARE THEY NOW?

Amelia has been living in the United States for almost twenty years, and she still does not have a green card. Her daughter, Margarita, has her green card, and her son, Enrique, is struggling to start his life over and avoid being deported.

I lost track of Ricardo and Jorge Alberto, the counterfeiters. I wouldn't be surprised if they were still at MacArthur Park in Los Angeles and one step ahead, technologically speaking, of the INS.

Sergio Arau is filming a feature film called *A Day without a Mexican* so that everyone has a chance to see it (and to see Mexicans in the United States).

The Mexicans I bumped into in Lectorum, the bookstore in New York, don't let a single December Twelfth go by without paying a visit to the Virgin of Guadalupe.

Zoe Baird, naturally, no longer works for the U.S. government and is earning a lot of money as a consultant. She no longer hires undocumented immigrants to work in her home either.

Rebeca is hoping to go to San Luis Potosí soon to see her two children. Her husband does not want to leave the United States, and they both toy with the possibility of bringing the entire family together in south Florida.

José Angel Pescador left the Mexican consulate in Los Angeles, and California has still not been reconquered by the Mexicans.

Several years have gone by, and I still have not found twenty Americans who could replace the members of the mariachi band in El Paso, Texas, who were deported, according to the INS, in order to "return their jobs to American workers."

Hotel prices in Albuquerque, New Mexico, went up when sixty-seven hotel housekeepers were arrested.

In Chicago, the young Mexican who told me that "those guys from the PRI are a bunch of crooks" still thinks that "those guys from the PRI are a bunch of crooks." Many of the 20 million Mexicans living abroad—whom the PRI majority in the Senate did not allow to vote in the presidential election on July 2, 2000—think the same way as the boy in Chicago.

Gabriel and Bertha Barrientos, the Mexican parents of the first child born in the new millennium, did not receive any of the presents promised them, and the mayor of New York stood them up. How is Angel? Just fine . . . and with a U.S. passport.

Heliodoro, who asked both the governor of California at the time, Pete Wilson, and the then president of Mexico, Carlos Salinas de Gortari, for help, was twice ignored.

The Mexican girl who wrote to President Clinton doesn't even know if her letter was ever read by anyone in the White House. She and her family returned to Puebla.

Elián—well, Elián will always be the boy-symbol, both in Cuba of the north and Cuba of the south.

I see my good friend Felipe almost every day at the television studio in Miami, and almost every day we "exchange ideas" and speak of Cuba.

Lázaro has not yet fully adapted to south Florida. He still feels like a dissident without a country. He has not, however, lost his enthusiasm for life or his faith that Cuba will change.

Doña Carla returned to Tegucigalpa, but she has her eyes set on New York or Miami.

Honduran José Lagos, Guatemalan Julio Villaseñor, Salvadoran Carlos Baquerano, and Nicaraguan Mario Lovo have a new mission:

to prevent any Central American who qualifies to remain in the United States legally from missing out on this opportunity because of laziness, fear, lack of information, or bureaucratic obstacles.

Every week, Mario Bruno nurtures my heart and my spirit.

Vieques is a daily reminder to Puerto Ricans that they are not Americans, and Juan Figueroa continues fighting so that no Puerto Rican is treated as a second-class citizen.

What about permanent status for Puerto Rico?

Fine, thank you.

The yawls packed with Dominicans continue to get stuck in the Mona Passage, and Víctor Morisete hopes that Dominicans in the United States are not getting stuck in poverty.

There is no peace in Colombia, and no one has come up with a better (or cheaper) idea than to sit down and negotiate an end to the violence.

The flooding in Venezuela has stopped, but now it is raining recycled Chavism.

The flow of Colombians and Venezuelans to Miami continues.

CNN grew tired of playing Christopher Columbus. During the 2000 presidential campaign, it assigned a special team of journalists to follow Hispanics everywhere.

California is the future, still.

Loretta Sánchez has solidified her well-earned seat in Congress, and Bob Dornan still does not understand how he lost two consecutive elections. He can no longer throw million-dollar tantrums.

Immigration laws in the United States are increasingly complicated, and immigrants are sending more and more money back to their native countries; and yes, immigrants continue to contribute more to this country than they take from it.

One of the most important research centers in Michigan bears the name of Juan Samora, and now Mexicans, dogs, and Indians can enter any park in the United States. Thank you, Julian, for the ticket.

This season, John Rocker stunned everyone with his pitching, but he struck out for being a racist.

The New York police officers who fired forty-one times at Amadou Diallo, killing him, are free. The officers in California who brutally beat Enrique Funes and Alicia Sotero are also free.

Spanglish is gaining ground on both English and Spanish. Spanglish goes hand in hand with the Internet.

Professor Ilan Stavans has finished compiling his Spanglish dictionary.

Marta left Mexico with her two girls.

Nicolás kicks a soccer ball like a miniature Pelé. *Goooool*.

Ricky Martin and other Hispanic performers are still better than the Latino politicians.

Chef Cristino is experimenting with new recipes. He still prefers *tortas* to caviar.

María Amparo still does not consider herself a novelist, even though her first book has sold around the world. In order to be a novelist, she says, you must have three novels.

Benito went back to painting. Congratulations, *bomberito*.

Paola does not feel like an immigrant in Spain or anywhere. She is Paola of the world.

Six million people continue to dream of amnesty.